THE HEALTHCARE INDUSTRY GUIDE TO THE OSHA

BLOODBORNE PATHOGENS STANDARD

Robert D. Moran and
Kathleen Katzeff

MAY 1992

Published By:

MORAN ASSOCIATES
919 18th Street, N.W.
Suite 800
Washington, D.C. 20006

ISBN: 0-9632296-8-0

Library of Congress Cataloging in Publication Data

Moran, Robert D. 1929 -
Katzeff, Kathleen 1963 -

THE HEALTHCARE INDUSTRY GUIDE TO THE OSHA BLOODBORNE PATHOGENS STANDARD
Includes Index.

1. Industrial safety - Law and legislation - United States.
2. Industrial hygiene - Law and legislation - United States.
3. United States. Occupational Safety and Health Administration.
I. Title

ABOUT THE AUTHORS:

Robert D. Moran is a former government official who headed the task force that planned the implementation of the Occupational Safety and Health Act and the formation of OSHA. He then served a 6-year term on the U.S. Occupational Safety and Health Review Commission and was its first Chairman. He is currently a Washington D.C. lawyer and management consultant specializing in occupational safety and health.

Kathleen Katzeff has been associated with George Washington University for 10 years where she currently works with the National Health Policy Forum. She holds Bachelor of Arts and Master of Health Services Administration degrees from the University.

ABOUT THE PUBLISHER:

MORAN ASSOCIATES is a full service consultant to management on occupational safety and health. It was established to help employers cope with OSHA requirements. The services it provides are listed on Page B-6. In 1991, it published THE OSHA 500, a guidebook to the OSHA recordkeeping, compliance program, and employee training standards.

If you would like to be included on the **MORAN ASSOCIATES** mailing list, see the last page of this book.

MORAN ASSOCIATES is located at 919 18th Street, N.W., Suite 800, Washington, D.C. 20006. Telephone: (202) 785-4949.

TABLE OF CONTENTS

ABOUT MORAN ASSOCIATES:

MORAN ASSOCIATES was established for the precise purpose of helping employers cope with the increasing complexity and gravity of OSHA regulations. Founded by **Robert D. Moran**, former Chairman of the Occupational Safety and Health Review Commission, Moran Associates offers specialized OSHA compliance consulting services.

In OSHA-related matters, the professional staff of Moran Associates is unmatched in experience, technical expertise and breadth of skills. We have helped businesses like yours address compliance problems - OSHA standards, costly penalties, civil lawsuits, even criminal charges - for over 14 years.

We are a results-oriented organization that constantly strives for the result most favorable to those who place their trust in us. Because we never forget that our clients must keep a close rein on their spending, Moran Associates is always ready to discuss costs, provide estimates, and operate within a budget.

SERVICES INCLUDE:

- Bi-monthly Newsletter: *OSHA CASEBOOK*
- Safety Program Organization & Development
- Legal Services
- On-site Management Training Programs
- Compliance Audits
- Written Compliance Programs
- Moran Hotline - providing information and answers ***during*** the OSHA inspection
- Representation in OSHA Rulemaking Procedings ***and*** in NIOSH Proceedings

To obtain further information, call or write:

MORAN ASSOCIATES
919 18th Street, N.W., Suite 800
Washington, D.C. 20006
(202) 785-4949 Fax: (202) 785-5351

THE HEALTHCARE INDUSTRY GUIDE TO THE OSHA BLOODBORNE PATHOGENS STANDARD

INTRODUCTION

INTRODUCTION

This book was written to help employers understand OSHA and its Bloodborne Pathogens Standard. It is intended to be a complete reference book on that particular standard and to serve as an introduction to OSHA for employers who have little or no familiarity with either the agency or its enabling statute, the Occupational Safety and Health Act of 1970.

There are six chapters in the book. The first two focus upon the OSH Act and the effect it has had -- and is having -- upon employers. The final four chapters are exclusively devoted to the OSHA Bloodborne Pathogens Standard.

There are 5 substantive appendices: A through E.

"A" is the text of the OSHA Bloodborne Pathogens Standard.

"B" is a suggested method for identifying employee injuries and illnesses in order to satisfy the OSHA recordkeeping requirements.

"C" is a 16-page document issued by OSHA in 1988 entitled: "Recommendations for Prevention of HIV Transmissions in Health-Care Settings."

"D" is 3 graphs (or tables) that show in graphic form the OSHA requirements for (1) Labelling, (2) Hepatitis B Vaccination, and (3) Post-Exposure Evaluation and Follow-up.

"E" is 4 one-page "Fact Sheets" on the following subjects: (1) Holding the Line on Contamination, (2) Personal Protective Equipment, (3) Hepatitis B Vaccination, and (4) Handling Sharps.

The 4 "Fact Sheets" were written by OSHA for the edification of employees. If you think they might be helpful to your employees, you can photocopy them from this book, or contact OSHA for copies.

The book is indexed in two ways: By subject matter, and by subsections of §1910.1030, the bloodborne pathogens standard.

Readers who want to get a fuller understanding of OSHA should read the book from the beginning. Those people, as well as others who simply want to use the book in order to learn more about the bloodborne pathogens standard, should read the instructions on ***How to Use This Book*** that follow.

HOW TO USE THIS BOOK

The Alphabetical Index at the end of the book (Appendix F) is arranged by subject matter. It will quickly lead you to the page numbers in this book where the subject of concern to you are discussed. If you are concerned about a particular section or subsection of the standard, consult it in the Section-by-Section Index (Appendix G). It will lead you to the pages of the book that discuss that particular section. You should use both indexes. That will generally provide you with more extensive information on a particular subject.

For example, if the subject of your interest is "ambulances" and the alphabetical index leads you to a discussion of subsection (d)(4) of the standard, you should also consult "(d)(4)" in the other index so you can learn about that requirement. If, on the other hand, you initially use the index because of your interest in one of the standard's subsections (for example "(f)(2)" covering vaccination), and it leads you to pages that mention things like "reasonably anticipated occupational exposure", you should also consult the alphabetical index for the terms "reasonably anticipated" and "occupational exposure."

For legal purposes, the bloodborne pathogens standard is designated: 29 C.F.R. §1910.1030. However, like all other OSHA standards, it has numerous sections and subsections (See the section on "How To Read An OSHA Standard" that follows.) In this book -- and in its index -- only the subsections are used. Thus, if you are interested in 29 C.F.R. §1910.1030(d)(4)(iii), look in the index under "(d)(4)(iii)." Here is another example: If the book mentions "section (f)(3)(ii)(C)" or any other such designation, that is simply an abbreviated way of writing: 29 C.F.R. §1910.1030(f)(3)(ii)(C), or whatever other "section" of the standard that may be mentioned.

When attempting to cope with OSHA requirements, you should never assume that you know the meaning of particular words or phrases. OSHA often uses them differently. There are many court cases, for example, that have resulted from OSHA's contention that a "roof" is the same thing as a "floor" or that the word "and" and the word "or" have the same meaning.

The text of the bloodborne pathogens standard is reproduced in Appendix A of this book. It is the only document that has legal force and effect. You should consult both the actual text of the standard as well as the explanation and discussions of its meaning. The latter can be found both in the book itself and in the material included in the Appendices.

HOW OSHA STANDARDS ARE CATALOGED

Most people have difficulty understanding OSHA standards. One court described them as a Byzantine pattern of regulation, and a Congressional Committee found that "the single most important problem of the Federal occupational safety and health program is the inability of the small businessman to learn what is expected of him."

That is all true. Nevertheless, you are obligated to observe applicable OSHA requirements and it will be helpful to acquire at least a rudimentary understanding of the scheme the agency utilizes for cataloging and publishing its requirements. Even if your interest is confined to the bloodborne pathogens standard, you will find that it requires compliance with other OSHA rules (recordkeeping, for example) and makes reference to other OSHA standards. Therefore, an explanation of the arrangement of those standard follows.

All OSHA standards are requirements of law. They are printed in Title 29 of the Code of Federal Regulations (To obtain a copy, see the section entitled: ***The OSHA Standards - How to Get Copies***). That is usually abbreviated as: "29 C.F.R.." The Code of Federal Regulations is the periodic publication and codification of all Federal agency regulations that initially appear in a daily issue of the Federal Register.

OSHA standards and regulations are in Parts 1901 through 1990 of Title 29, but only nine of them impose occupational safety and health obligations upon private sector employers. They are:

Part 1903	Inspections, citations and proposed penalties
Part 1904	Recording and reporting occupational injuries and illnesses
Part 1910	Occupational safety and health standards for ***General Industry***
Part 1915	Occupational safety and health standards for ***Shipyard Employment***
Part 1917	Occupational safety and health standards for ***Marine Terminals***
Part 1918	Occupational safety and health standards for ***Longshoring***
Part 1919	***Gear certification*** rules (maritime industry)
Part 1926	Occupational safety and health standards for ***Construction***

Part 1928 Occupational safety and health standards for *Agriculture*

If you read that list and are still wondering where to find the standards that apply to hospitals, physicians, dentists, funeral homes, bloodbanks, and similar operations, the answer is: Part 1910--General Industry. To OSHA, the term "general industry" means everything that doesn't fit under one of its other categories.

All of the sections of a particular "part" (of Title 29, Code of Federal Regulations) begin with the same four digits as that part. Thus part "1910" standards begin with §1910.1 and continue in numerical order. For example, §1910.1, §1910.2, §1910.3, etc. However, many of the sections have subsections, and they, in turn, have many additional subsections. The sequence in which they appear is explained later in the discussion entitled. *"How to Read an OSHA Standard."*

APPLICABILITY OF OSHA STANDARDS

Not all OSHA standards apply to all employers. Those that are codified in parts 1903 and 1904 apply to most employers. The OSHA standards in the remaining parts are ostensibly limited to the areas of business and industry suggested by their title. However, that is not always the case.

Some of the Part 1910 "General Industry" standards also apply in the construction, agriculture, and maritime industries. The rule of thumb applied by OSHA is this: *If an OSHA inspector observes a hazardous condition or practice at a construction (or maritime) worksite but there is no construction (or maritime) standard regulating the condition, he will cite you under the "general industry" standard that regulates that condition.* The authority for that OSHA practice is stated in 29 C.F.R. §1910.5(c): *any standard shall apply according to its terms to any employment and place of employment in any industry, even though particular standards are also prescribed for that industry.*

Thus, OSHA can cite an employer in the maritime industry or the construction industry for noncompliance with a "general industry" (Part 1910) standard in those situations where there is no applicable maritime or construction standard that regulates the cited condition or practice.

In most cases, the applicability of an OSHA standard can easily be ascertained from its text. In some cases, however, additional research may be necessary. For example, the particular standard requiring records for fixed fire extinguishing systems is listed as 29 C.F.R. §1910.160(b)(9). That is a 2-sentence standard that, if taken literally, applies to all fire extinguishing systems. However, §1910.160(b)(9) is a subsection of §1910.160. That standard begins with a section entitled "*scope and application,*" §1910.160(a)(1), which states, for example, that the standard does **not** apply to automatic sprinkler systems.

Many other OSHA standards are structured similarly. They begin with "*scope and application*" provisions. Regrettably, however, not all OSHA standards clearly specify their applicability.

The Bloodborne Pathogens Standard does have a "scope and application" provision, §1910.1030(a). It provides that the standard applies to all "occupational exposure" to "blood" or "other potentially infectious materials." All three of the terms in quotations are defined in the very next section of the standard, §1910.1030(b).

THE OSHA STANDARDS: HOW TO GET COPIES

There should be a copy of the OSHA standards at every place where employees work. They are bound in paperback books. If you want all OSHA standards and regulations, you will have to get six separate volumes, but if you only want the "general industry" standards, you need only 2 of those books. They are easy to obtain. OSHA inspectors routinely provide copies to employers as part of the inspection process. They can also be purchased commercially.

You can buy the C.F.R. books from the U.S. Government Printing Office directly, or from one of its bookstores. There are also some private publishers who sell copies of the OSHA standards in book form. In addition, each OSHA area office will provide a copy upon request. Consult the U.S. Government section of your telephone directory under the heading "Department of Labor" and the sub-heading "Occupational Safety and Health Administration."

The OSHA standards and regulations are also available on computer disk from various computer software merchants.

HOW TO READ AN OSHA STANDARD

Many OSHA standards are lengthy and complex. The difficulty of reading them is complicated by the use of small type to print them and the failure to separate each subsection by some readily identifiable method or reader-friendly format.

All OSHA standards, however, are arranged in the same format. Once that format is understood, locating particular subsections of a standard will be easier.

Publication of the Code of Federal Regulations (CFR) is the responsibility of the Director of the Office of the Federal Register. He decides where in the CFR each federal agencies' regulations will be published. He has assigned "Title 29" to OSHA. Thus each OSHA regulation is preceded by "29 C.F.R."

Individual parts of Title 29 are designated by a four digit number (for example, 1901, 1903, 1910, 1926). That "part" designation is the first four numbers of all OSHA standards. A period follows the first four digits.

Following that period, the standards are listed in numerical order beginning with number one. Thus 29 C.F.R. 1910.1 (or, as designated in this book, 29 C.F.R. §1910.1) refers to Title 29, Part 1910, section 1.

The number following the period is the designation given to a particular OSHA standard. It will be followed by a name. For example:

§1910.1030 Bloodborne Pathogens

There then will follow various subsections of the standard. They are designated by letters and numbers **all of which are in parenthesis.**

The first subsection is "(a)". For example §1910.1030(a). Other major subsections will be similarly designated in alphabetical order. For example §1910.1030(b), §1910.1030(c), etc. However, each of them often has its own subsections. And those subsections, in turn, have their own subsections.

The subsections are designated as follows:

First Group:	alphabetically by small letters as described above
Second Group:	numerically. For example (1), (2), (3), etc.
Third Group:	numerically by Roman numerals. For example (i), (ii), (iii), etc.
Fourth Group:	alphabetically by capital letters. For example (A), (B), (C), etc.

For subsequent groups (if necessary), the order listed above is repeated, but the letter or number is <u>underlined</u> (or italicized). For example (<u>a</u>), (<u>1</u>), etc.

An example to demonstrate the foregoing discussion follows.

Listed Below Are The Steps to be Taken to Locate:

29 C.F.R. §1910.1030(d)(4)(iv)(C)

1. Get a copy of Title 29, C.F.R., Parts 1900 to 1910

2. Locate §1910.1030. Bloodborne Pathogens

3. Begin with "(a)", then look to (b), (c), etc. until you find "(d)".

4. Find "(1)" under subsection "(d)". Then look for "(2)", "(3)" and "(4)"

5. Once you have located "(4)", look for Roman numeral "(i)", then for "(ii)," "(iii)", "(iv)"

6. Once you have located "(iv)", look for capital letter "(A)", then "(B)", then "(C)."

The format and sequence for all OSHA standards is the same. If those same steps are followed, you should be able to locate the particular subsection of the standard being sought.

DEFINITION OF TERMS

The text of the OSHA Bloodborne Pathogens Standard includes definitions for many of the terms used in the standard. You will find them in Appendix "A" of this book at page A-2. However, in order to assist readers who have difficulty with the fine print used in the Federal Register, those definitions are printed below in alphabetical order. The following also includes definitions of the terms "employer" and "employee", two terms that are not defined in the text of the standard.

> **"Blood"** means human blood, products made from human blood and human blood components. The term "human blood components" includes plasma, platelets, and serosanguineous fluids (e.g., exudates from wounds).
>
> **"Bloodborne Pathogens"**: While HBV and HIV are specifically identified in the standard, the term includes any pathogenic microorganism that is present in human blood and can infect and cause disease in persons who are exposed to blood containing the pathogen. Other examples include hepatitis C, malaria, syphilis, babesiosis, brucellosis, leptospirosis, arboviral infections, relapsing fever, Creutzfeld-Jakob disease, Human T-lymphotrophic Virus Type 1, and viral hemorrhagic fever.
>
> **"Clinical Laboratory"** means a workplace where diagnostic or other screening procedures are performed on blood or other potentially infectious materials.
>
> **"Contaminated"** means the presence or the reasonably anticipated presence of blood or other potentially infectious materials on item or surface.
>
> **"Contaminated Laundry"** means laundry which has been soiled with blood or other potentially infectious material or may contain sharps.

"Contaminated Sharps" means any contaminated object that can penetrate the skin including, but not limited to, needles, scalpels, broken glass, broken capillary tubes, and exposed ends of dental wires.

"Decontamination" means the use of physical or chemical means to remove, inactivate, or destroy bloodborne pathogens on a surface or item to the point where they are no longer capable of transmitting infectious particles and the surface or item is rendered safe for handling, use, or disposal.

"Employee" means a person in the employ of an "employer". Physicians who are members of a professional corporation are generally considered to be employees of that corporation. Physicians may also be treated as employees of the hospital where they work. A person who is a sole practitioner or a partner, however, is not an employee of his own practice or his partnership.

"Employer" means a person engaged in a business affecting commerce who has employees, but does not include the United States or any state or political subdivision of a state. Where physicians are organized into professional corporations, the corporation is the employer and the physicians are considered to be employees of the corporation.

"Engineering Controls" mean controls (e.g., sharps disposal containers, self-sheathing needles) that isolate or remove the bloodborne pathogens hazard from the workplace.

"Exposure Incident" means a specific eye, mouth, or other mucous membrane, non-intact skin, or parenteral contact with blood or other potentially infectious materials that results from the performance of an employee's duties.

"Handwashing Facilities" means a facility providing an adequate supply of running potable water, soap and single use towels or hot air drying machines.

"Licensed Healthcare Professional" is a person whose legally permitted scope of practice allows him or her to independently perform Hepatitis B Vaccination and Post-exposure Evaluation and Follow-up as provided in paragraph (f) of the OSHA standard.

"HBV" means hepatitis B virus.

"HIV" means human immunodeficiency virus.

"Occupational Exposure" means reasonably anticipated skin, eye, mucous membrane, or parenteral contact with blood or other potentially infectious materials that may result from the performance of an employee's duties.

"OPIM" See "Other Potentially Infectious Materials."

"Other Potentially Infectious Materials" means

1. The following human body fluids: semen, vaginal secretions, cerebrospinal fluid, amniotic fluid, saliva in dental procedures, any body fluid that is visibly contaminated with blood, and all body fluids in situations where it is difficult or impossible to differentiate between body fluid;

2. Any unfixed tissue or organ (other than intact skin) from a human (living or dead); and

3. HIV-containing cell or tissue cultures, organ cultures, and HIV- or HBV containing culture medium or other solutions; and blood, organs or other tissues from experimental animals infected with HIV and HBV.

"Parenteral" means piercing mucous membranes or the skin barrier through such events as neeldesticks, human bites, cuts, and abrasions.

"Personal Protective Equipment" is specialized clothing or equipment worn by an employee for protection against a hazard. General work clothes (e.g., uniforms, pants, shirts or blouses) not intended to function as protection against a hazard are not considered to be personal protective equipment.

"Production Facility" means a facility engaged in industrial-scale, large volume or high concentration production of HIV or HBV.

"Regulated Waste" means liquid or semi-liquid blood or other potentially infectious materials; contaminated items that would release blood or other potentially infectious materials in a liquid or semi-liquid state if compressed; items that are caked with dried blood or other potentially infectious material and are capable of releasing these materials during handling; contaminated sharps; and pathological and microbiological wastes containing blood or other potentially infectious materials.

"Research Laboratory" Means a laboratory producing or using research-laboratory- scale amounts of HIV and HBV. Research laboratories may produce high concentrations of HIV and HBV, but not in the volume found in production facilities.

"Sharps" <u>See</u> "Contaminated Sharps."

"Source Individual" means any individual, living or dead, whose blood or other potentially infectious materials may be a source of occupational exposure to the employee. Examples include, but are not limited to, hospital and clinic patients; clients in institutions for the developmentally disabled, trauma victims; clients of drug and alcohol treatment facilities; residents of hospices and nursing homes; human remains; and individuals who donate or sell blood or blood components.

"Sterilize" means the use of a physical or chemical procedure to destroy all microbial life including highly resistant bacterial endospore.

"Universal Precautions" is an approach to infection control. According to the concept of Universal Precautions, all human blood and certain human body fluids are treated as if known to be infectious for HIV, HBV, and other bloodborne pathogens.

"Work Practice Controls" means controls that reduce the likelihood of exposure by altering the manner in which a task is performed (e.g., prohibiting recapping of needle by a two-handed technique).

CHAPTER 1

THE OCCUPATIONAL SAFETY AND HEALTH ACT

The Occupational Safety and Health Act[1/] was enacted by Congress on December 29, 1970 and went into effect on April 28, 1971. It's text hasn't changed since then. Its impact upon employers has been very costly and it continues to have rather severe potential consequences. They are discussed in Chapter 2.

Only one amendment to the law was made during its first twenty years. That change, adopted as a part of the federal deficit-reduction package in November 1990, boosted the maximum penalty limits by a factor of seven and imposed a $5,000 *minimum* penalty for each willful violation.

The law was enacted in an effort to reduce workplace injuries and illnesses by establishing mandatory job safety and health standards and other requirements in order to enhance safe and healthful working conditions in places of employment throughout the United States.

The declared Congressional purpose and policy of the Act is "to assure so far as possible every working man and woman in the nation safe and healthful working conditions and to preserve our human resources."[2/]

1/ P.L. 91-596, 84 Stat. 1590, 29 U.S.C. §651 et seq.

2/ Section 2(b), 29 U.S.C. §651(b).

The OSH Act is administered and enforced by the Occupational Safety and Health Administration (OSHA). The acronym "OSHA" is used throughout this book to mean the "Occupational Safety and Health Administration," an agency of the United States Department of Labor. The Act delegated rulemaking and enforcement authority to the Secretary of Labor but the Secretary then created OSHA, to be headed by an Assistant Secretary, and redelegated his statutory authority to that official.

A. <u>COVERAGE</u>

The provisions of the law apply to every employer engaged in a business affecting commerce who has employees. The Bureau of Labor Statistics estimated that 4.2 million establishments employing some 57 million employees were subject to coverage in 1971. Those numbers have grown over the years as the working population has expanded. In 1991, there were approximately 6 million covered establishments.

The law applies in all 50 states, the District of Columbia, Puerto Rico, the Virgin Islands, American Samoa, Guam and other U.S. territories.[3/]

Federal and state employees are specifically excluded from coverage, but the Act permits the adoption of measures extending substantially similar requirements to them.[4/]

3/ Section 4(a), 29 U.S.C. §653(a).

4/ Section 3(5), 29 U.S.C. §652(5), excludes federal, state and local agencies from the definition of the term "employer." However, other sections of the Act authorize the federal and state governments to adopt occupational safety and health

The Act does not apply to persons covered under other existing occupational safety and health laws (such as the Federal Coal Mine Health and Safety Act) and under Section 274 of the Atomic Energy Act of 1954 as amended.[5/]

B. DUTIES OF EMPLOYERS AND EMPLOYEES

In general, the duty of each *employer* under the Act is to furnish each of his employees a place of employment, free from recognized hazards that are causing, or are likely to cause death or serious physical harm,[6/] to comply with the occupational safety and health standards promulgated under the Act,[7/] and to observe the OSHA recordkeeping requirements.

The duty of each *employee* is to comply with the occupational safety and health standards, and all rules, regulation and orders issued pursuant to the Act which are applicable to his own actions and conduct.[8/]

---

programs for the benefit of their employees. Sections 18 and 19, 29 U.S.C. §§667 and 668.

5/ Section 4(b)(1), 29 U.S.C. §653(b)(1). That exclusion has been the subject of considerable litigation. See the discussion in U.S. Air, Inc. v. OSAHRC, 689 F.2d 1191 (4th Cir. 1982), and Inspection of Norfolk Dredging Co., 783 F.2d 1526 (11th Cir. 1986).

6/ Section 5(a)(1), 29 U.S.C. §654(a)(1). That is the so-called "general duty clause" discussed in more detail later.

7/ Section 5(a)(2), 29 U.S.C. §654(a)(2). For OSHA purposes a "standard" is a requirement of law that must be observed by employers. It is virtually the same as a "regulation". OSHA standards are discussed infra.

8/ Section 5(b), 29 U.S.C. §654(b).

Employers who fail to comply with those obligations can be penalized by the government but there is no government sanction against noncomplying employees.[9/]

C. **THE GENERAL DUTY CLAUSE**

Congress intended that the Act would be principally enforced through specific standards that would tell employers what they must do to achieve a safe and healthful working environment. However, Congress added §5(a)(1), the so-called "general duty clause," in order to fill gaps that might exist in the standards. It was not expected to be cited very much and was intended to only cover hazardous conditions that are obvious and admitted by all concerned, but for which no specific standard then existed.

Although it appears that more employers have been cited under the general duty clause than Congress contemplated, the courts have curtailed its use to some extent by imposing a number of requirements that must be proved before a general duty clause violation can be established.[10/] As a result, it is not enough to simply show that a workplace hazard existed that caused death or serious physical harm to an employee. The proof that the Secretary of Labor must produce includes: (a) identification of

---

9/ Atlantic & Gulf Stevedores v. OSAHRC, 534 F.2d 541 (3d Cir. 1976).

10/ The leading case on general duty clause enforcement is National Realty and Construction Company v. OSAHRC, 489 F.2d 1257 (D.C. Cir., 1973). The rule of that case has been followed innumerable times. See, for example, Secretary of Labor v. Cerro Metal Products Division, 12 BNA OSHC 1821 (1986), and cases cited therein.

particular measures that the employer should have had in effect at the time the hazardous condition was present; (b) that such measures would be effective in counteracting the hazard, and (c) that it would be feasible to put such measures in effect. In the words of the court:

> *" . . . the Secretary [of Labor] must be constrained to specify the particular steps a cited employer should have taken to avoid citation, and to demonstrate the feasibility and likely utility of those measures."*[11/]

D. OCCUPATIONAL SAFETY AND HEALTH STANDARDS

Shortly after the law went into effect, the Secretary of Labor, under the authority Congress delegated to him, adopted thousands of occupational safety and health standards.[12/] In subsequent years, additional standards have been added. Some standards have been revised while others have been revoked. The Secretary's authority to adopt standards is a continuing one. Thus, new standards can be adopted in the future.

OSHA standards generally consist of rules for avoidance of hazards that have been proven by research and experience to be harmful to employee safety and health. The standards supposedly constitute an extensive compilation of wisdom. They sometimes apply to all employers. An example would be fire protection standards. A great many standards, however, apply only to

---

11/ National Realty, supra, 489 F.2d at 1268.

12/ 36 Federal Register 10466 et seq., May 29, 1971. All OSHA standards are codified in Title 29 of the Code of Federal Regulations (C.F.R.).

specific types of work -- such as driving a truck or handling compressed gases.

Two of the many thousands of occupational safety and health standards are listed below in order to demonstrate the form of such standards:

> **Example number one:** *"Aisles and passageways shall be kept clear and in good repair, with no obstruction across or in aisles that could create a hazard."*[13/]

> **Example number two:** *"Employees working in areas where there is a possible danger of head injury from impact, or from falling or flying objects, or from electrical shock and burns, shall be protected by protective helmets."*[14/]

It is the obligation of all employers and employees to familiarize themselves with those standards which apply to them and to observe them at all times.[15/]

E. ADOPTION OF STANDARDS

The Act provided the Secretary of Labor with authority to adopt standards in three different ways. That authority appears in sections 6(a), 6(b) and 6(c) of the Act.[16/] He made use of all of that authority in the past, but today the section 6(a) authority no longer exists and the section 6(c) authority has

---

13/ 29 C.F.R. §1910.23(b).

14/ 29 C.F.R. §1926.100(a).

15/ 29 U.S.C. §654.

16/ 29 U.S.C. §655(a), (b) and (c).

been so circumscribed by court decision that it has virtually fallen into disuse. Each of those three provisions is discussed below.

(1) Section 6(a) Standards

This authority no longer exists. It expired by its own terms on April 27, 1973, two years after the OSH Act went into effect. During the time it existed, however, it was the basis for adopting most of the standards that are in effect today.

Section 6(a) was limited to the adoption, as OSHA standards, of certain "national consensus standards" and "established Federal standards" that were in effect on December 29, 1970, the Act's enactment date. Both of those terms are defined in the law itself.[17/] No notice-and-comment rulemaking procedures were required for standards adopted under Section 6(a).[18/] The reason for that unusual leeway was to permit OSHA to get so-called "start-up" standards on the books as quickly as possible.

17/ *See* 29 U.S.C. §652(9) and §652(10). In general, national consensus standards were rules adopted by private organizations such as the National Fire Protection Association or the American National Standards Institute. An example would be the National Electrical Code. Established Federal standards, on the other hand, were standards promulgated by the government under some other Federal law. For example, the Walsh-Healey Public Contracts Act.

18/ That was a departure from the requirements of the Administrative Procedure Act, 5 U.S.C. §§551 *et seq*. That Act requires any Federal agency that has the power to adopt rules and regulations affecting the public to provide public notice of its *intent* to adopt a rule and allow sufficient time for the public to comment upon the proposed rule *before* a final rule can be put into effect.

To prevent the abuse of such power, however, the authority to adopt Section 6(a) standards was restricted to so-called "consensus" and "established Federal" standards and the power to adopt them as OSHA standards lasted only two years.[19/] However, the Secretary made considerable use of that authority during the two year period it existed and the vast majority of OSHA standards that are currently in effect were adopted under Section 6(a), 29 U.S.C. §655(a).

(2) Section 6(b) Standards

Section 6(b), 29 U.S.C. §655(b), is the authority for the adoption of all OSHA standards promulgated after April 28, 1973, except emergency temporary standards authorized by Section 6(c). It requires that advance notice of the intent to promulgate a standard must be published in the Federal Register, and the public must be given an opportunity to comment on the proposal as well as request a hearing thereon, before the proposal can be adopted as an OSHA standard. It is one of the Act's most detailed provisions and has been the subject of considerable litigation.[20/] Any OSHA standard that is adopted today must be

---

19/ For a good discussion of the Secretary's Section 6(a) authority and its limitations, see Diebold, Inc. v. Marshall, 585 F.2d 1327 (6th Cir. 1978).

20/ Two Supreme Court cases contain detailed discussions of section 6(b): Industrial Union Department v. American Petroleum Institute, 448 U.S. 607 (1980), and American Textile Manufacturers Institute v. Donovan, 452 U.S. 490 (1981).

promulgated under Section 6(b) if it is to remain in effect for longer than six months.

(3) Section 6(c) Standards

The Section 6(c), 29 U.S.C. §655(c), authority is very limited and rarely used. It permits the adoption of "emergency temporary standards" in those situations where the Secretary makes a satisfactory finding that (a) a "grave danger" exists as a result of employee exposure to toxic substances, harmful physical agents or "new hazards" and (b) an emergency standard is necessary to protect employees from such danger.[21/] No notice-and-comment rulemaking is required but a Section 6(c) standard will automatically expire six months after adoption unless, prior thereto, it is also promulgated under the Section 6(b) procedures discussed above.

(4) Variances From Standards

The Secretary, upon an employer application therefor, is authorized to grant temporary variances from standards in order to give the employer sufficient time to come into compliance if

---

21/ The difficulty of establishing the existence of those conditions is demonstrated by two decisions that invalidated OSHA attempts to adopt emergency temporary standards: Florida Peach Growers Association v. Department of labor, 489 F.2d 120 (5th Cir. 1974), and Asbestos Information Association v. OSHA, 727 F.2d 415 (5th Cir. 1984).

he can show a need and a protective plan of action.[22/] Variances may be granted without time limits if the Secretary finds that an employer is using safety measures that are as safe as those required in a standard. Affected employees must be given notice of each such application and an opportunity to participate in the variance-issuance process.[23/]

F. RECORDKEEPING REQUIREMENTS

In order to accurately describe the nature of the occupational safety and health problem, the Act requires each employer to maintain an accurate record of work-related deaths, injuries and illnesses. Minor injuries requiring only first aid treatment need not be recorded, but a record must be made if it involves medical treatment, loss of consciousness, restriction of work or motion, or transfer to another job.

The Act states that those records are to be made available to the Department of Labor and to the Department of Health and Human Services, either of which may require periodic reports thereon.[24/] However, there are judicial decisions holding that such records need not be disclosed in the absence of compulsory process[25/] such as a subpoena or a warrant.

22/ 29 U.S.C. §655(b)(6).

23/ 29 U.S.C §655(b)(6) and 655(d).

24/ Section 8(c)(2), 29 U.S.C. §657(c)(2). See also §24(a), 29 U.S.C. §673(a).

25/ See Secretary v. Taft Broadcasting Co., 12 BNA OSHC 1264 (1985), affirmed sub nom McLaughlin v. Kings Island Division, Taft Broadcasting Co., 849 F.2d 990 (6th Cir. 1988).

Employers are also required by the Act to maintain whatever additional records the Secretary may prescribe for enforcement purposes or for developing information regarding the cause and prevention of occupational accidents and illnesses,[26/] to maintain accurate records of employee exposures to potentially toxic materials or harmful physical agents that are required to be monitored or measured by OSHA standards,[27/] and to promptly advise any employee who has had such exposure of the same as well as the corrective action being taken.[28/]

The Secretary of Labor, in cooperation with the Secretary of Health and Human Services, is also authorized to issue regulations that will provide employees or their representatives with an opportunity to observe the employer's monitoring or measuring activities, to have access to the records thereof and to all records that indicate their own exposure to toxic materials or harmful physical agents.[29/]

The Act additionally authorizes the Secretary to adopt regulations requiring employers to conduct their own periodic

---

26/ Section 8(c)(1), 29 U.S.C. §657(c)(1). The injury/illness recordkeeping regulations are in Part 1904 of Title 29 C.F.R. See 29 C.F.R. §1904.1 et seq. Other recordkeeping requirements are included in various OSHA standards.

27/ Section 6(b)(7), 29 U.S.C. §655(b)(7). Such requirements are included in various OSHA standards. See, for example, 29 C.F.R. §1910.1001(m), the recordkeeping requirements of the asbestos standard, and 29 C.F.R. §1910.1030(h), the recordkeeping requirements of the bloodborne pathogens standard.

28/ Section 8(c)(3), 29 U.S.C. §657(c)(3).

29/ Id. The implementing regulation is 29 C.F.R. §1910.20.

inspections and to keep their employees informed of their protections and obligations under the law through posting of notices or other appropriate means. The information which employers may be required to give their employees may also include the provisions of applicable standards.[30/]

G. STATE PARTICIPATION

The Act allows the states to take over OSH Act administration and enforcement within their borders and encourages them to do so by providing them with monetary grants.[31/] A specific disclaimer of federal pre-emption is included in order to permit any state agency or court to assert jurisdiction under state law over any occupational safety or health issue with respect to which no federal standard is in effect.[32/]

Any state may assume responsibility for the development and enforcement of occupational safety and health standards under the Act if such state submits an approved plan (a "state plan") for

---

30/ Section 8(c)(1), 29 U.S.C. §657(c)(1). For an example of that, see the OSHA lead standard, 29 C.F.R. §1910.1025. It includes a requirement that the employer shall assure that each employee is informed of *"[t]he content of this standard and its appendices"*. 29 C.F.R. §1910.1025(l)(1)(v). The bloodborne pathogens standard requires that employers must provide their employees with training that must include an accessible copy of the standard's text and an explanation of its contents. 29 C.F.R. §1910.1030(g)(2)(vii)(a).

31/ Section 2(b)(11), 29 U.S.C. §651(b)(11).

32/ Section 18(a), 29 U.S.C. §667(a).

so doing to the Secretary of Labor.[33] The Secretary may approve such a plan under the following conditions:

1. An agency of the state must be designated or created to carry out the plan;

2. Standards (and the enforcement thereof) must be provided which create safe and healthful employment at least as effective as that otherwise provided for under the Act;

3. There must be adequate provisions for right of entry and inspection of workplaces;

4. Enforcement capacity must be demonstrated;

5. Adequate funds for administration must be assured;

6. Effective and comprehensive job safety and health programs for all public employees within the state must be established to the extent permitted by the particular state's law;

7. The state, and employers within the state, must make such reports as may be required by the Secretary of Labor.[34]

The Secretary of Labor is obligated to make a continuing evaluation of the manner in which each state plan is being carried out and to withdraw his approval thereof whenever there is a failure to comply substantially with any provision thereof.[35]

33/ Section 18(b), 29 U.S.C. §667(b).

34/ Section 18(c), 29 U.S.C. §667(c).

35/ Section 18(f), 29 U.S.C. §667(f).

In accordance with those provisions, twenty-one states and two territories currently administer and enforce the Act.[36/] For all intents and purposes, employers in those states are only subject to their state OSHA agency. The federal OSHA people play virtually no role at all there. Those jurisdictions currently have the authority to inspect private employers, cite them, adjudicate contested enforcement actions and adopt binding occupational safety and health standards and regulations. For the most part, OSHA itself does not do any of that in those places.

Nearly all of those states have standards that are _identical_ to the OSHA standards. Indeed, most of them simply re-publish those standards just as they appear in 29 C.F.R. Thus, for example, the bloodborne pathogens standard for Alaska, Arizona and most of the other "state plan" states (listed in n. 36, _supra_) would be designated as 29 C.F.R. §1910.1030 and contain the OSHA's standard's identical text.

There are two additional states (Connecticut and New York) where only state and local government agencies are within the state's OSHA authority. In all of the remaining states and territories, the state government plays no part in OSHA administration or enforcement except to provide consultative services upon request.

36/ Alaska, Arizona, California, Hawaii, Indiana, Iowa, Kentucky, Maryland, Michigan, Minnesota, Nevada, New Mexico, North Carolina, Oregon, Puerto Rico, South Carolina, Tennessee, Utah, Vermont, Virgin Islands, Virginia, Washington and Wyoming.

H. ENFORCEMENT

Employer compliance with OSHA standards, the recordkeeping requirements and the Act's general duty clause is enforced by means of on-site inspection of worksites by a force of approximately 2,500 state and federal OSHA inspectors who are stationed at more than a hundred different locations around the country.

The Act authorizes those inspectors to enter without delay, and at reasonable times, any establishment covered by the Act in order to inspect the premises and all pertinent conditions, structures, machines, apparatus, devices, equipment, and materials therein, and to question privately any employer, owner, operator, agent or employee.[37/] However, if the employer does not voluntarily consent to such an inspection, it cannot be conducted unless OSHA obtains a warrant authorizing it.[38/] OSHA is also authorized to issue administrative subpoenas to aid its inspections.[39/]

The Act permits the employer and a representative authorized by his employees to accompany the inspector during the physical inspection of any workplace for the purpose of aiding such an inspection.[40/]

37/ Sections 8(a) and (f), 29 U.S.C. §§657(a) and (f).

38/ Marshall v. Barlow, Inc., 436 U.S. 307 (1978).

39/ Section 8(b), 29 U.S.C. §657(b).

40/ Section 8(e), 29 U.S.C. §657(e).

The Secretary of Health and Human Services is also authorized to make inspections and question employers and employees in order to carry out those functions assigned to that agency under the Act.[41/] That authority has been delegated to, and is carried out by, the National Institute for Occupational Safety and Health (NIOSH). For additional discussion of that authority, see section K below.

(1) Citations and Proposed Penalties

Where an employer is believed to be in violation of the Act as a result of an OSHA inspection, he is issued a written citation describing the specific nature of the violation. The citation must fix a reasonable time for abatement of the violation, and each citation (or copies thereof) must be prominently posted by the employer at or near each place where a violation referred to in the citation occurred. Notices, in lieu of citation, may be issued for de minimis violations which have no direct or immediate relationship to safety or health.[42/]

If OSHA believes that the cited violation should be penalized, it must notify the employer by certified mail of the monetary penalty that it proposes to assess. The employer then

---

41/ Section 20(b), 29 U.S.C. §669(b). This authority has been used in the past for the purposes of conducting a so-called "health hazard evaluation" as set forth in section 20(a)(6), 29 U.S.C. §669(a)(6). See Establishment Inspection of Keokuk Steel Castings, 493 F. Supp. 842 (S.D. Iowa 1980), and General Motors Corp. v. NIOSH, 636 F.2d 163 (6th Cir. 1980).

42/ Section 9(a) and (b), 29 U.S.C. §§658(a) and (b).

has 15 working days within which to notify OSHA that he wishes to contest the citation or proposed assessment of penalty or both.[43/]

If a cited employer fails to notify OSHA within such time that he intends to contest the citation or proposed assessment of penalty, the citation and the amount of the proposed penalty become final, provided no employee files an objection to the time the citation allowed the employer to abate the cited violation (see "Abatement," in section H(3) below).

If the employer notifies OSHA within such time that he wishes to contest, OSHA must certify the matter to the Occupational Safety and Health Review Commission and the Commission must afford an opportunity for a hearing.[44/] The Commission has the power to affirm, modify or vacate any contested citation or proposed penalty. Orders of the Commission are final 30 days after issuance. Review of Commission orders may be obtained in the United States Court of Appeals.[45/]

(2) The Occupational Safety and Health Review Commission (OSHRC)

The Act created OSHRC as an independent agency of the federal government and gave it only one function -- to hear and

---

43/ Sections 10(a) and (c), 29 U.S.C. 659(a) and (c).

44/ Section 10(c), 29 U.S.C. §659(c).

45/ Sections 11(a) and (b), 29 U.S.C. §§660(a) and (b).

decide contested OSHA citations and penalty proposals.[46] The Commission is a two-tiered court system. At the lower level, it has a number of administrative law judges (ALJs) who hear contested citation cases and issue rulings. The ALJ decisions can be reviewed and changed by the 3-member presidentially-appointed Commission <u>if</u> a member so directs within 30 days of issuance of the ALJ decision. Commission decisions can be appealed to the United States Courts of Appeal.[47]

The Act provides that those who contest OSHA citations and penalty proposals are entitled to a fair and impartial hearing and decision on the contested matters. They receive just that from the Commission. Its record over the first twenty years of existence is one of impeccable fairness and impartiality between employers and OSHA. The Commission has fully sustained the OSHA charges in approximately one-fourth of its cases and has fully sustained the contesting employer in approximately one-third of its cases. In the remaining cases, some issues were decided in the employer's favor and others in OSHA's favor.

Perhaps more important than the results of its decisions is the fact that <u>all</u> of its decisions are in writing and contain detailed reasons why a particular disposition is being made.

<u>46</u>/ Sections 2(b)(3) and 12, 29 U.S.C. §651(b)(3) and 661.

<u>47</u>/ <u>See</u> n. 45, <u>supra</u>. It should be noted that an ALJ decision that is <u>not</u> ordered to be reviewed by a member of the Commission within the 30-day period allowed, will thereby automatically become a decision of the Commission. It can then be appealed to the appropriate Court of Appeals in exactly the same manner.

At the hearings conducted by Commission ALJs, the burden of proof is on OSHA to prove the validity of all citations that the employer has contested. When OSHA doesn't carry that burden -- and it often doesn't -- the citation will be vacated.

No matter how much adverse evidence OSHA presents to a Commission ALJ about an employer, the Commission will not impose any sanction or penalty greater than that set forth in the contested OSHA citation and penalty proposal. In other words, the "maximum sentence" an employer can receive in an OSHA enforcement proceeding is that listed upon the citation and penalty proposal. If the cited employer does not contest, that is exactly what he will receive.

When an employer *does* contest, the Commission is empowered to impose upon the employer:

1. The same sanction he would have received if he did not contest.

2. Something less than that.

3. No sanction at all.

The Employer who contests an OSHA citation may walk away scot-free as many employers have done and he may even be partially reimbursed for the fees and expenses he incurred in contesting the citation.[48]

48/ See the Equal Access to Justice Act, 5 U.S.C. §504, which among other things, authorizes reimbursement of the fees and expenses incurred by small businesses in defending against unjustified OSHA citations.

(3) Abatement

Each OSHA citation must prescribe a reasonable time for correction or abatement of the condition constituting the alleged violation.[49/] However, that time limit does not begin to run until a final order of the Review Commission, if the citation is contested by the employer in good faith and not solely for delay or avoidance of penalties.[50/]

Employees (or representatives of employees) also have the right to object to the period of time fixed in the citation for the abatement of a violation if, within 15 days after a citation is issued, an employee files a notice of contest with OSHA alleging that an unreasonable time was allowed for abatement. Review procedures similar to those discussed above apply when such a notice is filed.[51/]

A "Failure-To-Abate" violation of the Act exists in those situations where the time for correction of a violation has been established, either as a result of a previously uncontested citation, or the settlement or final adjudication of a prior contested citation; but the employer fails to abate within such time. In such a case, OSHA will notify the employer by certified mail of such failure and of the proposed penalty. That notice and penalty proposal will be final unless the employer contests the same by filing a notice of contest with OSHA within 15

49/ Section 9(a), 29 U.S.C. §658(a).

50/ Section 10(b) and 17(d), 29 U.S.C. §§659(b) and 666(d).

51/ Section 10(c), 29 U.S.C. §659(c).

working days.[52/] A failure-to-abate notification is essentially the same as a citation (but higher penalties are authorized) and an employer who contests it receives the same kind of hearing and adjudication discussed above.

Where an employer is under an abatement order for any reason and can establish that, despite a good faith effort to comply with the abatement requirements, abatement has not been completed because of factors beyond his reasonable control, OSHA can grant an extension. If it doesn't, the employer is entitled to a hearing before the Review Commission, which can issue an order affirming or modifying the abatement requirement.[53/]

(4) Monetary Penalties

Except in those rare instances where OSHA doesn't seek a monetary penalty, citations and failure-to-abate notices are accompanied by *proposed* penalties. If left uncontested, those proposals become fines and must be paid. If contested, however, the penalty proposals have no force or effect. The Review Commission will, after a hearing, decide what penalty, if any, will be assessed. The maximum amount of penalty authorized depends upon the nature of the violation.

Willful or repeated violations may incur fines of up to $70,000 for each violation, while serious or nonserious

---

52/ Section 10(b), 29 U.S.C. §659(b).

53/ Section 10(c), 29 U.S.C. §659(c). The procedures for invoking this process are set forth in 29 C.F.R. §2200.37.

violations may incur fines up to $7,000 for each violation.[54/] Any employer who fails to correct a previously-established violation within the time prescribed (a Failure-to-Abate) may be penalized up to $7,000 for each day the violation exists.[55/] Those penalty limits went into effect in 1991. Prior to that time, the maximum penalty limits were only one-seventh of the limits currently in effect.

(5) Criminal Sanctions

The Act also authorizes criminal penalties. A willful first violation by an employer which results in the death of any employee is punishable by a fine of up to $10,000 or imprisonment for up to six months. A second or subsequent conviction carries a penalty of up to $20,000 and up to one year in prison. Similar penalties are also included in the Act for false official statements and for giving unauthorized advance notice of any inspections to be conducted under the Act.[56/]

A state or local district attorney can also bring charges of murder, assault, battery and similar charges against an employer under the state's criminal law for acts that cause death, injury or illness to an employee. See, for example, New York v. Pymm, an October 25, 1989 decision of the Appellate Division, New York

---

54/ Sections 17(a), (b) and (c), 29 U.S.C. §§666(a), (b) and (c).

55/ Section 17(d), 29 U.S.C. §666(d).

56/ Section 17(e), (f) and (g), 29 U.S.C. §§666(e), (f) and (g).

Supreme Court, reported at 14 BNA OSHC 1297. Cases of that kind began to appear with some regularity in the late eighties and early nineties. Additional discussion of that phenomena appears in Chapter 2.

I. IMMINENT DANGERS

Any condition or practice in any place of employment that causes a danger to exist which could reasonably be expected to cause death or serious physical harm immediately or before the imminence of such danger can be eliminated through normal enforcement procedures, may be restrained by order of a United States District Court upon petition of the Secretary of Labor.

If the Secretary arbitrarily or capriciously fails to seek action to abate an imminent danger of such kind, a mandamus action to compel him to act may be maintained in the U.S. District Court by any employee who may be injured by reason of such failure.

AN OSHA inspector who concludes that imminent danger conditions or practices exist in any place of employment is obligated to inform the affected employees and employers of the danger and tell them that he is recommending to the Secretary of Labor that injunctive relief be sought.[57]

57/ Section 13, 29 U.S.C. §662.

J. PROTECTION FOR WHISTLEBLOWERS

No person may discharge or in any manner discriminate against any employee because he causes OSHA to inspect his employer's business, exercises any right under the Act, files a complaint or other proceeding, or because he testified or is about to testify in any proceeding under the Act.

Any employee who believes that he has been discharged or otherwise discriminated against in violation of that provision may, within 30 days of such action, file a complaint with OSHA. The Secretary is authorized to investigate the matter and to bring action in the U.S. District Court for appropriate relief. The Secretary must notify the complainant of his action on the complaint within 90 days of its receipt.[58/]

A number of court cases have discussed that provision of the Act. See, for example, Marshall v. Whirlpool Corporation,[59/] and the Supreme Court decision that affirmed the result reached in that case, Whirlpool Corporation v. Marshall.[60/]

K. NATIONAL INSTITUTE FOR OCCUPATIONAL SAFETY AND HEALTH (NIOSH)

A continuing program of research in the field of occupational safety and health, including the psychological factors involved, and the development of innovative methods,

---

58/ Section 11(c), 29 U.S.C. §660(c).

59/ 593 F.2d 715 (6th Cir. 1979).

60/ 445 U.S. 1 (1980).

techniques and approaches for dealing with occupational safety and health problems is the responsibility of NIOSH, an organization created by the Act as part of the Department of Health and Human Services.

NIOSH can conduct workplace inspections but it <u>cannot</u> issue citations or propose monetary penalties. It is authorized to:

1. Conduct such research and experimental programs as are necessary for the development of criteria for new and improved occupational safety and health standards and, on the basis of such research and experimentation, recommend new or improved OSHA standards to the Secretary of Labor.

2. To establish programs for medical examinations and tests as may be necessary to determine the incidence of occupational illness and the susceptibility of employees to such illnesses.

3. To conduct such special research, experiments and demonstrations as are necessary to explore new problems, including those created by new technology in occupational safety and health, which may require ameliorative action beyond that which is otherwise provided in the operating provisions of the Act.

4. To conduct research into the motivational and behavioral factors relating to the field of occupational safety and health.

A part of this program is the publication annually of a list of all known toxic substances and the concentrations at which toxicity is known to occur, as well as industry-wide studies on chronic or low-level exposure to a broad variety of industrial materials, processes, and stresses on the potential for illness, disease or loss of functional capacity in aging adults.

NIOSH may also require employers to measure, record and make reports on the exposure of employees to potentially toxic substances or harmful physical agents that might endanger their safety or health.

Upon the written request of any employer or authorized representative of employees, NIOSH is authorized to conduct on-site investigations in order to make determinations on whether any substance normally found in the place of employment has potentially toxic effects. That process, which has been used many times, is known as a "health hazard evaluation." The determinations made by NIOSH as the result of such an evaluation are printed in a report which is then submitted to both the employer and the affected employees as soon as possible. NIOSH has also made it a practice to submit such reports to OSHA. Resulting OSHA inspections and citations sometimes follow.

Information obtained by the Departments of Labor and HHS under the research provisions of the law is to be disseminated to employers and employees and organizations thereof.[61/]

L. OTHER PROVISIONS OF THE OSH ACT

When compared to other laws with the same general purpose, the OSH Act is relatively short. It is only 30 pages long.[62/] Its major provisions have been covered above but there are a number of others that are worth mentioning.

61/ Sections 20 and 22, 29 U.S.C. §§669 and 671.

62/ The 1990 amendments to the Clean Air Act, on the other hand, cover 380 pages.

(1) Training and Employee Education

The Act provides that the Secretary of HHS in consultation with the Secretary of Labor and other Federal agencies shall conduct -- either directly or through grants or contracts:

(1) Education programs to provide an adequate supply of qualified personnel to carry out the purposes of the Act, and

(2) Informational programs on the importance of and proper use of adequate safety and health equipment.

The Secretary of Labor, in consultation with the Secretary of HHS, is directed to:

(1) Provide for the establishment and supervision of programs for the education and training of employers and employees in the recognition, avoidance, and prevention of unsafe or unhealthful working conditions in employments covered by the Act, and

(2) Consult with and advise employers and employees, and organizations representing employers and employees, as to effective means of preventing occupational injuries and illnesses.

In addition, the Secretary of Labor is authorized to conduct, directly or by grants or contracts, short-term training of personnel engaged in work related to the Secretary's responsibilities under the Act.[63/]

(2) Statistical Programs

One of the Act's purposes is to obtain statistics that will "accurately describe the nature of the occupational safety and

63/ Section 21, 29 U.S.C. §670.

health problem."[64] In order to further that purpose, the Act provides that the Secretary of Labor, in consultation with the Secretary of HHS, shall develop and maintain an effective program of collection, compilation, and analysis of occupational safety and health statistics that will cover all employments whether or not subject to any other provisions of the Act.

The Secretary of Labor is also directed to compile accurate statistics on work injuries and illnesses including all disabling, serious, or significant injuries and illnesses, whether or not involving loss of time from work. Excluded from that requirement are injuries requiring only first aid treatment and which do not involve medical treatment, loss of consciousness, restriction of work or motion, or transfer to another job.

In order to carry out those responsibilities, the Act authorizes the Secretary of Labor to:

(1) Promote, encourage, or directly engage in programs of studies, information and communication concerning occupational safety and health statistics;

(2) Make grants to States or political subdivisions thereof in order to assist them in developing and administering programs dealing with occupational safety and health statistics; and

(3) Arrange, through grants or contracts, for the conduct of such research and investigations as give promise of furthering those objectives.[65]

64/ Section (2)(b)(12), 29 U.S.C. §651(b)(12).

65/ Section 24, 29 U.S.C. §673. The Federal share for each grant made pursuant to this authority can be as much as half of the State's total cost. Id.

(3) Annual Reports

The Act requires that both the Secretary of Labor and the Secretary of HHS shall prepare an annual report for submission to the President and Congress on the following matters:

(1) The progress toward achievement of the purpose of the Act.

(2) The needs and requirements in the field of occupational safety and health.

(3) Information regarding occupational safety and health standards, and criteria for such standards, developed during the preceding year.

(4) Evaluation of standards and criteria previously developed under the Act, defining areas of emphasis for new criteria and standards.

(5) Evaluation of the degree of observance of applicable occupational safety and health standards.

(6) A summary of inspection and enforcement activity undertaken.

(7) Analysis and evaluation of research activities for which results have been obtained under governmental or nongovernmental sponsorship.

(8) An analysis of major occupational diseases.

(9) Evaluation of available control and measurement technology for hazards for which standards or criteria have been developed during the preceding year.

(10) Description of cooperative efforts undertaken between Government agencies and other interested parties in the implementation of the Act during the preceding year.

(11) A progress report on the development of an adequate supply of trained manpower in the field of occupational safety and health, including estimates of future needs and the efforts being made by Government and others to meet those needs.

(12) List of all toxic substances in industrial usage for which labeling requirements, criteria, or standards have not yet been established.

(13) Such recommendations for additional legislation as are deemed necessary to protect the safety and health of the worker and improve the administration of the Act.[66/]

(4) Trade Secrets

All information reported to, or otherwise obtained by the Secretary or his representative in connection with any inspection or proceeding under the Act, which contains or might reveal a trade secret referred to 18 U.S.C. §1905, must be considered confidential, except that such information may be disclosed to other government officers or employees concerned with carrying out the Act or when relevant in any proceeding under the Act. In any such proceeding, the Secretary, the OSH Review Commission, or the court shall issue such orders as may be appropriate to protect the confidentiality of trade secrets.[67/]

(5) The Burden Upon Employers

The Act includes an interesting directive that a "minimum burden" shall be placed upon employers and indicates that small business should be treated somewhat differently than other businesses. It provides that any information obtained by the Secretary of Labor, the Secretary of HHS, or a State agency under

---

66/ Section 29, 29 U.S.C. §675.

67/ Section 15, 29 U.S.C. §665. Trade secret provisions also appear in some OSHA standards. See, for example, 29 C.F.R. §1910.1200(i) for the trade secret provisions of OSHA's hazard communication standard.

the Act shall be obtained with a minimum burden upon employers, especially those operating small businesses, and that: "Unnecessary duplication of efforts in obtaining information shall be reduced to the maximum extent feasible."[68/] So far as can be determined, little (if any) action to implement that provision of the law has been taken.

The administration and enforcement of the OSH Act has most assuredly been a burden upon employers during its first two decades and there does not seem to have been any commensurate benefit to employees. The next chapter of this book contains some additional discussion of those employer burdens.

68/ Section 8(d), 29 U.S.C. §657(d).

CHAPTER 2

OSHA COMPLIANCE AND THE CONSEQUENCES OF NONCOMPLIANCE

Virtually every employer in the country is obligated by law to observe thousands of occupational safety and health requirements, keep detailed injury/illness and other kinds of records, adopt various written programs, provide notifications, warnings, employee training programs, make sure employees are properly qualified, and do hundreds of other things in the interests of employee health and safety. OSHA's inspection results to date show that many of them are not doing it. Those that aren't are needlessly exposing themselves to potential trouble.

Until recently, people in the healthcare industries showed relatively little concern about OSHA. That all changed on March 6, 1992 when OSHA's new standard on Bloodborne Pathogens went into effect. Those industries are now on OSHA's target list. The purpose of this chapter is to acquaint them with OSHA and provide some guidance on what should be done.

There are many reasons for OSHA noncompliance. The principal or major reason, however, can be traced to a lack of savoir faire -- not knowing what to do. Its sad but true, nevertheless, that ignorance of the law is no excuse. One wit has facetiously commented that ignorance of the law is no excuse, and since OSHA will never tell you what the law is, your defenseless! There's some truth to that but there's some things you can do. They are covered later in this chapter.

The employers' obligations arise from the enactment of the Occupational Safety and Health Act of 1970 and the adoption since that time of innumerable OSHA standards, rules and regulations, as well as many state and local laws.

An employer who doesn't observe OSHA requirements could receive a citation and be fined. The size of those fines have been escalating dramatically. There have been recent reports of fines as high as four, five, six and seven million dollars arising out of a single OSHA inspection.

In 1990, Congress boosted the maximum OSHA penalty by a factor of seven. The maximum fine for a "nonserious" violation used to be $1,000. Now it is $7,000. For a single "willful" violation, the maximum was $10,000. Now its $70,000. When it made those changes, Congress said that it expected OSHA "to assess significantly higher penalties across-the-board." OSHA is fulfilling that expectation.

OSHA penalties can be high. But receiving a citation and penalty for OSHA noncompliance is a relatively minor misfortune when compared to the potential trouble that could evolve from an employer's failure to observe standard safety practices, precautions and warnings, as well as that frequently-stated, but often neglected, maxim: "Be prepared."

A. <u>OSHA PAPERWORK</u>

Potential sanctions and fines exist for <u>all</u> employers -- including those who never receive an OSHA inspection or citation. It arises from a number of sources, not the least of which is the very existence of the written documents required to be created and maintained by OSHA and by state and local hazard control laws. Those documents include MSDSs (material safety data sheets), hazard determinations, warning labels and notices, various written programs (such as a hazard communication program or an Injury and Illness Prevention Program), as well as other records and reports. On May 5, 1992, one more written program requirement went into effect: an Exposure Control Plan for blood and other potentially infectious materials.

All of them have one thing in common: They are in writing and, in the eyes of the law, they are documents. Few people need to be reminded of the power of documentary evidence. It has literally brought down emperors, kings, chiefs of state, financial wizards and business empires, not to mention those violent criminals who somehow managed to silence all eyewitnesses to their crimes but got caught by the ubiquitous IRS forms.

What may seem a document entirely innocent in its implications may in fact prove, in certain circumstances, to be dynamite. Former President Richard Nixon discovered that.

Some common questions being asked by employers are: Do I have all the written documents I'm supposed to have? Are they correct? Is there something there that could get me in trouble? Are there things I am supposed to be doing that I don't know about? Few employers are comfortable with their answers to those questions.

B. **STATE AND LOCAL ACTIVITIES**

The "enforcement" that strikes the most fear into the hearts of management officials is not coming from OSHA inspectors. Its coming from state and local prosecutors and grand juries. They aren't issuing OSHA citations. They're serving indictments for murder, manslaughter, reckless homicide and battery -- and a number of other crimes punishable by prison terms.

The involvement of local prosecutors in job-related deaths and injuries is expected to increase in the 1990s. Local district attorneys throughout the country are learning that it is politically popular to prosecute employers for employee exposure to job safety and health hazards.

In 1985, a politically ambitious county prosecutor obtained indictments against Chicago Magnet Wire Corporation and five of its corporate officials, charging each with multiple counts of aggravated battery and reckless conduct under the Illinois criminal code. The charges were based upon a union's complaints that the firm's use of toxic substances subjected employees to disease and disability. There was no evidence that the firm exceeded OSHA's permissible exposure limits for the substances. The fact that employees were being injured by the company's activities was a crime under Illinois law, according to the indictments' charges.

Although complex legal maneuvers delayed the trial for 5 or 6 years, the prosecutor got a lot of favorable publicity. He was elected Mayor of Chicago while the case was pending. That fact did not escape the attention of other politically ambitious prosecutors in other parts of the country. Despite the fact that the Chicago Magnet Wire case ended in acquittal in April 1991, local prosecutors remain convinced that there is "political hay to be made" in prosecuting employers and individual managers for job safety and health infractions.

In California, the state OSHA program includes a specific mandate to provide information to district attorneys in those cases that may warrant criminal prosecution. Other states are adopting similar provisions. Wisconsin law requires hospitals to notify the state medical examiner of each worker death. The medical examiner routinely provides such notices to the local district attorney. Milwaukee District Attorney E. Michael McCann told an AFL-CIO conference in December 1990 that he follows up on those notices and that: "We are able to arrive often within one hour to videotape the accident scene."

In January 1991, McCann obtained a guilty verdict on two counts of reckless homicide following a methane gas explosion on a Milwaukee water pollution abatement project. There have been similar cases in Michigan, Texas, New York and other states. During the first 6 months of 1991, OSHA referred 10 cases to the Department of Justice for possible criminal prosecution. That was the highest 6-month total in history,.

During the last decade, there were approximately 200 criminal prosecutions in California for safety-related crimes. Los Angeles County District Attorney, Ira Reiner, has been particularly aggressive in filing charges. His office has filed 35 OSHA-related criminal cases in recent years. Four people have served jail terms for involuntary manslaughter and 30 misdemeanors have been prosecuted. In July 1991, the Los Angeles D.A.'s office obtained a guilty plea to 32 criminal charges from a metal fabrication company based on employee exposure to airborne lead. The plea agreement included a $200,000 contribution by the company to a lead education and enforcement program which the DA's office hopes to use to catch more companies and obtain similar settlements in order to keep the program funded.

Reiner, who would like to be elected to statewide political office, utilizes "roll-out" teams to respond to reports of serious on-the-job injury or death. The team includes a CAL/OSHA inspector, an investigator from the District Attorney's office and sometimes a Deputy District Attorney. Long before legal counsel for the employer is even aware that an accident occurred, the team is often at the site -- conducting on-the-scene interviews, taking written and tape recorded statements from employees, supervisory personnel and other potential witnesses.

OSHA adopted a similar -- but much more comprehensive -- procedure in July 1991 when it promulgated a 49-page directive that sets forth its program for responding to what it describes as "Significant Events of Potentially Catastrophic Consequences."

In January 1991, California adopted a new Corporate Criminal Liability Act that requires employers to provide prompt notification of certain workplace hazards to both CAL/OSHA and affected employees. Corporate managers who fail to do so can receive a 3-year jail sentence and a $25,000 fine. A corporation can get a one million dollar fine for such an offense. Many expect that other states will adopt similar provisions.

There are at least a half dozen bills pending in Congress to add new criminal penalties against employers in an effort to strengthen OSHA enforcement. They have strong supporters. Organized labor is pushing for enactment and some of those bills are even supported by Bush Administration officials.

C. RECRIMINATIONS AGAINST EMPLOYERS

Jail terms for employers who are indifferent to job safety is a notion that is popular in Chicago, L.A., New York, and many other places throughout the country. It might even play in Peoria. People get upset when there is a chemical release, or stories about an employee who got AIDS from an occupational exposure, or reports of killed and disabled workers. They want someone to be punished. Elected prosecutors know that those people are likely voters.

Criminal penalties against corporate managers has been the practice in Europe for many years. After the 1985 Soviet nuclear explosion in Chernobyl, for example, several of its managers were sent to prison. Their crime? Permitting employees to work who were not qualified for their job assignments.

That charge is not unknown in this country. It seems that whenever an employee is killed or seriously injured on the job, someone will allege that his employer was at fault because the employee had not been properly trained, was being overworked, or forced to do a job for which he was not qualified.

Defending against such charges is not an easy task. Persons who have done so never cease to be amazed by the testimony of friends, relatives and co-workers. It always seems as though the deceased continually complained to them about his lack of skill, ability or training, but knew that he couldn't mention that to his boss if he wanted to continue working. And, of course, he had to keep working to support the poor, unfortunate little ones, etc., etc., and so forth.

An example of that phenomena was contained in a September 5, 1991 Washington Post report of a fire at a North Carolina chicken processing plant in which 25 employees died and 55 others were injured. The newspaper reported that employees of the Hamlet, North Carolina Imperial Food Products plant could not escape the fire because the doors were locked. It then quotes one employee who survived the fire as follows: *"No one complained to management about the hazard posed by locked doors. They were afraid that, if they did, they would get fired."*

Multiple manslaughter charges have resulted from similar cases in the past, including the 1911 Triangle Shirtwaist Company in New York and the 1941 Coconut Grove fire in Boston. A similar fate could be in store for the unfortunate managers of the Imperial Food Products plant.

D. <u>AFTER-THE-FACT CHARGES</u>

After-the-fact charges aren't confined to locked fire exits or to recklessly employing unqualified employees. Failure to observe MSDS (material safety data sheet) precautions as well as failure to include appropriate warnings on the MSDS and container labels are also popular.

There is currently a case where a permanently disabled employee is claiming that his condition results from his boss's failure to follow MSDS precautions. The MSDS for a product being used by the employee included a warning that the product should not be used near employees with pre-existing respiratory conditions <u>unless</u> those employees had first been given a respiratory function test. That test had not been given. Indeed, the boss hadn't noticed that statement on the MSDS and didn't know the employee had a respiratory condition. Too bad for him. The law imposes a duty to know those things.

A recently-published NIOSH survey faulted a food processor because the MSDS of a product it used didn't warn that it contained a substance that could aggravate pre-existing asthma conditions. There are many other cases based upon inadequate warnings.

In 1988, a D.C. jury awarded $3.5 million in damages to a construction worker who was exposed to an epoxy resin. The product's MSDS simply recommended that a "mask" be worn when using it. The plaintiff's lawyer, however, introduced a NIOSH report into evidence that recommended an "air-supplied respirator."

The foregoing is just a sample. New civil and criminal charges are being filed against employers every day. Most of them allege that the employer's wrong was his failure to observe warnings, or to follow proper safety procedures, or to fully protect employees from harm.

E. CAUGHT RED-HANDED

The employer who is supposed to have something in writing -- but doesn't have it -- is among the most vulnerable to attack. The failure to perform required OSHA paperwork is high on the list of the most-cited offenses.

Nearly all employers, for example, are required to have a written hazard communication program. Places that have power-operated machinery or equipment must have a written lockout/tagout program that sets forth their procedures for disabling machines during maintenance and servicing activities. Every California employer must have a written Injury and Illness Prevention Program. Other states are in the process of imposing similar requirements.

The newest such requirement went into effect on May 5, 1992. OSHA's Bloodborne Pathogens Standard requires that, if it is reasonably anticipated that employees will have contact with human blood, the place where those employees work must have a written Exposure Control Plan. It must list each job with "occupational exposures" and explains the means and methods their employer has adopted in order to satisfy the OSHA requirements. That means that each individual hospital, funeral home, doctor's office or other place where there is "occupational exposure" must have **its own** written plan. The HIV guidelines recommended by the Centers for Disease Control will not satisfy that OSHA requirement.

Several employers have received multi-million dollar penalties because they had too many occupational injury and disease cases, or because their OSHA paperwork was improper. Other employers have managed to avoid similar penalties simply by showing OSHA that it had a written program in effect.

Here is a list of a few other things that have to be in writing (although not all of them apply to all employers):

- Respiratory Protection Program
- Emergency Response Plan
- Housekeeping Program
- Chemical Hygiene Plan
- Hearing Conservation Program
- Fire Prevention Plan
- Accident Prevention Program

Of course, a large number of OSHA recordkeeping requirements also exist.

One problem for employers is that there is no list of all the things that have to be in writing. When an OSHA official was asked for such a list, he replied that OSHA itself didn't have one either. Since that time we have meticulously compiled one by painstaking research of the thousands of detailed OSHA standards. That list contains more than five hundred items.[69]

F. WORDS TO THE WISE

Many employer have periodic audits conducted of their OSHA compliance status. Based upon the most frequently observed areas that need attention, a few suggestions are offered below. They are additional to those mentioned above.

1. Notice Requirements

All work places must display an OSHA-supplied poster advising employees of their rights under the Act. There are also a number of standards requiring that employees be notified of other things, such as their right of access to medical records, the provisions of various OSHA standards, test results, and monitoring or measuring activities that their employer conducts for the presence of OSHA-regulated substances. A systematic method for observing those notification requirements will not only satisfy the OSHA requirements but will help employers defend against claims that employees were not properly warned or informed.

For example, adopt this rather simple 5-step system:

69/ In late 1991, that list of OSHA requirements was published in book form together with an alphabetical index and an explanation. It is available for sale to the public under the title: **The OSHA 500**. It has since proved to be one of the fastest selling OSHA books ever to be published.

(1). Have a sticker prepared (approximately 1 and 3/4 inches square) as follows:

Various OSHA regulations provide that copies of certain standards and regulations as well as notice of employee right of access to their medical and exposure records be provided to employees. The place where they are available is:

The person to contact is:

(2) Provide copies to each company workplace.

(3) Advise the person in charge at each workplace to obtain a copy of the book (or books) that contain all applicable OSHA standards and keep it in a place where it is available to employees who want to exercise their right to see copies of OSHA standards. [NOTE: Those books may already be in their possession. OSHA inspectors normally give them out during their inspections. If they don't have a copy, they can obtain one from any local OSHA office.]

(4) Instruct each company workplace to write two things on the sticker: 1. The place where the OSHA books will be kept. 2. The name of the person to be contacted for access to employee medical and exposure records.

(5) After those two things have been written on the sticker, the sticker should be put on each OSHA Job Safety and Health Protection poster (OSHA 2203) that is posted at their facility. Place the sticker on the blank spaces to the right of the list of cities and states in the "More Information" section of the poster. It will fit there. [NOTE: Such a poster is <u>required</u> to be posted. If none is, one should be obtained immediately from the local OSHA office.]

2. <u>Work Rules</u>

The OSH Act provides that <u>employees</u> must observe applicable OSHA requirements -- but it does not impose penalties for noncompliance. Employers, however, can and should penalize employees for OSHA noncompliance. To do so, they should adopt appropriate work rules. They should also have rules that require employees to immediately report to their supervisor: (1) any and all work hazards they perceive, and (2) any and all work injuries and illnesses they know of. Rules like that will help employers with their OSHA compliance when employees observe them, and in their defenses to claims and charges when employees do not observe them.

3. Recordkeeping

All employers must keep injury/illness records. Some of them must be recorded on OSHA forms. In order to know when an employee sustains an injury or illness and whether it needs to be recorded, there should be a systematic program in place so that none will be overlooked or ignored and the OSHA rules will be strictly observed. An example of such a program appears in Appendix B of this book.

There's also several hundred other OSHA recordkeeping and reporting requirements. Each depends upon the type of work done, the materials and equipment used and various other factors. Those regulations aren't easy to find. It was only by pouring over thousands of them that we were able to prepare a checklist that can be used to determine when and to whom they apply. It is included in our earlier book: The OSHA 500.

4. Employee Qualifications

There are numerous OSHA standards requiring that employees be trained in particular subjects or be "qualified" for particular jobs. A checklist to locate and identify them is a part of **THE OSHA 500**. But even in the absence of a specific standard that requires training, employers are frequently charged with "inadequate training" whenever a fatality or catastrophe occurs. Jail sentences for employers have been the result in some cases.

Certification that each employee is qualified for his job and documentation of each training session is essential to avoid such consequences and to satisfy legal requirements.

Another frequently-recommended protective measure is to include language on your company's application-for-employment Form stating that the applicant knows how to do the job he seeks as well as any hazards that may be associated with it. Once the applicant signs a Form containing that kind of statement, the employer will have at least some protection that could be used in the future in the event a claim is made against the employer based upon that person's alleged lack of qualifications.

5. Fatalities and Catastrophes

There are OSHA notification requirements whenever an employee is killed on the job or multiple hospitalizations result from a particular incident. More importantly, however, is the potential that the employer's response to the tragedy will add to the disaster or create adverse public relations. Employers should adopt contingency planning for such emergencies and conduct periodic practice sessions, just as should be the case for potential fires, hurricanes and similar disasters. Indeed, there are a number of OSHA standards that require it.

Some notable responses to catastrophes can serve as examples, i.e., Union Carbide's to the Bhopal tragedy, Johnson & Johnson to the Tylenol scare, Exxon's to the Alaskan oil spill and Perrier to the discovery of contaminated bottles of spring water. All of those cases involved corporate giants. For the smaller company's reaction to tragedy, keep tuned to your local television news programs and read the daily newspapers. You'll frequently see good examples of what <u>not</u> to do.

6. OSHA Inspections

Quite often the adverse consequences of an OSHA inspection are the result of the activities and statements of the <u>employers</u> representative during the inspection. That phenomenon can be avoided by adopting a plan in advance that specifies who will act for the employer during the inspection and making sure that he is properly educated and trained in his rights and responsibilities.

In one case nearly a hundred willful citations issued because the company safety director, when asked by the OSHA inspector why he had seen so many conditions that were OSHA violations, replied: "I'm only one person. I can't do it all." The OSHA inspector interpreted that statement as an admission by the company that the conditions he had in mind were, in fact, OSHA violations and that the company had consciously failed to devote sufficient resources to the identification and correction of the same. Perhaps that kind of trouble could have been avoided if the company representative had replied to the OSHA question by asking the inspector for a detailed itemization of his claim, or had simply responded: "That's your opinion."

7. OSHA Citations

No matter how harmless they may seem, every OSHA citation always carries the potential for future harm that is often not foreseen. An uncontested OSHA citation is frequently regarded as the moral equivalent of a guilty plea by courts, the media, persons with the responsibility for awarding contracts, competitors, and anyone who may want to tarnish the company's image. That problem is lessened when the citation is contested, then settled with an agreement containing "exculpatory" language that denies any employer wrongdoing, rather than simply letting the citation go uncontested.

Employers should adopt a firm company policy setting forth how OSHA citations will be handled rather than reacting on an *ad hoc* basis whenever a citation is received.

CHAPTER 3

OSHA'S INVOLVEMENT WITH BLOODBORNE PATHOGENS

Hepatitis B virus (HBV) has long been recognized as a pathogen capable of causing serious illness and death. Because the virus is transmitted through blood and certain body fluids, persons who handle them as part of their jobs have been at increased risk of contracting HBV. To the extent that those persons were "employees," they were potentially exposed to a workplace hazard. OSHA therefore turned its attention to the matter in the 1980's.

The human immunodeficiency virus (HIV) that causes AIDS, has only been recognized in the last decade. Because the transmission of HIV is considerably less efficient than HBV, the risk of HIV infection to employees who must handle blood and other potentially infectious materials is less than for HBV infection (i.e., HIV results in fewer seroconversions following exposure incidents.) The consequences of HIV infection are grave, however, because HIV causes the fatal disease AIDS.

A. <u>OSHA'S INITIAL ENFORCEMENT METHODS</u>

Although OSHA had no standard that was designed specifically to reduce occupational exposure to those viruses prior to 1992, the Agency had a number of regulations that applied in a general sort of way. For example, 29 C.F.R. §1910.132 requires employers to provide suitable personal protective equipment whenever a workplace hazard exists, and 29 C.F.R. §1910.145(f) requires that employers use accident prevention tags to warn of biological hazards.

In addition, section 5(a)(1), the General Duty Clause of the OSH Act, requires that each employer:

> "furnish to each of his employees employment and a place of employment which are free from recognized hazards that are causing or are likely to cause death or serious physical harm to his employees."

That provision of law does not define the term "recognized hazard" but over the past 20 years, it has been used by OSHA in an attempt to force employers to adopt a wide variety of changes in the interests of improved occupational safety and health.

During the 1980's and early 1990's, OSHA made use of those enforcement devices, as well as some of its other standards, in an effort to control employee exposure to bloodborne pathogens.

It issued a number of citations against various employers under the general duty clause. Those citations were accompanied by proposed measures that OSHA wanted those employers to implement in an effort to abate the cited hazard. They included Hepatitis B vaccination, employee training on the hazards of bloodborne pathogens as well as "universal precautions," and follow-up procedures after an HIV or HBV exposure incident.

OSHA also cited employers under 29 C.F.R. §1910.132(a), the standard requiring personal protective equipment, in an effort to force employers to require the use of gloves and gowns, among other things, where there was employee exposure to blood and potentially infectious body fluids.

The Agency used a number of other existing standards to force employers to make additional changes. Among them was 29 C.F.R. §1910.22(a), an OSHA standard requiring that places of employment be kept clean and in a sanitary condition. OSHA cited employers under that standard in order to get them to require the use of certain disinfectants following initial clean up of blood or potentially infectious body fluids.

OSHA also cited some employers under 29 C.F.R. §1910.141(a)(4)(i) and (ii), a waste disposal standard which requires the use of non-leaking waste containers and the removal of wastes in such a manner as to avoid creating a menace to health. OSHA used that standard in an effort to prohibit the recapping of needles by hand and to require the use of puncture-resistant sharp containers, among other things.

The OSHA standard that specifies accident prevention signs and tags, 29 C.F.R. §1910.145(f) was also utilized as an enforcement tool. It requires tags or other means of identification where employees are exposed to potentially hazardous conditions. OSHA maintained that it mandates "biological hazard tags" or "red bagging" for bags or other receptacles containing articles contaminated with potentially infectious material.

All of those standards had been on OSHA's books since the early 1970's. They had been used many times as the basis for citations against factory owners and similar employers in order to force them to require employee use of personal protective equipment like safety glasses or safety shoes, to get employers to clean up debris from the machine shop floor, or to place warning tags on defective machines or stairways that were out of service. OSHA had never previously used any of those standards against a biological hazard.

The standards mentioned above are broadly worded. Unlike many OSHA standards that must be observed irrespective of the existence of an actual hazard, they apply only where a "hazard" actually exists. When a cited employer contests such a citation, OSHA must prove that a reasonable person familiar with the circumstances surrounding the allegedly hazardous condition, including any facts unique to the cited employer's particular industry, would recognize a hazard warranting the use of the measures OSHA sought to impose. **General Dynamics Corp. v. OSHRC, 599 F.2d 453, 464 (1st Cir. 1979).** Proof of that kind is often difficult to obtain.

B. THE RULEMAKING PROCESS

In 1983, OSHA issued a set of voluntary guidelines designed to reduce the risk of occupational exposure to hepatitis B virus. The voluntary guidelines, which were sent to employers in the healthcare industry, included a description of the disease, recommended work practices, and recommendations for use of immune globulins and the hepatitis B vaccine. Employers were free to comply or ignore those guidelines because compliance was purely voluntary on the employer's part.

On September 19, 1986, an employee Union, the American Federation of State, County and Municipal Employees (AFSCME), petitioned OSHA to take action to reduce the risk of employees from exposure to certain infectious agents.

They requested that OSHA issue an emergency temporary standard (ETS) under section 6(c) of the Act. The Union also requested that OSHA immediately initiate a section 6(b) rulemaking that would require employers to provide the HBV vaccine at no cost to employees who were at risk of HBV infection and to require employers to follow work practice guidelines such as those issued by the Center for Disease Control.

AFSCME also requested that OSHA amend its Hazard Communication Standard in order to require a training program for employees exposed to infectious diseases, counseling for pregnant employees about diseases that have reproductive effects, and posting of isolation precautions in patient areas and in contaminated areas.

On September 22, 1986, three other Unions, the Service Employees International Union, the National Union of Hospital and Healthcare Employees, and RWDSU Local 1199-Drug, Hospital and Healthcare Union, petitioned the Agency to promulgate a standard to protect healthcare employees from the hazard posed by occupational exposure to hepatitis B virus. They requested that, as a minimum, the standard should contain all of the provisions in OSHA's 1983 guidelines with special emphasis on making workers aware of the benefits of vaccination. In addition, they asked

OSHA to immediately issue a directive stating that employers must provide the HBV vaccine free of charge to all high risk healthcare workers.

OSHA Assistant Secretary John A. Pendergrass, after determining that the available data did not meet the criteria for an ETS as set forth in section 6(c) of the Act, denied all of the Union petitions by letter dated October 22, 1987. OSHA further determined that the appropriate course of action was to publish an Advance Notice of Proposed Rulemaking (ANPR) in order to initiate rulemaking under section 6(b) of the Act and to collect further information.

Concurrently with the collection of such information, the Agency committed itself to enforcing its existing regulations and section 5(a)(1) of the Act (as described above) in healthcare settings. It also began an educational program in cooperation with the Department of Health and Human Services.

On October 30, 1987, the Departments of Labor and Health and Human Services published a Joint Advisory Notice entitled, "Protection Against Occupational Exposure to Hepatitis B Virus (HBV) and Human Immunodeficiency Virus (HIV)." 52 Federal Register 4181. In the cover letter to employers, Secretaries Brock and Bowen urged the "* * * widest possible adherence to the appropriate precautions as exemplified by the CDC guidelines and the Joint Advisory Notice." The letter, notice and a pamphlet written by OSHA for healthcare workers were mailed to more than

600,000 employers, employee representatives and trade and professional associations.

C. A STANDARD IS PROPOSED

On November 27, 1987, OSHA published in the Federal Register a notice announcing the initiation of the rulemaking process for a standard to regulate employee exposure to bloodborne pathogens. 52 Federal Register 45438. The Agency requested information relevant to reducing occupational exposure to HBV and HIV under section 6(b) of the OSH Act. The public was asked to comment on the scope of such a standard, the modes of controlling exposure, personal protective equipment, vaccination programs, management of exposure incidents, medical surveillance, training and education, generic standards, advances in hazard control, effectiveness of alternative approaches and the environmental effects. A sixty day period was set for comments, and those comments were to be submitted to the OSHA docket by January 26, 1988.

OSHA received an overwhelming response to the proposal. Over 350 comments were filed by interested parties including employers, unions, health professionals, trade representatives, professional associations, manufacturers, and federal, state and local government agencies, among others. The comments were both for and against the proposal. OSHA analyzed all of the comments and used the data that was submitted to prepare a proposed OSHA standard.

The proposed standard was published in the Federal Register on May 30, 1989. 54 Federal Register 23042. The agency allowed three months for the public to submit written comments on the new proposal. That time period was later expanded to a full year. OSHA also conducted public hearings in late 1989 and early 1990 in Washington, San Francisco, Chicago, Miami and New York City. Approximately 400 people participated in those hearings. More than three thousand written comments were also submitted on the proposed standard.

D. **THE STANDARD IS ADOPTED**

OSHA officials studied the comments, conducted additional studies through its own staff as well as outside consultants, and developed its final standard late in 1991. It was published in the Federal Register on December 6, 1991 and went into effect on March 6, 1992.

The publication of the standard was accompanied by a 174-page explanation of OSHA's reasoning. It included OSHA's analysis of why the standard was needed and its projected impact upon those employers and employees who must observe its requirements.

OSHA estimated that compliance with the standard would cost employers about $825 million, about 40% of which ($334 million) would be for the purchase of personal protective equipment such as gloves.

The agency further broke that cost estimate down by industry grouping and particular requirements of the standard. The results are shown in the following tabulation: Table E.S.-2, "Summary of Compliance Costs."

TABLE E.S.-2.—SUMMARY OF COMPLIANCE COSTS—GRAND TOTALS

Industry	Engineering/ work practices *	Vaccination/ post exposure follow-up	Exposure control plan	Housekeeping	PPE	Training	Recordkeeping	Totals
Offices of Physicians	$8,985,997	$14,770,091	$6,834,476	$7,169,447	$68,611,270	$34,826,736	$2,792,511	$143,990,528
Offices of Dentists	5,443,408	21,565,118	5,592,113	5,843,189	30,422,020	14,117,012	4,446,195	87,429,055
Nursing Homes	935,790	8,195,138	1,021,579	21,037,030	31,917,227	5,706,284	966,616	69,779,663
Medical and Dental Labs	1,242,593	792,155	288,191	3,534,680	4,559,722	1,780,771	123,287	12,321,399
Residential Care	81,202	1,128,257	157,935	539,902	905,583	1,401,437	146,073	4,360,390
Hospitals	68,781,203	26,745,404	1,614,393	56,414,706	138,972,636	25,773,835	3,611,521	321,913,697
Home Health	388,799	3,087,128	419,229	226,335	2,360,670	4,689,431	277,980	11,449,573
Hospices	9,978	196,713	42,398	22,183	104,442	196,925	20,948	593,588
Hemodialysis	271,929	241,668	50,930	42,356	1,320,193	302,054	77,834	2,306,964
Drug Rehabilitation	10,409	71,810	48,455	9,760	68,171	196,751	8,157	413,514
Government Clinics	790,219	1,451,787	709,439	516,634	3,893,062	3,047,676	248,574	10,657,912
Blood Plasma/ Tissue Center	1,193,678	299,277	47,543	90,434	1,949,073	331,395	100,778	4,012,178
Personnel Services	11,926	1,614,021	112,876	0	8,068,434	3,365,324	176,165	13,348,746
Funeral Services	50,208	1,503,382	1,110,339	579,318	2,423,908	2,981,395	194,599	8,843,149
Health Units in Industry	3,719,231	15,039,779	13,226,259	4,803,681	5,265,303	23,276,485	2,573,588	67,904,326
Research Labs	150,111	1,290,801	94,631	102,497	2,751,244	1,860,446	73,178	6,322,908
Linen Services	924	394,322	81,410	33,150	1,088,947	268,162	75,024	1,941,939
Medical Equipment Repair	213,104	276,128	70,078	618,485	4,543,377	253,503	38,581	6,013,256
Law Enforcement	195,410	2,237,428	322,123	52,344	3,311,809	4,189,199	545,597	10,853,911
Fire and Rescue	216,141	2,708,562	206,716	73,862	9,573,585	1,909,586	325,485	15,013,937
Correctional Facilities	93,437	1,322,391	114,886	153,978	1,581,115	1,438,951	211,278	4,916,036
Lifesaving	503	157,623	6,513	73,300	84,375	139,333	12,225	473,872
Schools	146,412	1,398,763	411,674	0	1,717,971	2,103,241	196,277	5,974,338
Waste Removal	0	222,960	3,256	0	1,383,200	249,083	10,681	1,869,180
Totals	97,523,109	106,710,705	32,587,446	101,937,270	326,877,357	134,405,018	17,253,151	812,703,560

* Includes $5,416,815 in recurring costs for leakproof containers.
Source: Occupational Safety and Health Administration, Office of Regulatory Analysis.

E. <u>COVERAGE OF THE STANDARD</u>

The bloodborne pathogens standard is <u>not</u> limited to employers in the healthcare industry. It applies to any employer with employees whose jobs subject them to occupational exposure to blood or other potentially infectious materials. As if to emphasize that point, OSHA has issued citations to factories and similar businesses that have an on-premises health unit because the company had not provided the plant nurse with hepatitis B vaccination.

OSHA maintains that the standard's coverage extends to any kind of business enterprise that has a first aid station, health unit, plant nurse or something similar, or has employees who regularly experience skin cuts.

In the process of developing the new standard, OSHA identified twenty-four employer groupings for special study and analysis because OSHA thinks that virtually every employer in those categories has employees with occupational exposure to blood. It has listed those 24 by standard industrial classification (SIC) number [70/] as follows:

Offices of Physicians (including ambulatory medical services)(SIC 801 and 803)

Dental Offices (SIC 802)

Hospitals (SIC 806)

70/ For statistical and census purposes, the federal government divides the kinds of places where people work into "industrial classifications." For example: automobile manufacturing, the hotel industry, etc. Each is assigned an "SIC" number. There are about 12,000 such categories. The full list and a definition of what kind of work is part of each category is published by the Office of Management and Budget (an agency of the White House) in a book of approximately 100 pages entitled: "Standard Industrial Classification Manual." That book is revised periodically to reflect the changing industrial composition of the economy.

Medical and Dental Laboratories (SIC 807)

Nursing Homes (SIC 805)

Residential Care Facilities (SIC 836)

Dialysis Centers (SIC 8092)

Drug Treatment Centers (SIC 8093)

Home Health Care (SIC 8082)

Hospices (various SIC codes)

Government Outpatient Facilities (SIC 9431)

Blood Collections and Processing (SIC 8099)

Health Clinics in Industrial Facilities (various SIC codes)

Personnel Services (SIC 7363)

Funeral Homes and Crematories (SIC 7261)

Research Laboratories (SICs 8221, 8731, 8733, and 283)

Linen Services (SIC 721)

Medical and Dental Equipment Repair (SICs 382, 384, and 7699)

Law Enforcement (SIC 9221)

Fire and Rescue (SIC 9224)

Correctional Institutions (SIC 9223)

Schools (SIC 9411)

Lifesaving (SIC 9229)

Regulated Waste Removal (SIC 4953)

F. <u>COSTS AND BENEFITS</u>

For each of those categories (except linen services, schools, lifesaving and regulated waste removal), OSHA made an estimate of the number of establishments that exist and the number of employees that OSHA believed to be "at risk" of occupational exposure to blood. The results of that estimate appears below in Table VII-1. "Industry Profile of Affected Establishments and Population at Risk [1990]."

TABLE VII-1.—INDUSTRY PROFILE OF AFFECTED ESTABLISHMENTS AND POPULATION AT RISK [1990]

SIC code	Type of establishment	Number of affected estab.	Population at risk
801; 803	Offices of Physicians.	122,104	640,681
802	Offices of Dentists.	100,174	316,237
805	Nursing Homes	12,200	485,303
806	Hospitals	6,197	2,386,165
807	Medical and Dental Labs.	4,425	62,854
808	Home Health	6,437	212,246
*	Hospices	651	10,856
8092	Hemodialysis	782	12,688
8093	Drug Rehabilitation.	744	6,722
9431	Government Clinics.	10,893	56,345
8099	Blood/Plasma/ Tissue Centers.	730	18,788
836	Residential Care.	2,425	49,102
7362	Personnel Services.	1,348	163,477
726	Funeral Services.	19,890	57,013
*	Health Units in Industry.	202,540	178,732
8221; 873; 283.	Research Labs	1,453	89,151
7218	Linen Services	1,250	50,000
384	Medical Equipment Repair.	1,076	6,185
9221	Law Enforcement**.	4,946	341,546
9224	Fire and Rescue***.	3,174	252,048
9223	Correctional Facilities.	1,895	120,224
9229	Lifesaving	100	5,000
9411	Schools	6,321	41,362
4953; 9511.	Waste Removal		13,300
Totals		511,755	5,576,026

* Includes various SIC codes.
** Includes state and local departments only.
*** Includes fire departments and private ambulance services.
Source: Occupational Safety and Health Administration, Office of Regulatory Analysis.

It should be noted that, in OSHA lexicon, the word **"establishment"** is a word of art. Those who don't realize that fact often confuse it with terms such as **business** or **industry**. It is important, therefore, to recognize and understand that difference. For OSHA purposes the word **"establishment"** means "a single physical location where business is conducted or where services or industrial operations are performed." 29 C.F.R. §1904.12(g)(1), emphasis added. For example, all hotels in the country would be classified as the "hotel industry" (SIC 7011). An individual hotel within that industry, such as the Palmer House or the Logan Airport Holiday Inn, is known as an **"establishment"** within the hotel industry.

In addition to its estimates of the cost of compliance and the number of employees "at risk", OSHA made an estimate of the "benefits" that it expects will result from the bloodborne pathogens standard. A summarization of that estimate follows:

> "In sum, compliance with the standard is estimated to prevent between 8,383 and 8,858 occupational and non-occupational cases of HBV infection per year, of which 2,096 to 2,214 would have resulted in acute symptoms, and 187 to 197 in death. Moreover, OSHA estimates that the standard will prevent between 253 and 578 employees from becoming HBV carriers, thereby halting the spread of this disease to others.
>
> In addition to hepatitis B, the provisions of the standard will greatly reduce workers' risk of contracting non-A, non-B hepatitis, acquired immune deficiency syndrome (AIDS), and other bloodborne diseases. The Centers for Disease Control (CDC) reports 24 documented cases of human immunodeficiency virus (HIV) infection in the U.S. which have resulted from occupational exposure. Four of these workers have developed AIDS."

56 Federal Register 64039, Dec. 6, 1991.

The foregoing is a rather brief recitation of how OSHA got involved with bloodborne pathogens and what the agency did about it for the 10-year period that preceeded its adoption of 29 C.F.R. §1910.1030, the standard regulating occupational exposure to bloodborne pathogens. The next three chapters of this book explain that standard in detail.

G. **INTERPRETING THE STANDARD**

Chapter 6 of this book includes the guideline and enforcement procedures for the standard that OSHA adopted on March 6, 1992 and issued to its inspectors. If you are inspected, those guidelines will be used by the OSHA inspector to conduct the inspection, determine your compliance or noncompliance and, if the latter, issue citations.

You can use those guidelines to help you come into compliance with the standard. You can also use the recommendations issued by OSHA in 1988 (Appendix C) and the OSHA materials that appear as Appendix D and Appendix E of this book.

In the event of a conflict, however, between any of them and the Chapter 6 Guidelines, you should rely upon the latter.

CHAPTER 4

THE BLOODBORNE PATHOGENS STANDARD

Although it took 174 pages in the Federal Register for OSHA to explain and justify the bloodborne pathogens standard, the text of the standard itself covers fewer than 8 pages. It appears as Appendix A of this book.

A. THE PRINCIPLE PROVISIONS

At the time it announced the standard's adoption, OSHA issued a news release that summarized its principal provisions in the following five paragraphs:

> *The standard requires employers to establish a written exposure control plan, identifying workers with occupational exposure to blood and other potentially infectious material and specifying means to protect and train them.*
>
> *It calls for engineering controls such as puncture-resistant containers for used needles; work practices such as handwashing to reduce contamination; and appropriate personal protective equipment such as gowns and gloves.*
>
> *There are also requirements for housekeeping covering decontamination procedures, a written schedule for cleaning, discarding of contaminated needles and other sharps and handling of regulated wastes. The standard specifies procedures for handling contaminated laundry. It addresses the increased risks faced by workers in HIV and HBV research laboratories and production facilities and includes additional protective measures such as specialized training for employees, limited access to contaminated areas and materials and special procedures and facilities for decontamination.*
>
> *The standard requires employers to offer, at their expense, voluntary hepatitis B vaccinations to all employees with occupational exposure and prescribes appropriate medical follow-up and counseling after an exposure incident. Employees who choose not to accept the vaccine must sign a declination form, but may be vaccinated at a later date if they change their minds.*
>
> *OSHA is also requiring appropriate labels and training to alert workers to the risks posed by bloodborne pathogens. Facilities that use concentrated viruses are also required*

to have warning signs. Employers must keep records of exposure incidents, post exposure follow-up, hepatitis B vaccinations and employee training.

B. OSHA SUMMARY OF THE STANDARD

At the same time that it announced its adoption of the standard, OSHA issued a "Fact Sheet" containing a more expansive summary of the standard's principal requirements. It is re-printed below:

PURPOSE: Limits occupational exposure to blood and other potentially infectious materials since any exposure could result in transmission of bloodborne pathogens which could lead to disease or death.

SCOPE: Covers all employees who could be "reasonably anticipated" as the result of performing their job duties to face contact with blood and other potentially infectious materials. OSHA has not attempted to list all occupations where exposures could occur. "Good Samaritan" acts such as assisting a co-worker with a nosebleed would not be considered occupational exposure.

Infectious materials include semen, vaginal secretions, cerebrospinal fluid, synovial fluid, pleural fluid, pericardial fluid, peritoneal fluid, amniotic fluid, saliva in dental procedures, any body fluid visibly contaminated with blood and all body fluids in situations where it is difficult or impossible to differentiate between body fluids. They also include any unfixed tissue or organ other than intact skin from a human (living or dead) and human immunodeficiency virus (HIV)-containing cell or tissue cultures, organ cultures and HIV or hepatitis B (HBV)-containing culture medium or other solutions as well as blood, organ or other tissue from experimental animals infected with HIV or HBV.

EXPOSURE CONTROL PLAN: Requires employers to identify, in writing, tasks and procedures as well as job classifications where occupational exposure to blood occurs--without regard to personal protective clothing and equipment. It must also set forth the schedule for implementing other provisions of the standard and specify the procedure for evaluating circumstances surrounding exposure incidents. The plan must be accessible to employees and available to OSHA. Employers must review and update it at least annually--more often if necessary to accommodate workplace changes.

METHODS OF COMPLIANCE: Mandates universal precautions, (treating body fluids/materials as if infectious) emphasizing engineering and work practice controls. The standard stresses handwashing and requires employers to provide facilities and ensure that employees use them following exposure to blood, It sets forth procedures to minimize needlesticks, minimize splashing and spraying of blood, ensure appropriate packaging of specimens and regulated wastes and decontaminate equipment or label it as contaminated before shipping to servicing facilities.

Employers must provide, at no cost, and require employees to use, appropriate personal protective equipment such as gloves, gowns, masks, mouthpieces and resuscitation bags and must clean, repair and replace these when necessary. Gloves are not necessarily required for routine phlebotomies in volunteer blood donation centers but must be made available to employees who want them.

The standard requires a written schedule for cleaning, identifying the method of decontamination to be used, in addition to cleaning following contact with blood or other potentially infectious materials. It specifies methods for disposing of contaminated sharps and sets forth standards for containers for these items and other regulated waste. Further, the standard includes provisions for handling contaminated laundry to minimize exposures.

HIV AND HBV RESEARCH LABORATORIES AND PRODUCTION FACILITIES: Calls for these facilities to follow standard microbiological practices and specifies additional practices intended to minimize exposures of employees working with concentrated viruses and reduce the risk of accidental exposure for other employees at the facility. These facilities must include required containment equipment and an autoclave for decontamination of regulated waste and must be constructed to limit risks and enable easy clean up. Additional training and experience requirements apply to workers in these facilities.

HEPATITIS B VACCINATION: Requires vaccinations to be made available to all employees who have occupational exposure to blood within 10 working days of assignment, at no cost, at a reasonable time and place, under the supervision of a licensed physician/licensed healthcare professional and according to the latest recommendations of the U.S. Public Health Service (USPHS). Prescreening may not be required as a condition of receiving the vaccine. Employees must sign a declination form if they choose not to be vaccinated, but may later opt to receive the vaccine at no cost to the employee. Should booster doses later be recommended by the USPHS, employees must be offered them.

POST-EXPOSURE EVALUATION AND FOLLOW-UP: Specifies procedures to be made available to all employees who have had an exposure incident plus any laboratory tests must be conducted by an accredited laboratory at no cost to the employee. Follow-up must include a confidential medical evaluation documenting the circumstances of exposure, identifying and testing the source individual if feasible, testing the exposed employee's blood if he/she consents, post-exposure prophylaxis, counseling and evaluation of reported illnesses. Healthcare professionals must be provided specified information to facilitate the evaluation and their written opinion on the need for hepatitis B vaccination following the exposure. Information such as the employee's ability to receive the hepatitis B vaccine must be supplied to the employer. All diagnoses must remain confidential.

HAZARD COMMUNICATION: Requires warning labels including the orange or orange-red biohazard symbol affixed to containers of regulated waste, refrigerators and freezers and other containers which are used to store or transport blood or other potentially infectious materials. Red bags or containers may be used instead of labeling. When a facility uses universal precautions in its handling of all specimens, labeling is not required within the facility. Likewise, when all laundry is handled with universal precautions, the laundry need not be labeled. Blood which has been tested and found free of HIV or HBV and released for clinical use, and regulated waste which has been decontaminated, need not be labeled. Signs must be used to identify restricted areas in HIV and HBV research laboratories and production facilities.

INFORMATION AND TRAINING: Mandates training within 90 days of effective date, initially upon assignment and annually--employees who have received appropriate training within the past year need only receive additional training in items not previously covered. Training must include making accessible a copy of the regulatory text of the standard and explanation of its contents, general discussion on bloodborne diseases and their transmission, exposure control plan, engineering and work practice controls, personal protective equipment, hepatitis B vaccine, response to emergencies involving blood, how to handle exposure incidents, the post-exposure evaluation and follow-up program, signs/labels/color-coding. There must be opportunity for questions and answers, and the trainer must be knowledgeable in the subject matter. Laboratory and production facility workers must receive additional specialized initial training.

RECORDKEEPING: Calls for medical records to be kept for each employee with occupational exposure for the duration of employment plus 30 years, must be confidential and must include name and social security number; hepatitis B vaccination status (including dates); results of any examinations, medical testing and follow-up procedures; a copy of the healthcare professional's written opinion; and a copy of information provided to the healthcare professional. Training records must be maintained for three years and must include dates, contents of the training program or a summary, trainer's name and qualifications, names and job titles of all person attending the sessions. Medical records must be made available to the subject employee, anyone with written consent of the employee, OSHA and NIOSH-- they are not available to the employer. Disposal of records must be in accord with OSHA's standard covering access to records.

C. UNDERSTANDING THE STANDARD

The legal designation of OSHA's bloodborne pathogens standard is 29 C.F.R. §1910.1030. That means that it will be published in Title 29 of the Code of Federal Regulations (C.F.R.) at section 1910.1030.

When a employer is cited for violating the standard, he will receive a citation that will allege that the employer violated "29 C.F.R. §1910.1030." The citation will probably identify a particular subsection of the standard allegedly violated. Each such subsection will be explained below.

The OSHA standard consists of 9 principle subsections: (a) through (i). They are designated §1910.1030(a), §1910.1030(b), etc. Each of them has a title to indicate the subsection's subject matter. For example, §1910.1030(b), **Definitions**. One reason many people have difficulty reading the text of an OSHA standard is that each subsection often has its own subsections. And those subsections, in turn, have their own subsections.

The subsections are designated as follows:

First Group: alphabetically by small letters as described in the preceeding paragraph.

Second Group: numerically. For example (1), (2), (3), etc.

Third Group: numerically by Roman numerals. For example (i), (ii), (iii), etc.

Fourth Group: alphabetically by capital letters. For example (A), (B), (C), etc.

For subsequent groups (if necessary), the order listed above is repeated but the letter or number is underlined. For example (a), (1), etc.

To illustrate that phenomena, the provision of the standard prohibiting a person from using his hands to pick up broken glassware that may be contaminated is designated:

§1910.1030(d)(4)(ii)(D)

Hopefully, that numerical system will become clearer when the standard is explained section by section and subsection by subsection. That explanation will now commence.

D. THE STANDARD IN ITS ENTIRETY--SECTION BY SECTION

The discussion that follows is divided into 9 parts (a) through (i). Those parts coincide with the 9 main subsections of the standard.

(A)

(a) §1910.1030(a). **Scope and Application** (Federal Register Page 64175, column 1).[72] This section is the only one of the 9 that does not have any subsections. It simply states in legal language the facilities that are obligated to observe the standard's requirements: Every place where there is "occupational exposure to blood or other potentially infectious materials."

(B)

(b) §1910.1030(b). **Definitions** (Federal Register Page 64175, column 1). This section defines in alphabetical order 26 of the terms that are used in the standard. When reading the standard, you should consult those definitions. Do not assume that you know the meaning of ordinary terms like "blood" or "sterilize". You may well be correct in that assumption but beware: OSHA frequently will define a term differently than its ordinary meaning. And, for OSHA purposes, the terms that are

---

72/ The Federal Register page number is listed for each of the 9 subsections simply as a convenience for the reader who wants to read its actual text. The text of the standard that appears in Appendix A of this book is a reprint from the Federal Register. The Federal Register page number appears at the top of each Federal Register page.

defined have only the meaning stated in the definition. Words that are not defined, however, must be interpreted by their plain and ordinary meaning.

(C)

(c) §1910.1030(c). **Exposure Control** (Federal Register page 64175, column 3). That section of the standard requires that employers adopt their own written exposure control plan. It must state how they will observe the standard's requirements, ensure that a copy of their Plan is accessible to their employees, and requires that it include a list of those jobs at each employer's workplace that involve "occupational exposure." It is divided into two principal subsections: (1) The written Exposure Control Plan, and (2) The Exposure Determination. They will be explained in reverse order.

The Exposure Determination is little more than a written list of jobs that have "occupational exposure" (a term defined in subsection "(b)" of the standard). If you know what those jobs are, you simply need to write them down, If you aren't sure, you'll have to conduct some inquiries or make a survey before you write them down.

The list of jobs must be separated into the following three categories:

A. Those in which <u>all</u> employees in the job classification have occupational exposure (operating room cleaning persons, for example).

B. Those in which only <u>some</u> employees have occupational exposure (nurses, for example).

C. The particular tasks and procedures, or groups of closely related tasks and procedures, in which occupational exposure occurs and that are performed by employees in job classification "B" (assisting surgeon during surgery, for example).

The same subsection also provides that the "exposure determination" shall be made without regard to the use of personal protective equipment. Consequently, OSHA regards a person as "exposed" even though--because of the use of impervious clothing--his skin cannot come into contact with blood.

An EXPOSURE CONTROL PLAN must be adopted by each employer who has one or more employees with occupational exposure. It must be in writing and it must also:

1. Contain the "exposure determination" list discussed above.

2. State the means and methods the employer will use to implement each requirement of the standard and the time-schedule for doing so.

3. Include a procedure for evaluating the circumstances surrounding each "exposure incident."

4. Be made accessible to affected employees.

5. Be reviewed and updated at least once a year and whenever there are changes in the "occupational exposure" situation.

6. Be made available to OSHA and NIOSH representatives on request.

(D)

(d) §1910.1030(d). **Methods of Compliance** (Federal Register Page 64176, column 1). That section of the standard provides for various "controls" that must be adopted. It is the longest single section of the standard. It is divided into four principle subsections, as follows:

1. Universal precautions (see the OSHA definition of that term).
2. Engineering and work practice controls.
3. Personal protective equipment.
4. Housekeeping.

In the next chapter of this book each subsection of each of those 4 subject matters is treated individually.

(E)

(e) §1910.1030(e). **HIV and HBV Research Laboratories and Production Facilities** (Federal Register Page 64178, column 2). This section only applies to those 2 particular types of operation. It does not apply anywhere else and, to further define its limited application, the standard plainly states that this section does not apply to clinical or diagnostic laboratories engaged solely in the <u>analysis</u> of blood, tissue or organs.

This section provides that the 2 particular types of operation to which it applies must observe all provisions of the standard <u>plus</u> the following 28 requirements:

1. All regulated waste shall either be incinerated or decontaminated by a method such as autoclaving that is known to effectively destroy bloodborne pathogens.

2. Laboratory doors shall be kept closed when work involving HIV or HBV is in progress.

3. Contaminated materials that are to be decontaminated at a site away from the work area shall be placed in a durable, leakproof, labeled or color-coded container that is closed before being removed from the work area.

4. Access to the work area shall be limited to authorized persons.

5. Written policies and procedures shall be established whereby only persons who have been advised of the potential biohazard, who meet any specific entry requirements, and who comply with all entry and exit procedures shall be allowed to enter the work areas and animal rooms.

6. When other potentially infectious materials or infected animals are present in the work area or containment module, a hazard warning sign incorporating the universal biohazard symbol shall be posted on all access doors. The hazard warning sign shall comply with subsection (g) of the standard (discussed below).

7. All activities involving other potentially infectious materials shall be conducted in biological safety cabinets or other physical-containment devices within the containment module.

8. No work with these other potentially infectious materials shall be conducted on the open bench.

9. Laboratory coats, gowns, smocks, uniforms, or other appropriate protective clothing shall be used in the work area and animal rooms.

10. Protective clothing shall not be worn outside of the work area and shall be decontaminated before being laundered.

11. Special care shall be taken to avoid skin contact with other potentially infectious materials.

12. Gloves shall be worn when handling infected animals and when making hand contact with other potentially infectious materials is unavoidable.

13. Before disposal, all waste from work areas and from animal rooms shall either be incinerated or decontaminated by a method such as autoclaving that is known to effectively destroy bloodborne pathogens.

14. Vacuum lines shall be protected with liquid disinfectant traps and high efficiency particulate air (HEPA) filters or filters of equivalent or superior efficiency.

15. The vacuum lines must be checked routinely and maintained or replaced as necessary.

16. Hypodermic needles and syringes shall be used only for parenteral injection and aspiration of fluids from laboratory animals and diaphragm bottles.

17. Only needle-locking syringes or disposable syringe-needle units (i.e., the needle is integral to the syringe) shall be used for the injection or aspiration of other potentially infectious materials.

18. Extreme caution shall be used when handling needles and syringes.

19. After being used, a needle shall not be bent, sheared, replaced in the sheath or guard, or removed from the syringe.

20. The needle and syringe shall be promptly placed in a puncture-resistant container and autoclaved or decontaminated before reuse or disposal.

21. All spills shall be immediately contained and cleaned up by appropriate professional staff or others properly trained and equipped to work with potentially concentrated infectious materials.

22. A spill or accident that results in an exposure incident shall be immediately reported to the laboratory director or other responsible person.

23. A biosafety manual shall be prepared or adopted and periodically reviewed and updated at least annually or more often if necessary.

24. Personnel shall be advised of potential hazards, shall be required to read instructions on practices and procedures, and shall be required to follow them.

25. Certified biological safety cabinets (Class I, II or III) or other appropriate combinations of personal protection or physical containment devices, such as special protective clothing, respirators, centrifuge safety cups, sealed centrifuge rotors, and containment caging for animals, shall be used for all activities with other potentially infectious materials that pose a threat of exposure to droplets, splashes, spills or aerosols.

26. Biological safety cabinets shall be certified when installed, whenever they are moved, and at least annually.

27. Signs bearing the "biohazard" legend depicted at Federal Register page 64180 must be posted at the entrance to each of the work areas. The signs must include the following:

    (a). Name of the infectious agent
    (b). Special requirements for entering the area.
    (c). The name and telephone number of the laboratory director or other responsible person.

28. The signs must be fluorescent orange-red or predominantly so, with lettering or symbols in a contrasting color.

In addition to the above, the following requirements apply only to HIV and HBV **research laboratories.**

1. Each laboratory shall contain a facility for hand washing and an eye wash facility which is readily available within the work area.

2. An autoclave for decontamination of regulated waste shall be available.

HIV and HBV **production facilities** must also comply with the following 10 requirements:

1. The work areas shall be separated from areas that are open to unrestricted traffic flow within the building.

2. Passage through two sets of doors shall be the basic requirement for entry into the work area from access corridors or other contiguous areas.

3. Physical separation of the high-containment work area from access corridors or other areas or activities may also be provided by a double-doored clothes-change room (showers may be included), airlock, or other access facility that requires passing through two sets of doors before entering the work area.

4. The surfaces of doors, walls, floors and ceilings in the work area shall be water resistant so that they can be easily cleaned. Penetrations in these surfaces shall be sealed or capable of being sealed to facilitate decontamination.

5. Each work area shall contain a sink for washing hands and a readily available eye wash facility. The sink shall be foot, elbow, or automatically operated and shall be located near the exit door of the work area.

6. Access doors to the work area or containment module shall be self-closing.

7. An autoclave for decontamination of regulated waste shall be available within or as near as possible to the work area.

8. A ducted exhaust-air ventilation system shall be provided. It must create directional airflow that draws air into the work area through the entry area.

9. The exhaust air shall not be recirculated to any other area of the building, shall be discharged to the outside, and shall be dispersed away from occupied areas and air intakes.

10. The proper direction of the airflow shall be verified (i.e., into the work area).

Persons who work in HIV or HBV research laboratories or in HIB or HBV productions facilities must be provided with the same instruction and training as all other employees covered by the standard (<u>see</u> the discussion of section "(g)" below). There are, however, six <u>additional</u> requirements for such persons. OSHA calls them employee training requirements, but some of them would more properly be designated as work rules.

They are as follows:

1. The employer shall assure that employees demonstrate proficiency in standard microbiological practices and techniques and in the practices and operations specific to the facility before being allowed to work with HIV or HBV.

2. The employer shall assure that employees have prior experience in the handling of human pathogens or tissue cultures before working with HIV of HBV.

3. The employer shall provide a training program to employees who have no prior experience in handling human pathogens.

4. Initial work activities shall not include the handling of infectious agents.

5. A progression or work activities shall be assigned as techniques are learned and proficiency is developed.

6. The employer shall assure that employees participate in work activities involving infectious agents only after proficiency has been demonstrated.

(F)

(f) §1910.1030(f) **Hepatitis B vaccination, post-exposure evaluation and follow-up** (Federal Register Page 64179, column 2). That section of the standard requires employers to: (1) Have their employees (who have "occupational exposure") vaccinated or get them to sign a form declining to be vaccinated, and (2) Provide certain evaluation and follow-up procedures upon learning of an employee who has had an "exposure incident." But there are a lot of details that must be observed. Here they are:

1. All medical evaluations and procedures including the hepatitis B vaccine and vaccination series and post-exposure evaluation and follow-up, including prophylaxis, must be:

   (a) Made available at no cost to the employee;

   (b) Made available to the employee at a reasonable time and place;

   (c) Performed by or under the supervision of a licensed physician or by or under the supervision of another licensed healthcare professional; and

(d) Provided according to recommendations of the U.S. Public Health Service current at the time the evaluations and procedures take place, except as specified below.

2. All laboratory tests must be conducted by an accredited laboratory at no cost to the employee.

3. Hepatitis B vaccination must be made available <u>after</u> the employee has received the required training (<u>See</u> paragraph "(g)" which is discussed below) and within 10 working days of initial assignment for those employees who have "occupational exposure" **unless** the employee has previously received the complete hepatitis B vaccination series, antibody testing has revealed that the employee is immune, **or** the vaccine is contraindicated for medical reasons.

4. The employer may <u>not</u> make participation in a prescreening program a prerequisite for receiving hepatitis B vaccination.

5. If the employee initially declines hepatitis B vaccination but at a later date (while still covered under the standard) decides to accept the vaccination, the employer shall make available hepatitis B vaccination at that time.

6. The employer shall assure that those employees who decline to accept hepatitis B vaccination sign the statement that appears as appendix A of the OSHA standard.

7. If a routine booster dose(s) of hepatitis B vaccine is recommended by the U.S. Public Health Service at a future date, such booster dose(s) shall be made available under the same rules stated above.

8. Whenever a report of an "exposure incident" is received, the employer shall make immediately available to the exposed employee a confidential medical evaluation and follow-up that at least include the following 11 elements:

(a) Documentation of the route(s) of exposure, and the circumstances under which the exposure incident occurred;

(b) Identification and documentation of the source individual, unless the employer can establish that identification is infeasible or prohibited by state or local law;

(c) The source individual's blood shall be tested as soon as feasible and after consent is obtained, in order to determine HBV and HIV infectivity. If consent is not obtained, the employer shall establish that legally required consent cannot be obtained.

(d) When the source individual's consent is not required by law, the source individual's blood, if available, shall be tested and the results documented.

(e) When the source individual is already known to be infected with HBV or HIV, testing for the source individual's known HBV or HIV status need not be repeated.

(f) Results of the source individual's testing shall be made available to the exposed employee, and the employee shall be informed of applicable laws and regulations concerning disclosure of the identity and infectious status of the source individual.

(g) The exposed employee's blood shall be collected and tested as soon as feasible after consent is obtained.

(h) If the employee consents to baseline blood collection, but does not give consent at that time for HIV serologic testing, the sample shall be preserved for at least 90 days. If, within 90 days of the exposure incident, the employee elects to have the baseline sample tested, such testing shall be done as soon as feasible.

(i) Post-exposure prophylaxis, when medically indicated, as recommended by the U.S. Public Health Service;

(j) Counseling

(k) Evaluation of reported illnesses.

9. A copy of the OSHA bloodborne pathogens standard must be provided to the healthcare professional responsible for the employee's Hepatitis B vaccination.

10. The employer shall ensure that the healthcare professional evaluating an employee after an "exposure incident" is provided the following information;

    (a) A copy of the OSHA standard;

    (b) A description of the exposed employee's duties as they relate to the exposure incident;

    (c) Documentation of the route(s) of exposure and circumstances under which exposure occurred;

    (d) Results of the source individual's blood testing, if available; and

    (e) All medical records relevant to the appropriate treatment of the employee including vaccination status which are the employer's responsibility to maitain. <u>See</u> the discussion of recordkeeping, section "(h)" below.

11. The employer must obtain and provide the employee with a copy of the evaluating healthcare professional's written opinion within 15 days of the completion of the evaluation.

12. The healthcare professional's written opinion for Hepatitis B vaccination shall be limited to whether Hepatitis B vaccination is indicated for an employee, and if the employee has received such vaccination.

13. The healthcare professional's written opinion for post-exposure evaluation and follow-up

shall be limited to the following information;

(a) That the employee has been informed of the results of the evaluation; and

(b) That the employee has been told about any medical conditions resulting from exposure to blood or other potentially infectious materials which require further evaluation or treatment.

14. All other findings of diagnoses shall remain confidential and shall not be included in the written report.

15. Medical records that are required must be maintained in accordance with section "(h)" of the standard. See the discussion of that section at pages 87-88, *infra*.

(G)

(g) §1910.1030(g). **Communication of hazards to employees** (Federal Register Page 64180, column 2). This section of the OSHA standard requires certain signs and labels as well as employee instructions and training. Those requirements are listed below:

1. Warning labels shall be affixed to containers of regulated waste, refrigerators and freezers containing blood or other potentially infectious material; and other containers used to store, transport or ship blood or other potentially infectious materials, except as provided below.

2. The labels must include the biohazard symbol. (It is shown in the copy of the standard that appears in Appendix A) at Federal Register page 64180).

3. The labels shall be fluorescent orange or orange-red or predominantly so, with lettering or symbols in a contrasting color.

4. The labels must be affixed as close as feasible to the container by string, wire, adhesive, or other method that prevents their loss or unintentional removal.

5. Red bags or red containers may be substituted for labels.

6. Containers of blood, blood components, or blood products that are labeled as to their contents and have been released for transfusion or other clinical use are **exempted** from the labeling requirements.

7. Individual containers or blood or other potentially infectious materials that are placed in a labeled container during storage, transport, shipment or disposal are **exempted** from the labeling requirement.

8. Labels required for contaminated equipment must meet the above requirements and they must also state which portions of the equipment remain contaminated.

9. Regulated waste that has been decontaminated need not be labeled or color-coded.

10. Employees with "occupational exposure" must be provided with instruction and training as follows:

    (a) The training must be given during working hours and be provided at no cost to the employees.

    (b) It must be given by June 4, 1992. For those employee's initially assigned <u>after</u> that date to tasks where "occupational exposure" may take place, the training must be given <u>at the time</u> of such initial exposure.

(c) The training must be repeated annually.

(d) For those employees who received training on bloodborne pathogens in the year preceding June 4, 1992, only training with respect to the provisions of the OSHA standard which were not included in such training need be provided.

(e) Annual training for all employees shall be provided within one year of their previous training.

(f) Additional training must be provided when changes such as modification of tasks or procedures or institution of new tasks or procedures affect the employees's "occupational exposure."

(g) The additional training may be limited to addressing the new exposures created.

11. The Training Program must meet the following requirements:

(a) Material appropriate in content and vocabulary to educational level, literacy, and language of employees shall be used.

(b) It must include an accessible copy of the text of the OSHA standard and an explanation of its contents;

(c) A general explanation of the epidemiology and symptoms of bloodborne diseases;

(d) An explanation of the modes of transmission of bloodborne pathogens;

(e) An explanation of the employer's exposure control plan and the means by which the employee can obtain a copy of the written plan;

(f) An explanation of the appropriate methods for recognizing tasks and other activities that may involve exposure to blood and other potentially infectious materials;

(g) An explanation of the use and limitations of methods that will prevent or reduce exposure including appropriate engineering controls, work practices, and personal protective equipment;

(h) Information on the types, proper use, location, removal, handling, decontamination and disposal of personal protective equipment;

(i) An explanation of the basis for selection of personal protective equipment;

(j) Information on the hepatitis B vaccine, including information on its efficacy, safety, method of administration, the benefits of being vaccinated, and that the vaccine and vaccination will be offered free of charge;

(k) Information on the appropriate actions to take and the persons to contact in an emergency involving blood or other potentially infectious materials;

(l) An explanation of the procedure to follow if an "exposure incident" occurs, including the method of reporting the incident and the medical follow-up that will be made available;

(m) Information on the post-exposure evaluation and follow-up that the employer is required to provide for the employee following an exposure incident;

(n) An explanation of the signs and labels and/or color-coding required by the OSHA standard. (see paragraphs 1 through 9 of this section "(g)", above).

(o) An opportunity for interactive questions and answers with the person conducting the training session.

12. The person conducting the training must be knowledgeable in the subject matter covered by the elements contained in the training program as it relates to the workplace that the training will address.

(H)

(h) §1910.1030(h). **Recordkeeping** (Federal Register Page 64181, column 2). The OSHA standard includes several recordkeeping requirements. They are stated below.

1. An accurate record must be maintained of each employee with an "occupational exposure." It must include:

   (a) The name and social security number of the employee;

   (b) A copy of the employee's hepatitis B vaccination status including the dates of all the hepatitis B vaccinations and any medical records relative to the employee's ability to receive vaccination as required by paragraph "(f)" of the OSHA standard.

   (c) A copy of all results of examinations, medical testing, and follow-up procedures required by the OSHA standard's paragraph "(f)".

   (d) The employer's copy of the healthcare professional's written opinion required by paragraph (f)(5) of the standard, and

   (e) A copy of the information that the employer provided to the healthcare professional as required by the standard's paragraph "(f)". <u>See</u> no. 10, under the discussion of §1910.1030(f), above

2. The records must be maintained in accordance with the provisions of the OSHA standard codified at 29 C.F.R. §1910.20, "Access to Employee Exposure and Medical Records."

3. Employee <u>medical</u> records must be kept confidential and must not be disclosed or reported without the employee's express written consent to any person within or outside the workplace except as required by law.

4. The records must be retained for at least the duration of employment plus 30 years.

5. Records of the employee's training must be kept for 3 years from the date on which the training occurred. They must contain the following information.

   (a) The dates of the training sessions;

   (b) The contents or a summary of the training sessions;

   (c) The names and qualifications of persons conducting the training; and

   (d) The names and job title of all persons attending the training sessions.

6. All such records must be made available upon request to OSHA and NIOSH representatives for examination and copying.

7. The employee <u>training</u> records must also be made available for examination and copying to employees and to designated representatives of employees, such as their local union representative.

8. An employee's <u>medical</u> records shall be provided to the employee (or anyone having the written consent of the employee) for examination and copying upon request.

9. Upon cessation of business, the records must be transferred to the successor employer. If there is no successor employer, NIOSH must be notified at least 3 months prior to the scheduled disposal of the records. The records must be transmitted to NIOSH if, during that 3-month period, NIOSH so orders.

(I)

(i) §1910.1030(i) **Dates** (Federal Register Page 64181, column 3). This section of the OSHA standard simply covers the various calendar dates upon which particular sections of the OSHA standard go into effect. Those dates differ for different provisions of the standard. They are as follows:

1. March 6, 1992 is the "effective date" of the standard but that doesn't mean that an employer must be in compliance with all its provisions on that date because some provisions do not go into effect until later, as stated below.

2. The written Exposure Control Plan must be completed on or before May 5, 1992.

3. The Employee Training and Information requirements go into effect on June 4, 1992.

4. Recordkeeping requirements also go into effect on June 4, 1992.

5. The following provisions of the standards go into effect on July 6, 1992:

    (a) Engineering and work practice controls

    (b) Personal protective equipment

    (c) Housekeeping

    (d) Hepatitis B vaccination and Post-Exposure Evaluation and Follow-up.

    (e) Labels and Signs

    (f) The requirements that apply only to HIV and HBV Research Laboratories and Production Facilities.

CHAPTER 5

PREPARATION OF A COMPLIANCE PLAN

The first step an employer must take in order to achieve compliance with OSHA's bloodborne pathogens standard is to analyze or survey the place of employment in order to find out all the tasks, procedures, occupations and job classifications where occupational exposure to blood occurs. The determination of whether or not there is "exposure" must be made without regard to the use of personal protective clothing and equipment.

A. MAKE A LIST

Once that kind of survey has been completed, or that kind of information has been acquired in some other manner, it must be committed to writing. You must create a written list of each position or job in your establishment, all or some of the duties of which involve potential exposure to human blood or other potentially infectious materials. If only some of the job's duties involve such exposure, those particular functions (or tasks) must be listed.

For example: Operating room attendant, dental assistant, obstetrician, the handling of contaminated sharps, transporting injured persons, etc.

The list must then be divided into the following three groups (of course, if everything on your list falls into a single category, you wouldn't have three groups):

1. Those job classifications in which **all** employees have occupational exposure. For example, operating room attendants.

2. Those job classifications in which only **some** employees have occupational exposure. For example, nurses.

3. In the latter case (no.2) the **specific tasks and procedures**, or groups of closely related tasks and procedures, which are associated with occupational exposure.

The following hypothetical example is offered in order to illustrate the "specific tasks and procedures" requirement. One of your job classifications in category no. 2 (only <u>some</u> employees in the classification have occupational exposure) is "laundry worker." In category no. 3, you would then list **the particular tasks** and procedures performed by your laundry workers **that are associated with occupational exposure.** One of them might be: unloading blood-contaminated laundry received from hospitals.

The particular tasks and procedures that are grouped must be related; i.e., they must share a common activity such as "vascular access procedures," "handling of contaminated sharps," or "handling of deceased persons," etc.

B. PREPARE A WRITTEN PLAN

After you have made up your list, it must be incorporated into your own written exposure control plan. The purpose of that requirement is to have at each "establishment" a written document that states the means and methods that will be used there in order to comply with each and every applicable provision of the OSHA bloodborne pathogens standard.

The Exposure Control Plan will have to be a fairly lengthy document. Many employers will probably choose to purchase a generic Plan because the elements of the Plan will not vary much from one place of employment to another, and because it may well be less expensive to purchase a ready-made Plan than to prepare one from scratch. If that course of action is chosen, the list of jobs in your establishment that involve "occupational exposure" could simply be attached to the ready-made Plan.

C. THE ELEMENTS OF AN EXPOSURE CONTROL PLAN

The Plan must cover all requirements of the OSHA standard and state what will be done at your establishment to implement those requirements.

What follows is an 11-part Plan that is offered as an example to show how that could be done.

1. *Exposure Determination*

As the result of an "exposure determination" which the OSHA standard required us to perform, we have identified and listed in Attachment A of this Exposure Control Plan those jobs, tasks and procedures in which occupational exposure may occur while at work here. Each has been marked with an A, B or C to conform with the categories defined on Attachment A. Persons holding those jobs will receive the training, protective equipment, vaccination, and other matters required by the OSHA standard. Employees will be individually advised by supervision of the requirements that apply to them.

For OSHA purposes, the "exposure determination" is made without regard to the use of personal protective equipment. In making our determination, we have followed OSHA's guidance. We will continue to review our exposure determinations and make additions to and deletions from the Attachment A list as appropriate.

2. *Control Methods*

Our Exposure Control Plan includes a combination of engineering and work practice controls as well as Personal Protective Equipment requirements.

We will observe the basic rule of exposure control known as "universal precautions." It requires that, in those situations where differentiation between body fluid types is difficult or impossible, ***all*** *body fluids shall be considered potentially infectious materials.*

An ***engineering control*** *is the use of available technology and devices to isolate or remove hazards from the worker. The engineering controls for this OSHA standard include but are not limited to: puncture-resistant sharps containers, splash guards, mechanical pipetting, and self-sheathing needles. The engineering controls that we have put in place will be examined and maintained or replaced on a regular basis to ensure their effectiveness.*

Our ***Personal Protective Equipment*** *controls are covered in Section 4 of this Plan.*

Work practice controls *are alterations in the manner in which a task is performed in an effort to reduce the likelihood of a worker's exposure to blood or other potentially infectious materials (OPIM). Those that we have adopted include the following:*

1. *There are handwashing facilities readily accessible to all affected employees and all workstations. Hands and other affected skin areas shall be washed with soap and water after removing gloves or other personal protective equipment and as soon as possible after contact with body fluids or OPIM.*
2. *All personal protective equipment (PPE) should be removed immediately, or as soon as possible upon leaving the work area, and placed in an appropriately*

designated area or container for storage, washing, decontamination, or disposal.

3. *Used needles and other sharps shall not be sheared, bent, broken, recapped, or resheathed by hand.*
4. *All procedures involving blood or other potentially infectious material shall be performed in such a manner as to minimize splashing and spraying.*

3. Work Rules

1. *Eating, drinking, smoking, applying cosmetics or lip balm, and handling contact lenses is prohibited in work areas where there is a reasonable likelihood of occupational exposure.*
2. *Food and drink shall not be kept in refrigerators, freezers, shelves, cabinets or on countertops or benchtops where blood or other potentially infectious materials are present.*
3. *All procedures involving blood or other potentially infectious materials shall be performed in such a manner as to minimize splashing, spraying, spattering, and generation of droplets of those substances.*
4. *Mouth pipetting/suctioning of blood or other potentially infectious material is prohibited.*
5. *Specimens of blood or other potentially infectious materials shall be placed in a container which prevents*

leakage during collection, handling, processing, storage, transport, or shipping.

(a) The container for storage transport, or shipping shall be labeled or color-coded in accordance with the rules for labels and signs set forth in Part 7 of this Plan (entitled: "Communication of Hazards"). It also must be closed prior to being stored, transported or shipped. When Universal Precautions are used in the handling of all specimens, the labeling/color-coding of specimens is not necessary ***provided*** *containers are recognizable as containing specimens. This exemption only applies while such specimens/containers remain within the facility. Labeling or color-coding in accordance with Part 7 is required when such specimens/containers leave the facility.*

(b) If outside contamination of the primary container occurs, the primary container shall be placed within a second container which prevents leakage during handling, processing, storage, transport, or shipping and will be labeled or color-coded according to the requirements listed in Part 7.

(c) If the specimen could puncture the primary container, the primary container shall be placed within a secondary container which is puncture-resistant in addition to the above characteristics.

6. *Equipment which may become contaminated with blood or other potentially infectious material shall be examined prior to servicing or shipping and shall be decontaminated as necessary, unless it can be demonstrated that decontamination of such equipment or portions of such equipment is not feasible.*

(a) A readily observable label as provided in Part 7 shall be attached to the equipment. It shall also state which portions remain contaminated.

(b) The above information shall be conveyed to all affected employees, the servicing representative, and/or the manufacturer, as appropriate, prior to

handling, servicing, or shipping so that appropriate precautions will be taken.

7. *During use, containers for contaminated sharps shall be:*

   (a) *Easily accessible to personnel and located as close as is feasible to the immediate area where sharps are used or can be reasonably anticipated to be found (e.g. laundries);*

   (b) *Maintained upright throughout use; and*

   (c) *Replaced routinely and not be allowed to overfill.*

8. *When moving containers of contaminated sharps from the area of use, the containers shall be:*

   (a) *Closed immediately prior to removal or replacement to prevent spillage or protrusion of contents during handling, storage, transport, or shipping;*

   (b) *Placed in a secondary container if leakage is possible. The second container shall be:*

      (A) *Closable;*

      (B) *Constructed to contain all contents and prevent leakage during handling, storage, transport, or shipping; and*

      (C) *Labeled or color-coded according to Part 7 of this Plan.*

9. *Reusable containers shall not be opened, emptied, or cleaned manually or in any other manner which would expose employees to the risk of percutaneous injury.*

4. Personal Protective Equipment Rules

Our Exposure Control Plan requires the use of Personal Protective Equipment (PPE). PPE is specialized clothing or equipment used by workers to protect themselves from direct exposure to blood or other potentially infectious materials. For purposes of this OSHA standard, PPE includes but is not limited to, gloves; gowns, laboratory coats, fluid-resistant aprons, head and foot coverings; face shields or masks and eye protection; mouthpieces, resuscitation bags, pocket masks, or other ventilation devices. They are to be used, as appropriate, when there is a potential for exposure to blood or other potentially infectious materials. Many such items are accompanied by written warnings, directions or instructions. They must be observed.

Those items of PPE that are appropriate for the work done here are available in a variety of sizes and readily accessible. Those persons required to wear them will be individually advised by their supervisor. We will provide for the cleaning, laundering or disposal of PPE and will repair or replace it as needed in order to maintain its effectiveness.

Surgical or examination gloves, however, must be replaced when visibly soiled. They shall not be washed or disinfected for re-use. Utility gloves, on the other hand, may be cleaned and disinfected for re-use if they show no signs of deterioration.

Any employee who has not been advised by his/her supervisor that any such item of PPE is required --but who desires to wear it while at work-- may obtain the desired PPE by requesting it from their immediate supervisor.

The following personal protective equipment rules apply:

1. *We will provide at no cost to any employee, appropriate personal protective equipment such as, but not limited to, gloves, gowns, laboratory coats, face shields or masks and eye protection, and mouthpieces, resuscitation bags, pocket masks, or other ventilation devices.*
2. *Personal protective equipment will be considered "appropriate" only if it does not permit blood or other potentially infectious material to pass through, to, or reach the employees work clothes, street clothes, undergarments, skin, eyes, mouth, or other mucous membranes under normal conditions of use --and for the duration of time that the protective equipment will be used.*
3. *Each supervisor must ensure that his/her subordinate employees use appropriate personal protective equipment* **unless** *that employee temporarily and briefly declines to use personal protective equipment when, under rare and extraordinary circumstances, it is the employee's professional judgement that in the specific instance at issue, its use would have prevented the delivery of health care or public safety services or would have posed an increased hazard to the safety of the worker*

or co-worker. When the employee makes this judgement, the circumstances shall be investigated and documented in order to determine whether changes can be instituted to prevent such occurrences in the future.

4. *Appropriate personal protective equipment in the appropriate sizes will be readily accessible at the worksite or will be issued to the employee who is to use it.*
5. *We will clean, launder, and dispose of all required personal protective equipment and shall repair or replace it as needed in order to maintain its effectiveness--at no cost to any employee.*
6. *If a garment(s) is penetrated by blood or other potentially infectious materials, the garment(s) shall be removed immediately or as soon as feasible.*
7. *All personal protective equipment shall be removed prior to leaving the work area.*
8. *When personal protective equipment is removed, it shall be placed in an appropriately designated area or container for storage, washing decontamination or disposal.*
9. *Masks in combination with eye protection devices, such as goggles or glasses with solid side shields, or chin-length face shields, shall be worn whenever splashes, spray, spatter, or droplets of blood or other potentially infectious materials may be generated and*

eye, nose, or mouth contamination can be reasonably anticipated.

10. *Appropriate protective clothing such as, but not limited to, gowns, aprons, lab coats, clinic jackets, or similar outer garments shall be worn in occupational exposure situations. The type and characteristics will depend upon the task and the degree of exposure anticipated.*

11. *Surgical caps or hoods and/or shoe covers or boots shall be worn in instances when gross contamination can reasonably be anticipated (e.g., autopsies, orthopaedic surgery).*

12. *Disposable gloves will be worn for procedures where body fluids are handled. The use of gloves is particularly important in the following circumstances:*

    (a) *If the worker has cuts, abraded skin, chapped hands, dermatitis, or similar conditions, and whenever it can be reasonably anticipated that the employee may have hand contact with blood, other potentially infectious materials, mucous membranes, and non-intact skin; and when handling or touching contaminated items or surfaces.*

    (b) *During instrumental examination of the oropharynx, gastrointestinal tract, and genitourinary tract*

    (c) *When examining abraded or non-intact skin or patients with active bleeding*

    (d) *During all cleaning and decontaminating procedures where body fluids and/or blood are present*

13. *Gloves must be of appropriate material, usually intact latex or intact vinyl, of appropriate quality for the*

procedures performed, and of appropriate size for the person who is to wear them.

14. *Surgical or examination gloves may not be reused.*
15. *General purpose utility gloves may be decontaminated and reused.*
16. *General purpose gloves shall not be used if they are peeling, cracked, or discolored or if they have punctures, tears, or other evidence of deterioration.*
17. *Hypoallergenic gloves, glove liners, powderless gloves, or other similar alternatives will be made readily accessible to those employees who are allergic to the gloves normally provided.*
18. *Gowns, including surgical gowns, shall be made of, or lined with, impervious material and shall protect all areas of exposed skin. In addition to the customary situations, gowns shall be worn whenever large amounts of blood are likely to be encountered.*
19. *The use of masks and protective eyewear or face shields is required when contamination of mucous membranes (eyes, mouth, or nose) with body fluids may occur through splashes or aerosolization of these fluids (such as surgical or dental procedures).*

5. *Vaccination, Post Evaluation and Follow-up*

1. *The hepatitis B vaccine and vaccination series and post-exposure evaluation and follow-up, including prophylaxis, is available at an accredited laboratory at no cost, to all employees whose jobs involve the risk of direct contact with blood or other potentially infectious material. EACH SUCH EMPLOYEE SHALL BE VACCINATED unless he/she specifically declines. An employee who declines the vaccination must execute a form similar to that attached to this Plan as Attachment B. Vaccination will also be available under the same circumstances to all employees who have had an exposure incident.*
2. *Vaccinations shall be given at a reasonable time and place under the supervision of a LICENSED HEALTH CARE PROFESSIONAL according to standard medical practices and the then current recommendations of the U.S. Public Health Service. The healthcare professional responsible for the employee's Hepatitis B vaccination shall be provided with a copy of the OSHA Bloodborne Pathogens standard.*
3. *For those employees who have occupational exposure, the vaccinations shall be given after the employee has received the training and education that is provided for in Part 10 of this Exposure Control Plan but within*

10 days of initial assignment unless (a) the employee has previously received the complete hepatitis B vaccination series, (b) antibody testing has revealed that the employee is immune, or (c) the vaccine is contraindicated for medical reasons.

4. *In no case shall participation in a prescreening program be made a prerequisite for receiving hepatitis B vaccination.*
5. *If an employee initially declines hepatitis B vaccination but at a later date while still covered under the OSHA standard, decides to accept the vaccination, hepatitis B vaccination will be made available at that time.*
6. *Those employees who decline to accept the hepatitis B vaccination must sign a statement to that effect. The required statement is printed as Attachment B.*
7. *If a routine booster dose(s) of hepatitis B vaccine is recommended by the U.S. Public Health Service at a future date, such booster dose(s) will be made available under the same circumstances stated above.*
8. *In the event of an exposure incident, a confidential medical evaluation and follow-up of the incident will be made available to the employee involved. It will include documentation of the route of exposure, HBV and HIV status of the source patient(s), if known and if permitted by law, and the circumstances under which the*

exposure occurred. The source patient(s) shall be notified of the incident and an attempt will be made to obtain consent to collect and test the source's blood in order to determine the presence of HIV and/or HBV infection. A blood sample shall be collected from the exposed worker as soon as possible after the exposure incident for determination of HIV and HBV status.

9. *The rules for handling exposure incidents are prescribed in subsections (f)(3) through (f)(6) of the OSHA standard, 29 C.F.R. §1910.1030(f)(3)-(6). Those rules will be strictly observed. They include the following:*

   (a) *Immediately following a report of an exposure incident a confidential medical evaluation and follow-up shall be made including at least the following elements:*

      (i) *Documentation of the route(s) of exposure, and the circumstances under which the exposure incident occurred:*

      (ii) *Identification and documentation of the source individual unless it can be established that identification is infeasible or prohibited by state or local law;*

   (b) *The source individual's blood shall be tested as soon as feasible and after consent is obtained in order to determine HBV and HIV infectivity. If consent is not obtained, it must be established that legally required consent cannot be obtained. When the source individual's consent is not required by law, the source individual's blood, if available, shall be tested and the results documented.*

   (c) *When the source individual is already known to be infected with HBV or HIV, testing for the source individual's known HBV or HIV status need not be repeated.*

(d) Results of the source individual's testing shall be made available to the exposed employee and the employee shall be informed of applicable laws and regulations concerning disclosure of the identity and infectious status of the source individual.

(e) The exposed employee's blood shall be collected and tested as soon as feasible after consent is obtained.

(f) If the employee consents to baseline blood collection, but does not give consent at that time for HIV serologic testing, the sample shall be preserved for at least 90 days. If, within 90 days of the exposure incident, the employee elects to have the baseline sample tested, such testing shall be done as soon as feasible.

(g) When medically indicated, there shall be post-exposure prophylaxis as recommended by the US Public Health Service; as well as Counseling; and Evaluation of reported illnesses.

(h) The healthcare professional evaluating the employee after an exposure incident will be provided with the following information:

- *A copy of The OSHA Bloodborne Pathogens Standard*
- *A description of the exposed employee's duties as they relate to the exposure incident*
- *Documentation of the route(s) of exposure and circumstances under which exposure occurred;*
- *Results of the source individual's blood testing, if available; and*
- *All medical records relevant to the appropriate treatment of the employee including vaccination status which it is our responsibility to maintain.*

(i) A copy of the evaluating healthcare professional's written opinion shall be obtained within 15 days of the completion of the evaluation.

(j) The healthcare professional's written opinion for Hepatitis B vaccination shall be limited to whether Hepatitis B vaccination is indicated for

an employee, and if the employee has received such vaccination.

(k) The healthcare professional's written opinion for post-exposure evaluation and follow-up shall be limited to the following information:

- *That the employee has been informed of the results of the evaluation; and*
- *That the employee has been told about any medical conditions resulting from exposure to blood or other potentially infectious materials which require further evaluation or treatment,*

(l) All other findings or diagnoses shall remain confidential and shall not be included in the written report.

(m) Medical records required by the OSHA Bloodborne Pathogens standard shall be maintained in accordance with the requirements of the OSHA standard on Access to Employee Exposure and Medical Records, 29 C.F.R. §1910.20.

6. Waste Disposal

1. *Contaminated needles and other contaminated sharps shall not be bent, recapped, or removed except where required by a specific medical procedure or in those situations where it can be demonstrated that there is no feasible alternative. In such cases recapping or needle removal must be accomplished through the use of a mechanical device or a one-handed technique.*
2. *Shearing or breaking of contaminated needles is prohibited.*
3. *Immediately or as soon as possible after use, contaminated reusable sharps shall be placed in appropriate containers until properly reprocessed. The*

containers for reusable sharps, as well as those that are to be discarded, shall be;

- *Puncture resistant*
- *Labeled or color-coded in accordance with Part 7 of this Plan*
- *Leakproof on the sides and bottom*

4. *Reusable sharps that are contaminated with blood or other potentially infectious materials shall not be stored or processed in a manner that requires employees to reach by hand into the containers where those sharps have been placed.*
5. *Disposal of all infectious waste shall be in accordance with applicable Federal, State, and local regulations.*
6. *All infectious waste shall be placed in closable, leakproof containers or bags that are color-coded, labeled and tagged.*
7. *Disposal syringes, needles, scalpel blades and other sharp items shall be placed in puncture-resistant containers for disposal.*
8. *Puncture-resistant sharps containers shall be easily accessible to workers and located in areas where they are commonly used.*
9. *Double-bagging prior to handling, storing, and/or transporting infectious waste is necessary if the outside of a bag is contaminated with blood or other potentially infectious materials.*

10. *Lab specimens of body fluids shall be transported in a container that will prevent leaking and disposed of in accordance with institutional policies and regulatory requirements.*

11. *Regulated waste shall be placed in containers which are:*

    (i) Closable

    (ii) Constructed to contain all contents and prevent leakage of fluids during handling, storage, transport or shipping;

    (iii) Labeled or color-coded in accordance with Part 7 of this Plan, and

    (iv) Closed prior to removal to prevent spillage or protrusion of contents during handling, storage, transport, or shipping.

12. *If outside contamination of the regulated waste container occurs, it shall be placed in a second container. The second container shall be:*

    (i) Closable

    (ii) Constructed to contain all contents and prevent leakage of fluids during handling, storage, transport or shipping;

    (iii) Labeled or color-coded in accordance with Part 7 of this plan; and

    (iv) Closed prior to removal to prevent spillage or protrusion of contents during handling, storage, transport, or shipping.

7. Communication of Hazards

1. *Warning labels or tags that comply with 29 C.F.R. §1910.145(f) shall be used to identify the presence of an actual or potential biological hazard. They shall be affixed to containers of regulated waste, refrigerators and freezers containing blood or other potentially infectious material; and other containers used to store, transport or ship blood or other potentially infectious materials, except as provided otherwise in this Part of our Exposure Control Plan.*
2. *The labels shall contain the word "BIOHAZARD" and the biological hazard symbol shown in Attachment C of this plan*
3. *The labels shall be fluorescent orange or orange-red or predominantly so, with lettering or symbols in a contrasting color.*
4. *Containers of blood, blood components, or blood products that are labeled as to their contents and have been released for transfusion or other clinical use are exempted from these labeling requirements.*
5. *Individual containers of blood or other potentially infectious materials that are placed in a labeled container during storage, transport, shipment or disposal are exempted from the labeling requirements.*

6. Labels required for contaminated equipment shall be in accordance with this part and shall also state which portions of the equipment remain contaminated.
7. Regulated waste that has been decontaminated need not be labeled or color-coded.
8. The word and message must be understandable to all employees who may be exposed to the identified hazard.
9. Labels/tags shall be an integral part of the container or affixed as close as feasible to the container by string, wire, or adhesive or other method that prevents their loss or unintentional removal.
10. Red bags or red containers may be substituted for labels.
11. All employees shall be informed of the meaning of the various labels, tags, and the color-coding system.

8. Housekeeping Practices

1. All work areas must be maintained in a clean and sanitary condition at all times.
2. An appropriate cleaning/decontamination schedule shall be adopted -- and followed-- for all rooms where body fluids are present. Schedules shall be as frequent as necessary depending on the area, the type of surface to be cleaned, and the amount and type of soil present.

3. *Housekeeping workers must wear appropriate PPE including general-purpose utility gloves during all cleaning of blood or other potentially infectious materials and during decontaminating procedures.*

4. *Initial clean-up of blood or other potentially infectious materials shall be followed with the use of an approved hospital disinfectant chemical germicide that is tuberculocidal or a solution of 5.25 percent sodium hypochlorite (household bleach) diluted between 1:10 and 1:100 with water.*

5. *Equipment contaminated with blood or other potentially infectious material shall be checked routinely and decontaminated if possible prior to servicing or shipping.*

6. *All equipment and environmental and working surface shall be cleaned and decontaminated after contact with blood or other potentially infectious materials.*

7. *Contaminated work surfaces shall be decontaminated with an appropriate disinfectant after completion of procedures; immediately or as soon as feasible when surfaces are overtly contaminated or after any spill of blood or other potentially infectious materials; and at the end of the work shift if the surface may have become contaminated since the last cleaning.*

8. *Protective coverings, such as plastic wrap, aluminum foil, or imperviously-backed absorbent paper used to*

cover equipment and environmental surfaces, shall be removed and replaced as soon as feasible when they become overtly contaminated or at the end of the workshift if they may have become contaminated during the shift.

9. *All bins, pails, cans and similar receptacles intended for reuse which have a reasonable likelihood for becoming contaminated with blood or other potentially infectious materials shall be inspected and decontaminated on a regularly scheduled basis and cleaned and decontaminated immediately or as soon as feasible upon visible contamination.*
10. *Broken glassware which may be contaminated shall not be picked up directly with the hands. It shall be cleaned up using mechanical means, such as brush and dust pan, tongs, or forceps.*

9. *Laundry Practices*

1. *Contaminated laundry shall be handled as little as possible with a minimum of agitation.*
2. *Contaminated laundry shall be bagged or containerized at the location where it was used and shall not be sorted or rinsed in the location of use.*
3. *Contaminated laundry shall be placed and transported in bags or containers labeled or color-coded in accordance*

with Part 7. When Universal Precautions are used in the handling of all soiled laundry, alternative labeling or color-coding is sufficient if it permits all employees to recognize the containers as requiring compliance with Universal Precautions.

4. *Whenever contaminated laundry is wet and presents a reasonable likelihood of soak-through of, or leakage from, the bag or container, the laundry shall be placed and transported in bags or containers which prevent soak-through and/or leakage of fluids to the exterior.*
5. *Employees who have contact with contaminated laundry must wear protective gloves and other appropriate personal protective equipment.*
6. *When contaminated laundry is shipped off-site to a second facility which does not utilize Universal Precautions in the handling of all laundry, the facility generating the contaminated laundry must place it in bags or containers which are labeled or color-coded in accordance with Part 7, above.*
7. *The material for the bags or containers used in laundry collection must prevent soak-through or leakage of fluids to the exterior, if the contaminated laundry is wet and presents a reasonable likelihood of soak-through or leakage. Not all contaminated laundry must be placed in such bags and containers --only laundry*

wet enough to leak or soak through and expose workers handling the bags/containers to blood or OPIM.

8. *Employees having direct contact with contaminated laundry must wear protective gloves and any other appropriate personal protective equipment, in order to prevent or reduce contact exposure to blood or OPIM. Any other personal protective equipment required must be determined on a case-by-case basis. Gowns, aprons, eyewear, and masks may be necessary to prevent employee exposure.*

9. *The generator of the laundry must have determined if the facility to which it is shipped utilizes universal precautions. If not, all bags or containers of contaminated laundry must be labeled or color-coded in accordance with Part 7, above. In this instance, if the generator of the laundry chooses to color-code rather than label, the color of the bag must be red.*

10. *The laundry workers must wear protective gloves and other appropriate personal protective equipment to prevent exposure to blood or other potentially infectious material during handling and sorting of linen.*

11. *Laundry that is contaminated with blood or other potentially infectious materials or that may contain contaminated needles or sharps shall be treated as if*

it were HBV/HIV infectious and handled as little as possible with a minimum of agitation.

12. Contaminated laundry shall be bagged at the location where it was used and shall not be sorted or rinsed in patient areas.

13. Contaminated laundry shall be placed and transported in bags that are labeled or color coded and that prevent liquid seepage if such a potential exists.

10. Training and Education of Employees

1. All employees with occupational exposure must participate in a training program which will be provided at no cost to affected employees during normal working hours.

2. The training will be provided as follows:

   (a) At the time of initial assignment to tasks where occupational exposure may take place;

   (b) Within 90 days after March 6, 1992, the effective date of the OSHA standard; and

   (c) At least annually thereafter.

3. For employees who have received training on bloodborne pathogens in the year preceding the effective date of the OSHA standard, only training with respect to the provisions of the standard which were not included need be provided.

4. Annual training for all employees shall be provided within one year of their previous training.

5. Additional training shall be provided when changes such as modification of tasks or procedures or institution of new tasks or procedures affect the employee's occupational exposure. The additional training may be limited to addressing the new exposures created.

6. Material appropriate in content and vocabulary to educational level, literacy, and language of employees shall be used.

7. The training program shall contain at a minimum the following elements:

   (a) An accessible copy of the regulatory text of the OSHA bloodborne pathogens standard and an explanation of its contents;

   (b) A general explanation of the epidemiology and symptoms of bloodborne diseases;

   (c) An explanation of the modes of transmission of bloodborne pathogens;

   (d) An explanation of our Exposure Control Plan and the means by which the employee can obtain a copy;

   (e) An explanation of the appropriate methods for recognizing tasks and other activities that may involve exposure to blood and other potentially infectious materials;

   (f) An explanation of the use and limitations of methods that will prevent or reduce exposure including appropriate engineering controls, work practices, and personal protective equipment;

   (g) Information on the types, proper use, location, removal, handling, decontamination and disposal of personal protective equipment;

(h) An explanation of the basis for selection of personal protective equipment;

(i) Information on the hepatitis B vaccine, including information on its efficacy, safety, method of administration, the benefits of being vaccinated, and that the vaccine and vaccination will be offered free of charge.

(j) Information on the appropriate actions to take and the person to contact in an emergency involving blood or other potentially infectious materials;

(k) An explanation of the procedure to follow if an exposure incident occurs, including the method of reporting the incident and the medical follow-up that will be made available;

(l) Information on the post-exposure evaluation and follow-up that we are required to provide for the employee following an exposure incident;

(m) An explanation of the signs and labels and/or color coding required by the OSHA bloodborne pathogens standard and Part 7 of our Exposure Control Plan.

(n) An opportunity for interactive questions and answers with the person conducting the training session.

(o) The person conducting the training will be knowledgeable in the subject matter covered by the elements contained in the training program as it relates to the particular work place that the training will address.

8. *Training records will be maintained for three years from the date on which the training occurred and will include the following:*

    (a) Dates of training sessions

    (b) Contents or summary of training program, including the trainers name and qualifications

    (c) Job titles and names of all persons attending the training session

9. *All training records shall be maintained for 3 years from the date on which the training occurred and must be made available upon request to OSHA and NIOSH as well as employee representatives, in accordance with 29 C.F.R. §1910.20, the OSHA records-access standard.*

11. Recordkeeping

1. *An accurate record of each worker's reported exposure incident to blood or other potentially infectious materials shall be established and maintained in accordance with applicable OSHA recordkeeping regulations. Such records shall be kept confidential and shall not be disclosed or reported to any person within or outside the workplace without the employee's express written consent except as may be required by law or OSHA regulation.*
2. *Needlestick injuries shall be included on the OSHA 200 occupational injury and illness log if medical treatment such as gamma globulin is administered by licensed medical personnel.*
3. *HBV and HIV shall be recorded on the OSHA 200 log if the illnesses can be traced back to an occupational injury or other exposure incident that occurred on the job.*

4. *Medical records will be kept for each employee with occupational exposure for the duration of employment plus 30 years.*

5. *Records will be maintained of Hepatitis B vaccination status (including all dates) on all employees.*

6 *The medical records that will be maintained will include the results of any examinations, testing results and follow-up procedures, as well as a copy of the health care professional's written opinion and a copy of the information that we provided to the health care professional (if any).*

7. *The employee medical records shall include:*

   (a) *The name and social security number of the employee*

   (b) *A copy of the employee's hepatitis B vaccination status including the dates of the hepatitis B vaccinations and any medical records relative to the employee's ability to receive vaccination,*

   (c) *A copy of all results of examinations, medical testing, and follow-up procedures;*

   (d) *The employer's copy of the healthcare professional's written opinion; and*

   (e) *A copy of the information provided to the healthcare professional.*

D. <u>THE USE OF AN EXPOSURE CONTROL PLAN</u>

The foregoing covers most of the matters that you would have to include in your own individual exposure control plan. You also must make sure that you strictly observe the things you put in writing. Failure to do so will raise an inference that you are attempting to deceive OSHA by putting one thing in writing but doing things differently in actual practice. That frequently is the basis for a willful OSHA citation.

Your employees must know the elements of your written Plan and it must be readily accessible to them. That can be accomplished in any one of a number of ways. You could print it and distribute it to employees separately, or as part of an employee information pamphlet. You could post it on the bulletin board, or you could simply keep a copy on file while making sure that employees are on notice of that fact and that it is available for them to review. That could be done as part of your employee training program, for example. There are many other ways to accomplish the foregoing. It can be done differently at each establishment.

CHAPTER 6

OSHA'S GUIDELINES AND ENFORCEMENT PROCEDURES FOR THE BLOODBORNE PATHOGENS STANDARD

This chapter will include a reprint of the entire 71-page text of the instructions that OSHA has provided to its inspectors for interpreting and enforcing the bloodborne pathogens standard. Those instructions were issued on March 6, 1992 and are designated: "OSHA Instruction CPL 2-2.44C."

A. THE ROLE PLAYED BY THE OSHA INSTRUCTION

The purpose of an OSHA Instruction is to explain a particular OSHA standard to those government agents who are responsible for enforcing it, and to advise them **how** the standard should be enforced. Those government agents, although frequently referred to as "OSHA Inspectors," are known within OSHA itself as "Compliance Safety and Health Officers," a title that is often abbreviated as "CSHO."

Every employer who is concerned about being inspected should read the OSHA Instruction because that is what the inspector will use for guidance when making the inspection. There are some OSHA inspectors who do not even read the standard itself. They read only the OSHA Instruction and assume that it accurately reflects the standard. Often, however, that is not the case.

For example, one section of the standard states that:

> "Engineering controls shall be examined and maintained or replaced on a regular schedule to ensure their effectiveness."

§1910.1030(d)(2)(ii). Although that section does not mention "inspections" or "monitoring," the OSHA Instruction states that it requires the employer to conduct "regularly scheduled inspections" or adopt an "effective monitoring system." Emphasis added. The following is quoted from the OSHA Instruction (see pp. 142-143, infra):

> "Section (d)(2)(ii). This section requires that engineering controls be examined and maintained or replaced on a regular schedule to ensure their effectiveness. Regularly scheduled inspections are required to confirm, for instance, that engineering controls as protective shields have not been removed or broken, that sharps disposal containers are being replaced in sufficiently frequent intervals and that other physical, mechanical or replacement-dependent controls are functioning as intended.
>
> **CITATION GUIDELINES.** It is the employer's responsibility to regularly examine and repair and/or replace engineering controls as often as necessary to ensure that each control is maintained and that it provides the protection intended. If the compliance officer finds that there is no system for regular checking of the engineering controls, section (d)(2)(ii) shall be cited.
>
> - If there is a check system, but the compliance officer finds, for example, that the biosafety cabinet is not functional, filters are overloaded (in research laboratories or production facilities), disposal containers are overfilled, or a hematron splash shield is broken or missing, section (d)(2)(ii) shall be cited if an effective monitoring system would have uncovered the deficiency.
>
> - Additionally, if there is unprotected employee exposure, section (d)(2)(i) shall be cited for failure to use personal protective equipment after institution of engineering controls."

B. THE OSHA INSTRUCTION'S SEQUENTIAL ARRANGEMENT

The OSHA Instruction is a step-by-step, section-by-section guideline to the standard. It begins on page 133, infra, with subsection "(a)" -- which could be more correctly identified as 29 C.F.R. §1910.1030(a) -- and continues in alphabetical order, concluding with the subsection "(i)", the standard's final subsection (29 C.F.R. §1910.1030(i)) at page 195 of this book.

You can use the above guidance to locate any particular subsection that may interest you. It may be easier, however to use the index at the back of this book. Every section and subsection of the standard that is mentioned at any place in this book is listed, followed by each page of the book that mentions it.

OSHA has arbitrarily assigned a letter/number system to each paragraph of the OSHA Instruction for their own internal ease of reference. However, it's not that easy to follow because, as the subsections become more numerous, you can't always be sure of the principle section or subsection of which the matter is a part. To help with that problem, the following guidance is provided.

1. The OSHA Instruction is divided into 14 sections. Each begins with a capital letter. They are in alphabetical order: A through N. However, the guidelines and enforcement policies for the entire standard are grouped into only one such section, section M. That section is divided into numerous subsections.

2. The subsections are in numerical order, beginning with 1.

3. Subsections of a numbered subsection are in alphabetical order, beginning with "a."

4. When additional subsections are used, they will have numbers in parenthesis, beginning with "(1)"--then small letters in parenthesis, beginning with "(a)."

5. For example, the "job classifications" discussion in the middle of page 138, <u>infra</u>, is section M.3.a.(2).(a).

C. <u>SOME HIGHLIGHTS OF THE OSHA INSTRUCTION</u>

Because it has been learned from past experience that all employers will not read the entire text of the OSHA Instruction, a few of its highlights will be described below.

1. **OSHA Inspections.** As a rule, employers are quite interested in knowing whether or not (and when) they will be inspected. OSHA uses a very involved, somewhat complex system for selecting inspection targets. It would take dozens of pages to explain it. If you want that kind of explanation, contact the publisher of this book, for references to explanatory articles.

   There are, however, two events that will nearly always lead to an OSHA inspection: (1) A complaint or referral made to OSHA by one of your employees or by a representative of another public agency (for example, a municipal health agency), and (2) An accident, fire, explosion or similar event that is reported in the media.

2. **What the Inspector Looks For.** The first thing OSHA will want to look at during an inspection will be your written Exposure Control Plan. That is stated in section H of the OSHA Instruction (pp.130-132). OSHA will also question some of your employees privately to see if the standard is being observed. If OSHA is satisfied that your Exposure Control Plan is in order and the employee interviews do not indicate noncompliance, its unlikely that OSHA will proceed any further with the inspection. However, if the reason for the inspection is a complaint or an accident, OSHA will investigate all the surrounding circumstances.

3. **Recordkeeping/Exposure Incidents.** Section J of the OSHA Instruction (page 132) explains the circumstances under which an "exposure incident" must be recorded under the OSHA recordkeeping requirements. You should

read that section if an "exposure incident" should occur. If you want further information on OSHA's recordkeeping requirements, you will need another book. You should contact the publisher of this book and order a copy of "The OSHA 500." It explains everything you will need to know about OSHA recordkeeping.

4. **Definitions.** The standard itself defines 26 terms that are used in the standard. See 29 C.F.R. §1910.1030(b). It appears on the first page of Appendix A of this book. Section M.2. of the OSHA Instruction, however, defines 7 of those same terms somewhat differently. See pp. 136-137, infra. For the most part, however, those definitions are more expansive rather than in conflict with those contained in the standard itself.

5. **The "Work Area".** In many different places, the standard requires that certain things must be done (or not done) in the "work area" but that is one term that the standard itself does not define. The OSHA Instruction, however, **does** define the term in section M.4.b.(5). (See pp. 146-147, infra). If you are concerned with a provision of the standard that uses the term "work area", consult that definition.

D. THE OSHA INSTRUCTION

The complete text of OSHA Instruction CPL 2-2.44C, March 6, 1992, Subject: "Enforcement Procedures for the Occupational Exposure to Bloodborne Pathogens Standard, 29 C.F.R. §1910.1030," begins on the next page and continues for the 70 pages that follow it.

U.S. Department of Labor

Assistant Secretary for
Occupational Safety and Health
Washington, D.C. 20210

OSHA Instruction CPL 2-2.44C
MAR 6 1992
Office of Health Compliance Assistance

SUBJECT: Enforcement Procedures for the Occupational Exposure to Bloodborne Pathogens Standard, 29 CFR 1910.1030

A. Purpose. This instruction establishes policies and provides clarifications to ensure uniform inspection procedures are followed when conducting inspections to enforce the Occupational Exposure to Bloodborne Pathogens Standard.

B. Scope. This instruction applies OSHA-wide.

C. Cancellation. This instruction cancels OSHA Instruction CPL 2-2.44B, February 27, 1990, (except as noted at M.9. of this instruction).

D. References.

1. OSHA Instruction CPL 2.45B, June 15, 1989, the Revised Field Operations Manual (FOM).

2. OSHA Instruction ADM 1-1.12B, December 29, 1989, the Integrated Management Information System (IMIS) Forms Manual.

3. Centers for Disease Control Morbidity and Mortality Weekly Report: "Recommendations for Prevention of HIV Transmission in Health Care Settings." August 1987; Vol. 36, No. S-2.

4. Centers for Disease Control Morbidity and Mortality Weekly Report: 1988 Agent Summary Statement for Human Immunodeficiency Virus and Report on Laboratory-Acquired Infection with Human Immunodeficiency Virus. April 1, 1988; Vol. 37, No. S-4.

5. Centers for Disease Control Morbidity and Mortality Weekly Report: "Guidelines for Prevention of Transmission of HIV and HBV to Health Care and Public Safety Workers." June 23, 1989; Vol. 38, No. S-6.

6. Centers for Disease Control Morbidity and Mortality Weekly Report: "Update: Universal Precautions for the Prevention of Transmission of HIV, HBV and Other Bloodborne Pathogens in Health Care Settings." June 24, 1988; Vol. 37, No. 24.

7. Centers for Disease Control Morbidity and Mortality Weekly Report: "Public Health Service Statement on Management of Occupational Exposure to Human Immunodeficiency Virus, Including Consideration Regarding Zidovudine Postexposure Use." January 1990; Vol. 139, No. RR2. (See Appendix A.)

8. Centers for Disease Control Morbidity and Mortality Weekly Report: "Protection Against Viral Hepatitis, Recommendations of the Immunization Practices Advisory Committee." February 1990; Vol. 39, No. S-2. (See Appendix B.)

9. U.S. Department of Health and Human Services: "Biosafety in Microbiological and Biomedical Laboratories," Publication No. (NIH) 88-8395, May 1988.

E. Action. OSHA Regional Administrators and Area Directors shall use the guidelines in this instruction to ensure uniform enforcement of the Bloodborne Pathogens Standard. The Directorate of Compliance Programs will provide support as necessary to assist the Regional Administrators and Area Directors in enforcing the Bloodborne Pathogens Standard.

F. Federal Program Change. This instruction describes a Federal program change which affects State programs. Each Regional Administrator shall:

1. Ensure that this change is promptly forwarded to each State designee, using a format consistent with the Plan Change Two-Way Memorandum in Appendix P of OSHA Instruction STP 2.22A CH-3.

2. Explain the technical content of this change to the State designee as requested..

3. Ensure that State designees are asked to acknowledge receipt of this Federal program change in writing to the Regional Administrator as soon as the State's intention is known, but not later than 70 calendar days after the date of issuance (10 days for mailing and 60 days for response). This acknowledgment must include the State's intention to follow OSHA's policies and procedures described in this instruction, or a description of the State's alternative policy and/or procedure which is "at least as effective" as the Federal policy.

4. Ensure that the State designees submit a plan supplement, in accordance with OSHA Instruction STP 2.22A, Ch-3, as appropriate, following the established schedule that is agreed upon by the State and Regional Administrator to submit non-Field Operations Manual/ Technical Manual Federal Program Changes.

   a. If a State intends to follow the revised inspection procedures described in this instruction, the State must submit either a revised version of this instruction, adapted as appropriate to reference State law, regulations and administrative structure, or a cover sheet describing how references in this instruction correspond to the State's structure. The State's acknowledgment letter may fulfill the plan supplement requirement if the appropriate documentation is provided.

   b. If the State adopts an alternative to Federal enforcement inspection procedures, the State's plan supplement must identify and provide a rationale for all substantial differences from Federal procedures in order for OSHA to judge whether a different State procedure is as effective as the comparable procedure.

5. After Regional review of the State plan supplement and resolution of any comments thereon, forward the State submission to the National Office in accordance with established procedures. The Regional Administrator shall provide a judgment on the relative effectiveness of each substantial difference in the State plan change and an overall assessment thereon with a recommendation for approval or disapproval by the Assistant Secretary.

6. Advise State designees that the State is also responsible for extending coverage under its procedures for addressing occupational exposure to bloodborne pathogens to the public sector, such as police, firefighters, ambulance and other emergency response employees.

7. Review policies, instructions and guidelines issued by the State to determine that this change has been communicated to State program personnel.

G. Background. In September 1986, OSHA was petitioned by various unions representing health care employees to develop an emergency temporary standard to protect employees from occupational exposure to bloodborne diseases. The agency decided to pursue the development of a Section 6(b) of the Act standard and published a proposed rule on May 30, 1989.

1. The agency also concluded that the risk of contracting the hepatitis B virus (HBV) and human immunodeficiency virus (HIV) among members of various occupations within the health care sector required an immediate response and therefore issued OSHA Instruction CPL 2-2.44, January 19, 1988. That instruction was canceled by CPL 2-2.44A, August 15, 1988, and subsequently, CPL 2-2.44B was issued February 27, 1990.

2. On December 6, 1991, the agency issued its final regulation on occupational exposure to bloodborne pathogens (29 CFR 1910.1030). Based on a review of the information in the rulemaking record, OSHA has determined that employees face a significant health risk as the result of occupational exposure to blood and other potentially infectious materials (OPIM) because they may contain bloodborne pathogens. These pathogens include HBV which causes Hepatitis B, a serious liver disease, and HIV, which causes Acquired Immunodeficiency Syndrome (AIDS). The agency further concludes that this hazard can be minimized or eliminated using a combination of engineering and work practice controls, personal protective clothing and equipment, training, medical surveillance, hepatitis B vaccination, signs and labels, and other provisions.

H. Inspection Scheduling, and Scope.

1. Inspection scheduling shall be conducted in accordance with the procedures outlined in the FOM, Chapter II, and for Federal agencies, Chapter XIII, except as modified in paragraphs 2., 3., and 4. below.

2. All inspections, programmed or unprogrammed, shall include, if appropriate, a review of the employer's exposure control plan and employee interviews to assess compliance with the standard.

3. Expansion of an inspection to areas involving the hazard of occupational exposure to body fluids

(including onsite health care units and emergency response or first aid personnel) shall be performed when:

a. The exposure control plan or employee interviews indicate deficiencies in complying with OSHA requirements, as set forth in 29 CFR 1910.1030 or this instruction.

b. Relevant formal employee complaints are received which are specifically related to occupational exposure to blood or OPIM.

c. A fatality/catastrophe inspection is conducted as the result of occupational exposure to blood or OPIM.

4. Regional Offices may develop and implement local emphasis programs as a supplement to complaint-generated inspection activities. (See the FOM, Chapter II.)

I. <u>General Inspection Procedures</u>. The procedures given in the FOM, Chapter III, shall be followed except as modified in the following sections:

1. Where appropriate, the facility administrator, infection control director or occupational health nurse, "in service" education (i.e., training) director, and head of central services and/or housekeeping shall be included in the opening conference or interviewed early in the inspection.

2. If the facility maintains a file of "incident reports" or a first aid log on injuries (e.g., needlesticks), this shall be reviewed as it may contain injuries not included on the OSHA 200 log.

3. Compliance officers shall take necessary precautions to avoid direct contact with body fluids and shall not participate in activities that will require them to come into contact with body fluids, needles or other sharp instruments contaminated with blood. To evaluate such activities, compliance officers normally shall establish the existence of hazards and adequacy of work practices through employee interviews and shall observe them at a safe distance.

4. On occasions when entry into potentially hazardous areas are judged necessary, the compliance officer shall be properly equipped as required by the facility as well as by his/her own professional judgment, after consultation with the supervisor.

5. Compliance officers shall use appropriate caution when entering patient care areas of the facility. When such visits are judged necessary for determining actual conditions in the facility, the privacy of patients shall be respected. Photographs of patients normally will not be necessary and in no event shall identifiable photographs be taken without their consent.

J. Recording of Exposure Incidents. For OSHA 200 recordkeeping purposes, an occupational bloodborne pathogens exposure incident (e.g., needlestick, laceration, or splash) shall be classified as an injury since it is usually the result of an instantaneous event or exposure. It shall be recorded if it meets one of the following recordability requirements:

1. The incident is a work-related injury that involves loss of consciousness, transfer to another job, or restriction of work or motion.

2. The incident results in the recommendation of medical treatment beyond first aid (e.g., gamma globulin, hepatitis B immune globulin, hepatitis B vaccine, or zidovudine) regardless of dosage.

3. The incident results in a diagnosis of seroconversion. The serological status of the employee shall not be recorded on the OSHA 200. If a case of seroconversion is known, it shall be recorded on the OSHA 200 as an injury (e.g., "needlestick" rather than "seroconversion") in the following manner:

   a. If the date of the event or exposure is known, the original injury shall be recorded with the date of the event or exposure in column B.

   b. If there are multiple events or exposures, the most recent injury shall be recorded with the date that seroconversion is determined in column B.

K. Multi-Employer Worksite. The following citation guidelines apply in multi-employer worksites (See FOM, Chapter V, F.):

1. Employers shall be cited for violations of the standard to which their own employees are exposed.

2. They shall also be cited for violations to which employees of other employers on their premises are exposed to the extent that they control the hazard. For example, they shall be cited for not providing personal protective equipment to unprotected employees of other employers on their premises.

3. Physicians who are members of professional corporations are generally considered to be employees of that corporation. Therefore, the corporation may be cited for violations affecting those physicians, such as failure to provide the hepatitis B vaccine. Also, the hospitals where they work may be cited for violations to which they are exposed.

4. No citation shall be issued where the only persons exposed are physicians who are sole practitioners or partners, and thus not employees under the Occupational Safety and Health Act.

L. Federal Agency Facilities. Agencies of the Federal Government are covered by this instruction.

M. Clarification of the Standard on Occupational Exposure to Bloodborne Pathogens, 29 CFR 1910.1030. The guidance that follows relates to specific provisions of 29 CFR 1910.1030 and is provided to assist compliance officers in conducting inspections where the standard may be applicable:

NOTE: Compliance officers shall refer to 29 CFR 1910.1030 regulatory text and preamble for further information.

1. **Scope and Application - 29 CFR 1910.1030(a).** This section defines the range of employees covered by the standard.

   a. Since there is no population that is risk free for HIV or HBV infectivity, any employee who has occupational exposure to blood or other potentially infectious material will be included within the scope of this standard.

b. Although a list is included below of a number of job classifications that may be associated with tasks that have occupational exposure to blood and other potentially infectious materials, **the scope of this standard is in no way limited to employees in these jobs.** The hazard of exposure to infectious materials affects employees in many types of employment and is not restricted to the health care industry. At the same time, **employees in the following jobs are not automatically covered unless they have occupational exposure:**

- Physicians, physician's assistants, nurses, nurse practitioners, and other health care employees in clinics and physicians' offices;
- Employees of clinical and diagnostic laboratories;
- Housekeepers in health care facilities;
- Personnel in hospital laundries or commercial laundries that service health care or public safety institutions;
- Tissue bank personnel;
- Employees in blood banks and plasma centers who collect, transport, and test blood;
- Freestanding clinic employees (e.g., hemodialysis clinics, urgent care clinics, health maintenance organization (HMO) clinics, and family planning clinics);
- Employees in clinics in industrial, educational, and correctional facilities (e.g., those who collect blood, and clean and dress wounds);
- Employees assigned to provide emergency first aid;

- o Dentists, dental hygienists, dental assistants and dental laboratory technicians;
- o Staff of institutions for the developmentally disabled;
- o Hospice employees;
- o Home health care workers;
- o Staff of nursing homes and long-term care facilities;
- o Employees of funeral homes and mortuaries;
- o HIV and HBV research laboratory and production facility workers;
- o Employees handling regulated waste;
- o Medical equipment service and repair personnel;
- o Emergency medical technicians, paramedics, and other emergency medical service providers; and
- o Firefighters, law enforcement personnel, and correctional officers (employees in the private sector, the Federal Government, or a State or local government in a State that has an OSHA-approved State plan).

INSPECTION GUIDELINES. The scope section of this standard states that it "applies to all occupational exposure to blood or other potentially infectious materials as defined by paragraph (b)." The compliance officer must take careful note of the phrase "as defined by paragraph (b)" when determining coverage. Definitions of particular importance that the compliance officer must clearly understand before beginning an inspection are: Blood, Bloodborne Pathogens, Contaminated, Exposure Incident, Occupational Exposure, Other Potentially Infectious Materials, and Regulated Waste. These will be of use in determining if an employee in either a health care or a non-health care setting is covered by this standard.

NOTES:

1. Part-time, temporary, and health care workers known as "per diem" employees are covered by this standard.

2. If an employee is trained in first aid and designated by the employer as responsible for rendering medical assistance as part of his/her job duties, that employee is covered by the standard.

3. Employees in the construction and maritime industries who have occupational exposure to blood or OPIM are covered by the standard.

2. **Definitions - 29 CFR 1910.1030(b).** The following provides further clarifications of some definitions found in this section:

   a. **"Blood":** The term "human blood components" includes plasma, platelets, and serosanguineous fluids (e.g., exudates from wounds).

   b. **"Bloodborne Pathogens":** While HBV and HIV are specifically identified in the standard, the term includes any pathogenic microorganism that is present in human blood and can infect and cause disease in persons who are exposed to blood containing the pathogen. Other examples include hepatitis C, malaria, syphilis, babesiosis, brucellosis, leptospirosis, arboviral infections, relapsing fever, Creutzfeld-Jakob disease, Human T-lymphotrophic Virus Type 1, and viral hemorrhagic fever.

   c. **"Exposure Incident":** "Non-intact skin" includes skin with dermatitis, hang-nails, cuts, abrasions, chafing, etc.

   d. **"Occupational Exposure":** The term "reasonably anticipated" includes the potential for exposure as well as actual exposure. Lack of history of blood exposures among first aid personnel of a particular manufacturing site, for instance, does not preclude coverage.

NOTE: This definition does not cover "good Samaritan" acts which result in exposure to blood or other potentially infectious materials from assisting a fellow employee, although OSHA encourages employers to offer follow-up procedures in such cases.

e. **"Other Potentially Infectious Materials"(OPIM):** Coverage under this definition also extends to blood and tissues of animals who are deliberately infected with HIV or HBV.

f. **"Parenteral":** This definition includes human bites that break the skin, which are most likely to occur in violent situations such as may be encountered by prison personnel and police and in emergency rooms or psychiatric wards.

g. **"Regulated Waste":** This definition is covered in detail at M.4.d.(3) of this instruction.

3. **Exposure Control Plan - 29 CFR 1910.1030(c).** This section requires the employer to identify those tasks and procedures in which occupational exposure may occur and to identify the positions whose duties include those tasks and procedures identified with occupational exposure. The exposure control plan required by section (c)(1) is a key provision of the standard because it requires the employer to identify the individuals who will receive the training, protective equipment, vaccination, and other benefits of the standard.

INSPECTION AND CITATION GUIDELINES. The compliance officer shall review the facility's written exposure control plan. While the plan may be part of a larger document, such as one addressing all health and safety hazards in the workplace, in order for the plan to be accessible to employees, it must be a cohesive entity by itself or there must be a guiding document which states the overall policy goals and references the elements of existing separate policies that comprise the plan.

- The compliance officer shall determine whether the plan is reviewed annually and updated to reflect significant modifications in tasks or procedures which may result in occupational exposure as required in section (c)(1)(iv).

- The content of the exposure control plan shall be reviewed for at least the following elements:

a. **Sections (c)(1)(ii)(A) and (c)(2)(i).** The exposure determination requires employers to identify and document:

(1) Those job classifications in which all employees have occupational exposure, and

(2) Those job classifications in which some employees have occupational exposure.

(a) In the latter case, the specific tasks and procedures, or groups of closely related tasks and procedures, which are associated with occupational exposure must be delineated. For example, only some of the employees in a hospital laundry room might be assigned the task of handling contaminated laundry.

(b) The tasks and procedures that are grouped must be related; i.e., they must share a common activity such as "vascular access procedures," "handling of contaminated sharps," or "handling of deceased persons," etc.

(3) The exposure determination shall have been made without taking into consideration the use of personal protective clothing or equipment.

b. **Section (c)(1)(ii)(B).** The schedule and method of implementation for sections (d)-(h) in a manner appropriate to the circumstances of the particular workplace must be addressed in the exposure control plan. An annotated copy of the final standard may be adequate for small facilities. An employer may state on a copy of the final standard when and how he/she will implement the provisions of the standard. Larger facilities could develop a broad facility-wide program incorporating provisions from the standard that apply to their establishments.

c. **Section (c)(1)(ii)(C).** The exposure control plan shall include the procedure for evaluating the circumstances surrounding exposure incidents, including an evaluation of the policies and "failures of control" at the time of the exposure incident. Also to be considered are the engineering controls and work practices in place, as well as protective equipment or clothing used, at the time of the exposure incident.

d. **Section (c)(1)(iii).** The location of the plan may be adapted to the circumstances of a particular workplace provided that the employee can access a copy at the workplace, during the workshift (e.g., if the plan is maintained solely on computer, employees must be trained to operate the computer). In accordance with 29 CFR 1910.20, a hard copy of the exposure control plan shall be made available to the employee within 15 working days of the employee's request.

e. **Sections (c)(2)(i)(A) and (B).** As previously discussed in the exposure control plan, the employer is required to list the job classifications covered by the plan. The list is part of the exposure determination. If a job classification, task, or procedure with occupational exposure is omitted from the list, but all employees in the job or performing the task or procedure have been included in all other aspects of the plan (i.e., vaccinations, training, etc.), it is to be considered an other-than-serious violation.

4. **Methods of Compliance - 29 CFR 1910.1030(d).** Section (d) sets forth the methods by which employers shall protect their employees from the hazards of bloodborne pathogens and comply with this standard through the use of universal precautions, engineering controls, work practice controls, personal protective equipment, proper housekeeping and handling of regulated waste.

a. **Universal Precautions - (d)(1).** Universal precautions is OSHA's accepted method of control to protect employees from exposure to all human blood and OPIM. The term "universal precautions" refers to a concept of bloodborne disease control which requires that all human blood and OPIM be treated as if known to be infectious for HIV, HBV, or other bloodborne pathogens regardless of the perceived "low risk" of a patient or patient population.

(1) Another method of infection control is called Body Substance Isolation (BSI). This method defines **all** body fluids and substances as infectious. BSI incorporates not only the fluids and materials covered by this standard but expands coverage to include all body fluids and substances.

(2) BSI is an acceptable alternative to universal precautions provided facilities utilizing BSI adhere to all other provisions of this standard.

CITATION GUIDELINES. If the employer has a policy of treating the blood or OPIM of some patients as potentially infectious and the blood or OPIM of others (e.g., the elderly or children) as not infectious, a violation of this provision exists.

M.4.b. **Engineering Controls and Work Practices - (d)(2).** This section requires the employer to institute engineering and work practice controls as the primary means of eliminating or minimizing employee exposure. In those circumstances in which occupational exposure remains after institution of engineering and work practice controls, employers must provide, and ensure that employees use, personal protective equipment as additional protection.

INSPECTION GUIDELINES. The compliance officer shall determine through interviews or observation of work involving the use of needles whether proper engineering controls and work practices, such as immediate disposal of used needles into a sharps container, are used.

- Most preferable is the use of devices which offer an alternative to needles being used to perform the procedure. Examples of such devices include stopcocks (on-off switch), needle-protected systems or needleless systems which can be used in place of open needles to connect intravenous lines. Other devices which are integral to the syringe, such as self-sheathing needles, allow both hands to remain behind the needle and require very little manipulation to isolate the needle safely.

- When a health care worker must recap, such as during intermittent administration of various drugs during certain procedures, and when it is not feasible to use self-sheathing needle syringes, the employee must use some type of device that protects the hand or allows a safe one-handed recapping method. A proper one-handed scoop method is a work practice which may also be used in these circumstances. (See M.4.b.(3)(b) of this instruction on section **(d)(2)(vii)** for details.)

- The compliance officer shall evaluate the work practices used by health care providers to determine that they ensure the effectiveness of engineering controls. For example, some devices provide a fixed barrier between the hands and the needle after use. While some finger/hand shields available on the market offer full protection of the hand holding the needle sheath from accidental puncture, some do not. They may leave much of the hand area uncovered and are not considered acceptable protection for use in a two-handed recapping procedure. Both the shield and the cap must be constructed so that an employee is not exposed to puncture from a needle protruding from the side or end of the cap.

- The compliance officer should note that sharps may include more than the traditional needles or scalpels. They also include anything that might produce a puncture wound which would expose employees to blood or OPIM (e.g., the ends of contaminated orthodontia wires or broken glass).

CITATION GUIDELINES. Section **(d)(2)** shall be cited for failure to use engineering/work practice controls. A citation for the appropriate section of **(g)(2)(vii)** shall be grouped with it, if the compliance officer determines that inadequate training caused the failure to use such controls.

- Citations shall be issued if engineering or work practice controls are not used to eliminate or minimize employee exposure.

- While employers do not automatically have to institute the most sophisticated engineering controls (e.g., needleless IV connectors, self-sheathing needles), it is the employer's responsibility to evaluate the effectiveness of existing controls and to review the feasibility of instituting more advanced engineering controls.

M.4.b.(1) **Section (d)(2)(ii).** This section requires that engineering controls be examined and maintained or replaced on a regular schedule to ensure their effectiveness. Regularly scheduled inspections are required to confirm, for instance, that engineering controls such as protective shields have not been removed or broken, that sharps disposal containers are being replaced in sufficiently frequent intervals and that other physical, mechanical or replacement-dependent controls are functioning as intended.

CITATION GUIDELINES. It is the employer's responsibility to regularly examine and repair and/or replace engineering controls as often as necessary to ensure that each control is maintained and that it provides the protection intended. If the compliance officer finds that there is no system for regular checking of the engineering controls, section **(d)(2)(ii)** shall be cited.

- If there is a check system, but the compliance officer finds, for example, that the biosafety cabinet is not functional, filters are overloaded (in research laboratories or production facilities), disposal containers are overfilled, or a hematron splash shield is broken or missing, section **(d)(2)(ii)** shall be cited if an effective monitoring system would have uncovered the deficiency.

- Additionally, if there is unprotected employee exposure, section **(d)(2)(i)** shall be cited for failure to use personal protective equipment after institution of engineering controls.

M.4.b.(2) **Sections (d)(2)(iii) through (d)(2)(vi).** These sections require employers to provide handwashing facilities which are readily accessible to employees. Handwashing with soap and at least tepid running water must be performed as soon as feasible, particularly in cases of gross contamination, to adequately flush contaminated material from the skin.

(a) **Section (d)(2)(iv).** This section allows the use of alternative handwashing methods as an interim measure when soap and water are not a feasible means of washing the hands or other parts of the body. Antiseptic hand cleaner, in conjunction with clean cloth or paper towels, or antiseptic towelettes are examples of alternative methods.

<u>1</u> When these types of alternatives are used, employees shall wash their hands (or other affected area) with soap and running water as soon as feasible thereafter.

<u>2</u> The compliance officer may see these types of alternative washing methods used by ambulance-based

paramedics and emergency medical technicians (EMT's), firefighters, police, and mobile blood collection personnel who are exposed to blood or OPIM with no means of washing up with running water.

M.4.b.(2)(b) **Section (d)(2)(v).** This section requires employers to ensure that employees wash their hands immediately or as soon as feasible after removal of gloves or other PPE. There is no requirement for handwashing upon leaving the work area unless contact with blood or OPIM has occurred or gloves/PPE have been removed.

CITATION GUIDELINES. If the compliance officer finds that required handwashing facilities are not being provided, section **(d)(2)(iii)** shall be cited unless the employer demonstrates that handwashing facilities are not feasible. If infeasibility is demonstrated, section **(d)(2)(iv)** shall be cited when the required alternatives are not used. If handwashing is not performed by the employees after exposures or removal of gloves, sections **(d)(2)(iv), (v), or (vi)** shall be cited. This may be grouped with the pertinent training sections of **(g)(2)** if employees have not been adequately trained in handwashing procedures.

- At a fixed establishment, if employees need to perform handwashing, they must have a location for washing available at a reasonable distance from their normal work area; i.e., no further than what would be considered reasonable for location of restrooms.

- If an employee must thread his/her way through doorways and/or stairs to wash with appropriate frequency so that there is a reasonable chance of resultant environmental surface contamination, a violation of section **(d)(2)(iii)** exists.

M.4.b.(3) **Section (d)(2)(vii).** Shearing or breaking of contaminated needles is completely prohibited by this section. Bending, recapping, or removing contaminated needles by hand is prohibited as a general practice. However, certain circumstances may exist in which these actions are necessary; e.g., when performing blood gas analyses, inoculating a blood culture bottle, administering incremental doses of a medication such as an anesthetic to the same patient, or removing the needle from a phlebotomy collection apparatus (e.g., vacutainer).

(a) In these procedures, if the employer can demonstrate that no alternative is feasible or that such action is required by a specific medical procedure, recapping is allowed by some method other than the traditional two-handed procedure; e.g., by means of resheathing instruments or forceps.

(b) The use of the properly performed one-hand scoop method (in which the hand holding the sharp is used to scoop up the cap from a flat surface) for recapping is a recognized and acceptable method; however, the scoop method must be performed in a safe manner and must be limited to situations in which recapping is necessary.

(c) An acceptable means of demonstrating that no alternative is feasible would be a written justification included as part of the exposure control plan and stating that the particular medical procedure requires, for example, the bending of the needle and the use of forceps to accomplish this.

(4) **Section (d)(2)(viii).** Since reusable sharps, such as large bore needles, scalpels, and saws, pose the same percutaneous exposure hazard as disposable sharps, they must be contained in a manner that eliminates or

minimizes the hazard until they are reprocessed. Therefore, the containers for reusable sharps must meet the same requirements as containers for disposable sharps (See M.4.d.(3)(b) of this instruction on section **(d)(4)(iii)(A)(1).**), with the exception that they are not required to be closable since it is anticipated that containers used for collecting and holding reusable sharps will, themselves, be reused. (See M.4.d.(2)(e) of this instruction on section **(d)(4)(ii)(E)** for the manner in which these reusable sharps are to be stored and processed, and M.4.d.(3)(g) on section **(d)(4)(iii)(A)(4)** on the requirements for cleaning and processing of these reusable containers.)

M.4.b.(5) **Sections (d)(2)(ix) and (x).** These sections are intended primarily to eliminate or minimize indirect transmission of HBV from contaminated environmental surfaces.

(a) Hand cream is not considered a "cosmetic" and is permitted. It should be noted that:

1 Some petroleum-based hand creams can adversely affect glove integrity, and

2 The handwashing requirements of section **(d)(2)(v)** and **(d)(2)(vi)** shall be followed.

(b) The term "work area" means the area where work involving exposure or potential exposure to blood or OPIM exists, along with the potential contamination of surfaces. Employees are permitted to eat and drink in an ambulance cab, for example, as long as the employer has implemented procedures to permit employees to wash up and change contaminated clothing prior to entering the ambulance cab, and to ensure that patients and contaminated material remain behind the separating partition.

INSPECTION GUIDELINES. In addition to direct contamination of food or drink by blood or OPIM, the compliance officer must keep in mind that containers of food and beverage may also become contaminated, resulting in unsuspected contamination of the hands. The key to this section is whether food and drink may be contaminated by such processes as leakage/spilling of specimen containers, contact with contaminated items, or the performance of activities (e.g., laboratory analysis) that could generate splashes, sprays, or droplets of blood or OPIM.

CITATION GUIDELINES. Deficiencies of sections **(d)(2)(iv)** through **(x)** shall be cited in conjunction with the appropriate section of **(g)(2)** if inadequate training exists.

M.4.b.(6) **Section (d)(2)(xi).** The intent of this section is not only to decrease the chances of direct employee exposure through spraying or splashing of infectious materials onto employees, but also to reduce contamination of surfaces in the general work area.

(a) Surgical power tools, lasers, and electrocautery devices may generate aerosols. However, OSHA does not believe that the data currently support the mandatory use of respiratory protection for exposure to aerosols, nor is there an effective engineering control to address aerosol exposure or approved respirator and filter cartridges.

(b) Particularly hazardous is the use of sprays, brushes, and high pressure in equipment lines.

(c) Typically, spattering or generation of droplets would necessitate use of eye protection and mask or a face shield. (See M.4.c.(8) of this instruction on section **(d)(3)(x)**.)

CITATION GUIDELINES. A citation shall normally be issued for section **(d)(2)-(xi)** if cleaning procedures unnecessarily cause splashing, spraying, spattering, and generation of droplets of blood or OPIM.

M.4.b.(7) **Section (d)(2)(xii).** While this section prohibits mouth pipetting/suctioning, the agency allows a recognized emergency care method of clearing an infant's airways called "DeLee suctioning" in the following situation:

(a) In an emergency,

(b) When no other method is available; and

(c) Provided that a trap which prevents suctioned fluid from reaching the employee's mouth is inserted in-line between the infant and the employee.

(8) **Sections (d)(2)(xiii)-(d)(2)(xiii)(C).** These sections deal with the containerization and labeling of specimens with the intent to eliminate or minimize the possibility of inadvertent employee contact with blood or OPIM which have leaked out of the container, contaminated exterior surfaces of the container, and/or surrounding surfaces. The labeling requirement warns employees that these substances are present so that proper handling precautions can be taken.

(a) The labeling exemption listed in section **(d)(2)(xiii)(A)** applies to facilities which handle **all** specimens (not just those specimens which contain blood or OPIM) with universal precautions.

1 This exemption applies only while these specimens remain within the facility.

2 All employees who will have contact with the specimens must be trained to handle all specimens with universal precautions.

3 If the specimens leave the facility (e.g., during transport, shipment, or disposal) a label or red color-coding would be required.

M.4.b.(8)(b) Extracted teeth are subject to the containerization and labeling provisions of the standard.

(c) The use of pneumatic tube systems for transport of small materials in hospitals now includes transmittal of laboratory specimens and other more fragile items. The primary concern in the transportation of clinical specimens in a pneumatic tube system is leakage of the specimen into the carrier and potentially into the system tubing. Some systems have virtually eliminated breakage as a cause of leakage by means of padded inserts for carriers and soft delivery of the carrier. Leakage generally results from improper packaging and/or the use of primary containers that do not prevent leakage during transport.

1 All workers who might potentially open a carrier shall be trained to regard the contents as biohazardous in nature. Employees who open biohazard carriers shall wear gloves in accordance with section (d)(3) when removing specimens from the tube system carrier, as it may be contaminated with leakage. They shall be trained in decontamination of the carrier and, if need be, the

tube system in accordance with section **(g)(2)**.

2 All precautions and standards for manual transport of specimens also apply to the automated transport of specimens (e.g., containerization and tagging/labeling).

INSPECTION GUIDELINES. The compliance officer must observe or document work practices to determine whether a secondary container is being used when necessary. If a bloody glove contaminates the outside of a primary container while the employee is placing a specimen, the employee would need to use a secondary container. Also, primary containers which may be punctured by their contents, including such items as pointed bone slivers, must be placed in a puncture-resistant secondary container.

M.4.b.(9) **Section (d)(2)(xiv).** When it is not possible to decontaminate equipment prior to servicing or shipping (e.g., highly technical or sensitive equipment and/or limited access to contaminated parts), at least partial decontamination, such as flushing lines and wiping the exterior, shall be accomplished.

INSPECTION AND CITATION GUIDELINES. The compliance officer shall ensure that the employer's program makes provision for the required equipment labels. A label shall be attached to equipment stating which portions of the equipment remain contaminated in order to inform downstream servicing/repair employees of the hazard and precautions they need to take.

(a) Before citing **(d)(2)(xiv)**, the compliance officer shall document that equipment is being shipped and/or serviced.

(b) Compliance officers shall observe or document work practices used when employees are decontaminating equipment. (See M.4.b.(6) of this instruction on section **(d)(2)(xi)** for use of high pressure equipment.)

(c) When decontaminating reusable equipment that is heavily soiled, the employee will have to perform some prewashing before proceeding with decontamination because most disinfectants/sterilants cannot sufficiently penetrate the organic material that may remain on such heavily soiled equipment. (See M.4.d.-(2)(e) of this instruction for details.)

M.4.c. **Personal Protective Equipment - (d)(3).** PPE must be used to prevent blood or OPIM from passing through to, or contacting the employees' work or street clothes, undergarments, skin, eyes, mouth, or other mucous membranes, unless engineering controls and work practices have eliminated occupational exposure.

(1) **Section (d)(3)(i).** The type and amount of PPE shall be chosen to protect against contact with blood or OPIM based upon the type of exposure and quantity of these substances which can be reasonably anticipated to be encountered during the performance of a task or procedure.

INSPECTION AND CITATION GUIDELINES. The financial responsibility for purchasing and providing PPE rests with the employer. The employer is not obligated under this standard to provide general work clothes to employees, but is responsible for providing PPE. If laboratory coats or uniforms are intended to protect the employee's body from contamination, they are to be provided by the employer.

(a) Laboratory coats, uniforms and the like that are used as PPE shall be laundered by the employer and not sent home with the employee for cleaning. (See M.4.c.(4) of this instruction on section (d)(3)(iv).)

M.4.c.(1)(b) Scrubs are usually worn in a manner similar to street clothing, and normally should be covered by appropriate gowns, aprons or laboratory coats when splashes to skin or clothing are anticipated.

1 If a pullover scrub (as opposed to scrubs with snap closures) becomes minimally contaminated, employees should be trained in accordance with section (g)(2)(vii)(G) to remove the pull-over scrub in such a way as to avoid contact with the outer surface; e.g., rolling up the garment as it is pulled toward the head for removal.

2 However, if the amount of blood exposure is such that the blood penetrates the scrub and contaminates the inner surface, not only is it impossible to remove the scrub without exposure to blood, but the penetration itself would constitute exposure. It may be prudent to train employees to cut such a contaminated scrub to aid removal and prevent exposure to the face.

(c) A gown which is frequently ripped or falls apart under normal use would not be considered "appropriate PPE".

(d) Resuscitator devices are to be readily available and accessible to employees who can reasonably be expected to resuscitate a patient.

1 Emergency ventilation devices also fall under the scope of PPE and hence must be provided by the employer for use in resuscitation (e.g., masks, mouthpieces,

resuscitation bags, shields/overlay barriers).

M.4.c.(1)(d)2 Improper use of these devices shall be cited as a violation of section **(d)(3)(ii).** In addition, section **(g)(2)(vii)(G)** which requires employees to be trained in the types, proper use, location, etc., of the PPE shall be cited if inadequate training exists. Improper use includes failure to follow the manufacturer's instructions and/or accepted medical practice.

NOTE: The American Society for Testing Materials is currently (at the publication date of this document) testing and evaluating methods to be used for assessing the quality of PPE that is available for medical use.

(2) **Section (d)(3)(ii).** This section requires the use of PPE. It also provides for a limited exemption from the use of PPE, based on situations in which use of PPE would prevent the proper delivery of health care or public safety services, or would pose an increased hazard to the personal safety of the worker. The following represents examples of when such a situation could occur:

(a) A sudden change in patient status occurs such as when an apparently stable patient unexpectedly begins to hemorrhage profusely, putting the patient's life in immediate jeopardy;

(b) A firefighter rescues an individual who is not breathing from a burning building and discovers that his/her resuscitation equipment is lost/damaged and he/she must administer CPR;

M.4.c.(2)(c) A bleeding suspect unexpectedly attacks a police officer with a knife, threatening the safety of the officer and/or co-workers.

NOTE: An employee's decision not to use PPE is to be made on a case-by-case basis and must have been prompted by legitimate and truly extenuating circumstances. In such cases, no citation shall be issued when the employee temporarily and briefly abandons use of PPE. This does not relieve the employer of the responsibility to ensure that PPE is readily accessible at all times. The employer shall document why PPE was not used in each case and evaluate the circumstances surrounding the incident to reduce the likelihood of a future (unprotected) incident.

CITATION GUIDELINES. Section **(d)(3)(ii)** shall be cited if PPE is not being used properly. Improper use would include wearing the wrong PPE (e.g., wearing a laboratory coat when a rubber apron is needed) or wearing the wrong size PPE.

- In addition, section **(g)(2)(vii)(G)** shall also be cited if the employees have not been adequately trained.

- Unless all elements of the exemption, including the documentation requirement are met, the employer shall not receive the benefit of this exemption and section **(d)(3)(ii)** shall be cited.

(3) **Section (d)(3)(iii).** This section requires that the employer provide PPE in appropriate sizes and accessible locations. In addition, hypoallergenic gloves, glove liners,

powderless gloves, or other similar alternatives shall be readily accessible to those employees who are allergic to the gloves normally provided. The compliance officer shall review the employer's program and, through employee interviews, ensure that these provisions have been met.

CITATION GUIDELINES. If PPE is not provided, the compliance officer shall cite section **(d)(3)(i)**. If PPE is not readily available, the compliance officer shall cite section **(d)(3)(iii)**. For example, the clothing of paramedics out on an emergency call may become blood-soaked. If they are unable to change before the next emergency call because a second set of clothing is located at the ambulance's home base, and the ambulance does not return to base for prolonged periods, a violation of section **(d)(3)(iii)** would exist.

- If it is common practice that PPE is not utilized during certain situations or procedures where exposure to blood or OPIM is anticipated, then a violation of section **(d)(3)(ii)** would exist. If inaccessibility of PPE exists, section **(d)(3)(iii)** shall also be cited.

M.4.c.(4) **Section (d)(3)(iv).** It is the employer's responsibility not only to provide PPE, but to clean, maintain, and/or dispose of it.

(a) While many employees have traditionally provided and laundered their own uniforms or laboratory coats or the like, if the item's intended function is to act as PPE, then it is the employer's responsibility to provide, clean, repair, replace, and/or dispose of it.

(b) Home laundering is not permitted since the employer cannot guarantee that proper handling or laundering procedures are being followed; it could also lead to the migration of contaminants to the home.

(c) If the employee wishes to choose, wear, and maintain his/her own uniform or laboratory coat, then he/she would need to don additional employer-handled and employer-controlled PPE when performing tasks where it is reasonable to anticipate exposure to blood or OPIM.

CITATION GUIDELINES. If PPE is not cleaned/ laundered/disposed of by the employer, or if the employer cleans the PPE but there is a charge to the employee, then section **(d)(3)(iv)** shall be cited. If PPE is not repaired and/or replaced by the employer at no cost to the employee then section **(d)(3)(v)** shall be cited.

- If PPE is not removed when penetrated by blood or OPIM, the compliance officer shall cite section **(d)(3)(vi)**.

- If the PPE is not changed, and additional PPE was available, section **(g)(2)(vii)(G)** may also be cited if employees have not been adequately trained.

M.4.c.(5) **Section (d)(3)(vii).** To minimize migration of contamination beyond the work area, employees who are provided designated lunchrooms or break rooms are permitted to eat/ drink/smoke in these areas as long as the employees wash up and change any contaminated clothing prior to entry.

INSPECTION AND CITATION GUIDELINES. The "work area" shall be evaluated on a case-by-case basis. While it is not the intent of the standard to require employees to change PPE when traveling, for example, from one hospital laboratory area to another, the compliance officer shall evaluate on a case-by-case basis whether the employee received adequate training in accordance with section **(g)(2)(vii)(F)** to ensure that no surface contamination occurs during the employee's movement. A violation would exist for the following:

- An employee wearing contaminated gloves exits from a pathology laboratory to use a public telephone located in a public hallway of the hospital. Under such circumstances, it can be reasonably anticipated that another employee, without benefit of gloves or knowledge of the potential surface contamination, could use the phone and unwittingly become contaminated.

M.4.c.(6) **Section (d)(3)(ix)(A)-(C).** These sections discuss the use of gloves. Gloves of appropriate sizes must be made available in accordance with section **(d)(3)(iii)**. Studies have shown that gloves provide a barrier, but that neither vinyl nor latex procedure gloves are completely impermeable. Thus, hand-washing after glove removal is required.

(a) While disposable gloves shall be replaced as soon as practical when contaminated, obviously some critical procedures (i.e., surgery, delivery) cannot be interrupted to change gloves. The key words to evaluate are "practical" and "feasible".

(b) Disinfecting agents may cause deterioration of the glove material; washing with surfactants could result in "wicking" or enhanced pentration of liquids into the glove via undetected pores thereby transporting potentially infectious materials into contact with the hand. For this reason, disposable (single use) gloves may not be washed and reused.

(c) The compliance officer should note that certain solutions, such as iodine, may cause discoloration of gloves without affecting their integrity and function.

(d) At a minimum gloves shall be used where there is reasonable anticipation of employee hand contact with blood, OPIM, mucous membranes, or nonintact skin; when performing vascular access procedures; or when handling or touching contaminated surfaces or items.

M.4.c.(7) **Section (d)(3)(ix)(D).** The exemption regarding the use of gloves during phlebotomy procedures applies only to employees of volunteer donor blood collection centers, and does not apply to phlebotomy conducted in other settings such as plasmapherisis centers or hospitals.

INSPECTION GUIDELINES. Where an employer in a volunteer donor blood collection center does not require routine gloving for all phlebotomies, the compliance officer shall document that the employer has fulfilled the requirements of sections **(d)(3)(ix)(D)(1) through (d)(3)(ix)(D)(4)(iii)**, and that employees have received the training necessary to make an informed decision on the wearing of gloves.

CITATION GUIDELINES. Section **(d)(3)(ix)(D)** shall not be cited. Rather, the other sections of **(d)(3)** shall be cited if such an employer violates them and if the employer has not demonstrated fulfillment of all the requirements of the exemptions.

(8) **Section (d)(3)(x).** This section requires protection for the mucous membranes of the face and upper respiratory tract from droplet spattering. Minimum protection would consist of a mask in conjunction with eye glasses with solid side shields or a chin length face shield.

(a) The employer would not necessarily have to provide prescription eyewear for employees. They could provide and mandate the use of side shields, goggles, and/or protective face shields, and provide proper training in decontamination procedures.

(b) During microsurgery, when it is not reasonably anticipated that there would be any spattering, it would not constitute a violation for the surgeon, while observing surgery through a microscope, not to wear other eye protection.

M.4.c.(9) **Sections (d)(3)(xi)-(xii).** Use of protective body clothing, such as gowns, aprons, laboratory coats, clinic jackets, surgical caps, or shoe covers, and the degree to which such PPE must resist penetration, are performance based. The employer must evaluate the task and the type of exposure expected and, based on the determination, select the "appropriate" personal protective clothing in accordance with section **(d)(3)(i).** For example, laboratory coats or gowns with long sleeves shall be used for procedures in which exposure of the forearm to blood or OPIM is reasonably anticipated to occur.

INSPECTION GUIDELINES. The compliance officer will need to evaluate the task being performed and the degree of anticipated exposure by direct observation, employee interview, or review of written standard operating procedures.

NOTE: There are no currently available standardized methods of testing and classification of performance specifications for resistance of clothing to biological hazards.

d. **Housekeeping - (d)(4).** The term "worksite" in this section refers not only to permanent fixed facilities such as hospitals, dental/medical offices, clinics, etc., but also covers temporary non-fixed workplaces. Examples of such facilities include but are not limited to ambulances, bloodmobiles, temporary blood collection centers, and any other non-fixed worksites which have a reasonable possibility of becoming contaminated with blood or OPIM.

M.4.d.(1) **Section (d)(4)(i).** Cleaning schedules and methods will vary according to the factors outlined in this section. While extraordinary attempts to disinfect or sterilize environmental surfaces such as walls or floors are rarely indicated, routine cleaning and removal of soil are required.

(a) The employer must determine and implement an appropriate written schedule of cleaning and decontamination based upon the location within the facility (e.g., surgical operatory versus patient room), type of surface to be cleaned (e.g., hard-surfaced flooring versus carpeting), type of soil present (e.g., gross contamination versus minor splattering), and tasks and procedures being performed (e.g., laboratory analyses versus normal patient care).

(b) The particular disinfectant used, as well as the frequency with which it is used, will depend upon the circumstances in which the housekeeping task occurs.

INSPECTION AND CITATION GUIDELINES. Compliance officers should consult the Environmental Protection Agency (EPA) lists of registered sterilants (representing the highest level of antimicrobial activity which destroys all viruses), tuberculocidal disinfectants (effective against tuberculosis bacteria and the specific viruses named on the product label as well as the hepatitis B virus), and antimicrobials with HIV efficacy claims for verification that the disinfectant used is appropriate. These lists are available from the Regional bloodborne pathogens coordinators.

NOTE: Products registered by the EPA as HIV-effective are not necessarily tuberculocidal and are therefore not necessarily effective against HBV which is more resistant to inactivation than is HIV. To determine the overall effectiveness of a particular product with an HIV-efficacy claim for use in a cleanup where HBV or other bloodborne pathogens are also of concern, the compliance officer must compare the listing of HIV-effective products with the other two listings to check if they overlap for the product of interest.

M.4.d.(2) **Section (d)(4)(ii).** Since environmental contamination is an effective method of disease transmission for HBV (the CDC states that HBV can survive for at least one week in dried blood on environmental surfaces or contaminated needles and instruments), section (d)(4)(ii) provides the minimum requirements for the cleaning and decontamination of equipment and environmental and working surfaces that come into contact with blood or OPIM.

(a) In section (d)(4)(ii)(A), cleaning of contaminated work surfaces after completion of procedures is required to ensure that employees are not unwittingly exposed to blood or OPIM remaining on a surface from previous procedures.

1 Where procedures are performed on a continual basis throughout a shift or a day, as may be the case with a clinical laboratory technician performing blood analyses, it is not the agency's intent for the work surface to be decontaminated before the technician can proceed to the next analysis; rather for contaminated work surfaces to be decontaminated after the procedures are completed which, in the above example, would include a set of analyses. The completion of procedures

might also occur when the employee is going to leave the work area for a period of time.

M.4.d.(2)(a)2 Decontamination is not automatically required after each patient care procedure, rather only after procedures resulting in surface contamination.

3 There may be some instances in which "immediate" decontamination of overt contamination and spills may not be practical as with, for example, an operating table during surgery.

4 The third instance of mandated work surface decontamination is to be performed at the end of the work shift if the work surface may have become contaminated since the last cleaning by, for example, setting down contaminated instruments or specimens. This requirement is based upon the existence of a contaminated work surface rather than a particular worksite location. It does not, for example, encompass desks, countertops, and so forth that remain uncontaminated.

(b) The use of protective coverings described in section **(d)(4)(ii)(B)** is an acceptable alternative for protecting items and surfaces against contamination and is particularly useful in situations in which a piece of equipment would be difficult to decontaminate but could be protected by a cover.

1 If this option is chosen, the covering must be removed and replaced at the stated minimum intervals; e.g., as soon as feasible following overt contamination or at the end of a

workshift if they may have become contaminated during the shift.

M.4.d.(2)(b) 2 More stringent decontamination rules, such as cleaning equipment or changing coverings between patients, may be prudent infection control policy but do not fall under OSHA's jurisdictional mandate to safeguard employee (not patient) health.

(c) Section d(4)(ii)(C) requires both the inspection and decontamination on a regularly scheduled basis of cans, bins, pails, and so forth which are intended for reuse.

1 Since these containers may be used in a manner which presents the potential for their becoming contaminated with blood or OPIM, they must be cleaned immediately or as soon as feasible upon visible contamination. For example, a reusable metal trash can may be lined with a disposable plastic regulated waste bag which leaks and contaminates the can. In addition, regular decontamination will prevent the can from leaking, spilling, or contaminating the outside of successive bags.

2 Disinfection of these containers is not necessary to ensure their safety for their intended use; it may be possible to achieve their proper decontamination by means of a soap and water wash.

(d) Since contaminated broken glass is capable of inflicting percutaneous injury and direct inoculation of bloodborne pathogens into the bloodstream, section (d)(4)(ii)(D) stipulates that broken glassware which may be contaminated shall not be picked up directly with the hands. The tools which are used in cleanup must be properly decontaminated or discarded after use and the broken glass placed in a sharps container and employees must be given specific information and training with respect to this task in accordance with the requirements of section **(g)(2)**. Vacuum cleaners are not appropriate for cleanup of contaminated broken glass.

M.4.d.(2)(e) Section **(d)(4)(ii)(E)** prohibits employers from allowing employees to place their hands into containers whose contents include reusable sharps contaminated with blood or OPIM. (See M.4.d.(3)(g) of this instruction on section **(d)(4)(iii)(A)(4)**.)

NOTE: The final standard recognizes that proper decontamination of reusable equipment, such as glassware or hand instruments, cannot be achieved in the presence of organic debris (e.g., blood) as it interferes with the efficacy of the disinfecting/sterilizing process and the number of products which can successfully penetrate a heavy bioburden is limited.

(f) Violations of sections **(d)(4)(ii)** and **(d)(4)(ii)(A)-(E)** may result from a failure to adequately train employees in proper housekeeping procedures. If the compliance officer determines this is the case, violations should be grouped with the appropriate section(s) of **(g)(2)**.

(3) **Regulated Waste - (d)(4)(iii).** This section requires regulated waste to be properly contained and disposed of, so as not to become a means of transmission of disease to workers.

M.4.d.(3)(a) To eliminate the implication that OSHA has determined the "infectivity" of certain medical wastes, the bloodborne pathogens standard uses the term "regulated waste" to refer to the following categories of waste which require special handling, at a minimum:

1 Liquid or semi-liquid blood or OPIM.

2 Items contaminated with blood or OPIM and which would release these substances in a liquid or semi-liquid state if compressed.

3 Items that are caked with dried blood or OPIM and are capable of releasing these materials during handling.

4 Contaminated sharps.

5 Pathological and microbiological wastes containing blood or OPIM.

INSPECTION AND CITATION GUIDELINES. The compliance officer shall not use the actual volume of blood as the determining factor as to whether or not a particular material is to be considered regulated waste since 10 ml of blood on a disposable bed sheet would appear as a spot (not regulated waste) while the same amount of blood on a cotton ball would likely cause saturation and dripping (regulated waste). Similarly, an item may adequately contain these materials when in a static state yet liberate them when compacted in the waste container.

- Rather, the potential for dripping of liquid blood or OPIM, or flaking off of dried blood or OPIM should be considered.

- Under no circumstances should a bag of waste be squeezed or shaken to determine this. The compliance officer shall exercise professional judgment to make a determination based on visual factors such as a pool of liquid in the bottom of the container or dried blood flaking or falling off during handling, or based on employee interviews.

NOTES:

1. The compliance officer should keep in mind that while OSHA specifies certain features of the regulated waste containers, including appropriate tagging, the ultimate disposal method (landfilling, incinerating, and so forth) for medical waste falls under the purview of the EPA and possibly State and local regulations.

2. The EPA's Standard for the Tracking and Management of Medical Waste and a number of State regulations consider used needles to be regulated medical waste regardless of the presence of infectious agents. Failing information to the contrary, the compliance officer should consider a used needle to be contaminated.

M.4.d.(3)(b) **Section (d)(4)(iii)(A)(1).** The construction of the sharps containers must meet at least four criteria, two of which will be easily discernible. The compliance officer shall examine a container, preferably empty, to check that it is closable and color-coded or labeled.

1 Sharps containers are made from a variety of products, from cardboard to plastic. As long as they meet the definition of a sharps container, the compliance officer should

consider them to be acceptable no matter what the composition.

M.4.d.(3)(b)2 At the time of publication of this instruction, the American Biological Safety Association was in the process of developing a standard for puncture-resistance of sharps disposal containers.

a If questions arise, the compliance officer shall consult the manufacturer's literature or contact the manufacturer directly to determine if the container is leak-proof on the sides and bottom, as well as puncture resistant.

b If the container is considered puncture-resistant by the manufacturer, but there is evidence, through observation or employee statements that sharps have been protruding through a container, section (d)(4)(iii)(A)(1)(ii) shall be cited.

3 The sharps container should not create additional hazards. Some sharps containers have unwinders that are used to separate needles from syringes.

a If this situation is encountered, the compliance officer shall determine if the circumstances warrant needle removal. If they do not, section (d)(2)(vii)(A) which prohibits needle removal unless no alternative is feasible or it is required by a specific medical procedure, shall be cited.

b If needle removal must be accomplished, the employee shall be trained in the correct procedure as required by **(g)(2)(vii)(F)**.

M.4.d.(3)(b)4 The needle sheath is **not** to be considered a "waste container" because it is viewed as a temporary measure. Self-sheathing needle products must be disposed of in a sharps container.

a Some self-sheathing devices contain a fast-curing colored liquid adhesive which is released inside the sheath after completion of administration of a substance through the needle. This product is intended to permanently adhere all components of the syringe needle and needle sheath, rendering the syringe and needle assembly inoperable and incapable of causing injury.

b These devices shall still be disposed of in sharps containers since there is no guarantee of correct usage or proper functioning of the device.

5 Duct tape may be used to secure a sharps container lid but is not acceptable if it serves as the lid itself.

(c) **Section (d)(4)(iii)(A)(2)(i).** The compliance officer shall ensure that the sharps container is as close as feasible to where sharps are used or can be reasonably anticipated to be found.

M.4.d.(3)(c)1 If an employee must travel to a remote location to discard a sharp, it will increase the possibility of an accidental needlestick and increase the chances that needles and sharps will be improperly discarded and create potential hazards for other staff members.

a Areas such as correctional facilities, psychiatric units, or pediatric units may have difficulty placing containers in the immediate use area. If a mobile cart is used by health care workers in these units, an alternative would be to lock a sharps container in the cart.

b The determination of whether or not the container is as close as feasible shall be made on a case-by-case basis. After interviewing employees, if the compliance officer believes there is a better location for the container, management shall be given the opportunity to explain the present location of the container. The acceptability of the new site shall also be discussed. The compliance officer shall then decide if a violation of this section exists.

2 Laundries shall also have sharps containers easily accessible due to the incidence of needles being mixed with laundry. Facilities that handle shipments of waste which may contain contaminated sharps, shall also have sharps containers available in the event a

package accidentally opens and releases sharps.

M.4.d.(3)(d) **Section (d)(4)(iii)(A)(2)(iii).** The compliance officer shall ensure the employer's exposure control plan specifies how and when the sharps containers will be replaced and that the program is followed.

1 The employer's plan must include the method by which sharps containers will be determined to need to be replaced, such as sharps containers which have a transparent window or are at a height which allows employees to see if the container needs to be replaced.

2 If the employer has a plan but it is not followed, a citation for inadequate training on work practices, (g)(2)(vii)(F), shall be grouped with this section if a training violation exists.

(e) **Section (d)(4)(iii)(A)(3)(i) and (ii).** If work practice violations of these sections exist (e.g., not closing the container prior to movement or not placing the container in a secondary container if leakage is possible), they shall be grouped with **(g)(2)(vii)(F)** if employees have not received adequate training.

(f) **Section (d)(4)(iii)(A)(3)(ii)(B).** It is reasonable to presume that some sharps containers will contain residual liquids. If the container cannot be sealed to prevent leakage, it must be placed in a secondary container.

(g) **Section (d)(4)(iii)(A)(4).** A reusable sharps container system will be acceptable if it does not expose employees to the risk of percutaneous injury. No system involving the manual opening, emptying, or cleaning of the containers will be allowed. The only acceptable system is a fully automated container cleaning system that eliminates employee exposure to sharps.

M.4.d.(3)(h) **Section (d)(4)(iii)(B).** While this section requires that regulated waste containers be closable, simply being closed does not ensure that wastes will be contained. Waste-containing bags may break and spill their contents, including liquid blood, while, for example, being loaded onto incinerator hoppers, thus contaminating both the employees and the work area.

1 Also, small medical offices which generate only a small volume of regulated waste may place that waste in a large holding container until the container is filled. In such a case, the design of the container must be such that it is able to retain the waste over an extended period of time between pickups by a specialized waste service.

2 The compliance officer should, therefore, check for visual signs of leakage of fluids during handling, storage, transport, or shipping.

3 Any failures to comply with the container construction requirements would be cited under this section. If the compliance officer determines that the employee was not properly trained to recognize the problem or use the containers correctly, a citation for the appropriate section of (g)(2) should be grouped with violations of paragraph (d).

M.4.d.(3)(i) **Sections (d)(4)(iii)(B)(1)(iii) and (2)(iii).** Regulated waste containers are required to be labeled with the biohazard symbol or color coded to warn employees who may have contact with the containers of the potential hazard posed by their contents.

1 Even if a facility considers all of its waste to be regulated waste, the waste containers must still bear the required label or color-coding in order to protect new employees, who would not normally come into contact with wastes, and employees from outside the facility. This requirement is in contrast to the labeling alternative allowed when laundries use universal precautions for the handling of all soiled laundry. (See M.4.d.-(4)(a) of this instruction on section (d)(4)(iv)(A)(2).)

2 Regulated waste that has been decontaminated need not be labeled or color-coded. The compliance officer in such a case shall verify that the employer's exposure control plan states the decontamination procedures to be followed.

a In order to ensure that the decontamination process is successful, the employer must monitor factors such as the content, volume, density, configuration, and organic content of the load of waste. (See M.7.a.(2) of this instruction on section (g)(1)(i)(I).)

b The temperature needed for the complete breakdown of plastics, as required by EPA, is sufficient to decontaminate regulated waste.

M.4.d.(3)(i)2 c Autoclave efficiency can be verified by means of biological or chemical indicators. While most disposal bags used will contain an indicative color strip, if this is not the case a review may be made of the documentation kept for the sterilizer. Such documentation should include (1) date, time, and operator of each run, (2) type and approximate amount of waste tracked, (3) post-treatment reading of temperature-sensitive tape, (4) dates and results of calibration of the sterilizer, and (5) results of routine spore testing.

d For a more detailed discussion of chemical decontamination, see guidelines at M.4.d.(1) of this instruction.

3 Although these sections contain label requirements, failure to label can also be cited under section (g)(1)(i).

(j) **Section (d)(4)(iii)(B)(2).** A second container is required to be used when outside contamination of the first waste container occurs. This provision does not require routine double-bagging but rather requires double-bagging in such circumstances as a waste container being splashed with blood during surgery or autopsy, when a container has been handled by an employee with bloody gloves, or when a waste bag leaks blood or OPIM onto an adjacent bag.

M.4.d.(4) **Laundry - (d)(4)(iv).** This section reduces employee exposure to bloodborne pathogens by reducing the amount of manual handling of contaminated laundry. Restricting the sorting to the laundry area will also reduce contamination of additional surfaces.

INSPECTION AND CITATION GUIDELINES. Sections (d)(4)(iv)(A) and (A)(1) limit the handling of laundry to removal and bagging or containerization. The compliance officer shall check the laundry collection program as well as the training of the employees assigned to these tasks.

(a) **Section (d)(4)(iv)(A)(2).** The employer has been given the choice, by this section, to either:

1 Label or color-code according to section **(g)(1)(i)**, or

2 Utilize universal precautions in the handling of all soiled (i.e., used) laundry.

a If universal precautions are used for handling all soiled laundry, the employer may use an alternative color or label for the bags/containers, as long as all employees are trained to recognize them as containing soiled laundry which requires the use of universal precautions.

b Training violations would be cited under the appropriate section of **(g)(2)(vii)**.

3 Refer to M.4.d.(4)(d) on section **(d)(4)(iv)(C)** for labeling when laundry is shipped off-site.

M.4.d.(4)(b) **Section (d)(4)(iv)(A)(3).** The material for the bags or containers used in laundry collection must prevent soak-through or leakage of fluids to the exterior, if the contaminated laundry is wet and presents a reasonable likelihood of soak-through or leakage. Not all contaminated laundry must be placed in such bags or containers, only laundry wet enough to leak or soak through and expose workers handling the bags/ containers to blood or OPIM.

(c) **Section (d)(4)(iv)(B).** Employees having direct contact with contaminated laundry must wear protective gloves and any other appropriate personal protective equipment, in order to prevent or reduce contact exposure to blood or OPIM. Any other personal protective equipment required must be determined on a case-by-case basis. Gowns, aprons, eyewear, and masks may be necessary to prevent employee exposure.

(d) **Section (d)(4)(iv)(C).** The generator of the laundry must have determined if the facility to which it is shipped utilizes universal precautions. If not, all bags or containers of contaminated laundry must be labeled or color-coded in accordance with section (g)(1)(i). In this instance, if the generator of the laundry chooses to color-code rather than label, the color of the bag must be red.

INSPECTION AND CITATION GUIDELINES. The compliance officer shall check the employer's program to determine if laundry is shipped to another facility for cleaning and shall evaluate the methods used to ship contaminated laundry (CL) to a facility that does not utilize universal precautions in the handling of all soiled laundry. The following are unacceptable shipment methods and constitute violations of this section:

M.4.d.(4)(d)1 The CL is not shipped labeled or in a red bag. Section **(d)(4)(iv)(C)** would be cited and grouped with the applicable subsection of **(g)(1)(i)**.

2 The CL is shipped with an improper label. Section **(d)(4)(iv)(C)** would be cited and grouped with the applicable subsections of **(g)(1)-(i)(B),(C)**, and/or **(D)**.

3 The CL is shipped in a bag color-coded for in-house use (in a color other than red). Section **(d)(4)(iv)(C)** would be cited and grouped with section **(g)(1)(i)(E)**.

5. **HIV and HBV Research Laboratories and Production Facilities - 29 CFR 1910.1030(e).** This section includes additional requirements that must be met by research laboratories and production facilities engaged in the culture, production, concentration, and manipulation of HIV and HBV.

- **"Research laboratory"** means a laboratory which produces or uses research laboratory scale amounts of HIV or HBV. Although research laboratories may not have the volume found in production facilities, they deal with solutions containing higher viral titers than those normally found in patients' blood. Academic research laboratories are included in this definition. Laboratories that conduct research unrelated to HIV or HBV on blood and other body fluids, or who use unconcentrated blood or blood components as the source of HIV or HBV, are not considered research laboratories for the purpose of this section.

- **"Production facilities"** are those engaged in industrial scale, large volume, or high concentration production of HIV or HBV.

NOTES: 1. Employers in such a facilities remain responsible for complying with the entire standard. Requirements stated elsewhere in the standard are not repeated.

2. These requirements are based largely on information from published guidelines of the Centers for Disease Control (CDC) and the National Institutes of Health (NIH) (See D.9. of this instruction, "Biosafety in Microbiological and Biomedical Laboratories.")

INSPECTION AND CITATION GUIDELINES. The compliance officer shall review the covered facility's plan, interview a sufficient number of employees, and observe work practices as necessary to determine if the requirements of this section are met. Care shall be taken to ensure the compliance officer understands the special practices and precautions in place at the facility, so that the compliance officer is not placed at risk. Specific requirements include:

a. **Section (e)(2)(i).** The term "regulated waste" refers to the OSHA definition as found in section (b) of this standard. The purpose of decontaminating regulated waste is to prevent the accidental exposure of other employees to the concentrated virus.

b. **Sections (e)(2)(ii)(A) through (M).** Sections (A), (C), and (D) limit access to the laboratory and warn of the hazards associated with bloodborne pathogens. The compliance officer must review the written policies and procedures to determine if they are adequate to ensure that unauthorized individuals are not placed at risk nor that they can distract or otherwise interfere with the work of the authorized employees. Interviews with employees should be used to determine if the policies are followed.

   (1) **Section (e)(2)(ii)(E).** The "other physical containment device" must be sufficient to ensure that virus-containing material will be kept away from the worker's mucous membranes, unprotected skin, and breathing zone.

(2) **Sections (e)(2)(ii)(H) and (I).** These sections prevent the spread of contamination to other work areas. Section (I) allows for an alternative to a HEPA filter as long as it is of equivalent or superior efficiency. HEPA filters may be ineffective in humid atmospheres.

(a) The employer must also have made provisions for routine maintenance and/or replacement of all filters and traps.

(b) If the compliance officer suspects that the engineering controls are failing to prevent the spread of the virus, the manufacturer should be contacted to establish the limits and required maintenance of the filters and traps.

(3) **Section (e)(2)(ii)(J).** The compliance officer shall determine if the use of needles and syringes is kept to a minimum and that they are properly handled as required, paying particular attention to establishing if the puncture-resistant containers are properly autoclaved or decontaminated before being discarded, reused, or incinerated.

(4) **Section (e)(2)(ii)(M).** This section ensures that any necessary additional procedures are developed to protect employees in situations unique to a research/production facility. The biosafety manual required by this section shall be reviewed and updated annually or more often if necessary. The facility will thus be required to review its procedures and determine if they are adequate to protect workers.

c. **Section (e)(2)(iii).** Specific containment equipment is required by this section to minimize or eliminate exposure to the viruses.

(1) If the compliance officer determines that biological safety cabinets (BSC) have been chosen as the means of containment, they must be certified (Class I, Class II, or Class

III) when installed or moved, and at least annually.

(a) The compliance officer shall check that a dated tag is affixed to the BSC indicating who performed the certification. Alternatively, a certification report attesting to a minimum inward face velocity of at least 75 linear feet per minute and the integrity of the HEPA filters shall be reviewed by the compliance officer. The report must be dated and signed by the trained technician performing the measurements and integrity tests.

(b) See Appendix C for details on biological safety cabinets.

(2) In the alternative, appropriate combinations of PPE or physical containment devices (examples listed in the standard) will be accepted.

d. **Sections (e)(3)(i) and (e)(4)(iii).** The hand-washing facility must be supplied with at least tepid water, soap, and hand towels. The eyewash must supply a sufficient quantity of water to completely flush the eyes. A 15-minute supply of continuous free-flowing water is acceptable. The hands must be free to hold the eyelids open to aid in the complete flushing of the eyes. Portable facilities are acceptable only if they meet these requirements.

e. **Section (e)(4)** covers additional requirements for production facilities only. The requirement in section **(e)(4)(v)** minimizes the potential for accidental exposure to other employees from the transport of culture fluids, plastic ware, and other contaminated equipment.

f. **Training Requirements - (e)(5).** The additional training requirements are specified in section **(g)(2)(ix).** Any violations found would be cited under that section of the standard. (See M.7.b.-(5) of this instruction for details.)

6. **Hepatitis B Vaccination and Post Exposure Evaluation and Followup - 29 CFR 1910.1030(f).** This section provides a means to protect employees from infection caused by the hepatitis B virus by requiring employers to make the hepatitis B vaccination available to employees with occupational exposure to blood or OPIM. It also ensures that employees receive appropriate medical followup after each specific exposure incident. Appendix D provides general algorithms for these requirements.

   a. **General - (f)(1).** This section refers to the hepatitis B vaccination as both the hepatitis B vaccine and vaccination series. These are to be made available to all occupationally exposed employees. In addition, a post-exposure evaluation and followup procedures are to be made available to all employees who experience an exposure incident. While it is OSHA's intent to have the employer remove, as much as possible, obstacles to the employee's acceptance of the vaccine, the term "made available" emphasizes that it is the employee's option to participate in the vaccination and followup programs.

   INSPECTION GUIDELINES. The compliance officer shall examine the employer's program to determine if the vaccination series and post-exposure followup procedures meet the requirements of section **(f)(1)(ii).**

   (1) **Section (f)(1)(ii)(A).** The term "no cost to the employee" means no "out of pocket" expense to the employee.

      (a) The employer may not require the employee to use his/her health care insurance to pay for the series unless the employer pays all of the cost of the health insurance and unless there is no cost to the employee in the form of deductibles, co-payments, or other expenses. Even partial employee contribution to the insurance premium means the employee could be affected by a rise in the total premium caused by insurance company reaction to widespread hepatitis

B vaccinations and is therefore unacceptable.

(b) The employer may not institute a program in which the employee pays the original cost of the vaccine and is reimbursed by the employer if she/he remains employed for a specified period of time.

(c) An "amortization contract" which requires employees to reimburse the employer for the cost of the vaccination should they leave his/her employ prior to a specified period of time is similarly prohibited.

(2) **Section (f)(1)(ii)(B).** The term "reasonable time and place" requires the medical procedures and evaluations to be convenient to the employee. They shall be offered during normally scheduled work hours. If participation requires travel away from the worksite, the employer must bear the cost.

(3) **Section (f)(1)(ii)(C).** The compliance officer may have to contact the Regional bloodborne pathogens coordinator to determine if the State board of nursing licensing allows licensed health care professionals other than physicians to carry out the procedures and evaluations required by section (f).

(4) **Section (f)(1)(ii)(D).** This section takes into consideration the changing nature of medical treatment relating to bloodborne pathogens. The CDC is the U.S. Public Health Service (USPHS) agency responsible for issuing guidelines and making recommendations regarding infectious agents. OSHA will accept the CDC guidelines current at the time of the evaluation or procedure. Copies of the current guidelines can be obtained by contacting the Regional bloodborne pathogens coordinator or CDC. (See Appendices A and B.)

NOTE: This section requires that the current USPHS/CDC guidelines be followed for all vaccinations, evaluations, and followup procedures. Any additional requirements (such as obtaining a written health care professional's opinion) specified in section **(f)** must also be met.

(5) **Section (f)(1)(iii)** requires that all laboratory tests be conducted by an accredited laboratory. The compliance officer must determine by means of employer documentation (e.g., certificate) that the laboratory is accredited by a national accrediting body (such as CDC or College of American Pathologists) or equivalent State agency which participates in a recognized quality assurance program.

b. **Hepatitis B Vaccination - (f)(2).** The compliance officer shall determine whether or not all occupationally exposed employees have the hepatitis B vaccination series made available to them after training required by section **(g)(2)-(vii)(I)** and within 10 working days of their initial assignment. The term "made available" includes the health care professional's evaluation and arranging for the administration of the first dose of the hepatitis B vaccination series to begin within the 10 days. This includes all employees with reasonably anticipated occupational exposure, regardless of how often the exposure may occur. Part-time and temporary employees are included in this coverage. The vaccine does not have to be made available if the employer documents (1) the exemption(s) set forth in section **(f)(2)**, or (2) the signature of the employee on the mandatory declination form. (See **Appendix A** of **29 CFR 1910.1030.)**

(1) **Section (f)(2)(i)** states the circumstances under which an employer is exempted from making the vaccination available. If, (a) the complete hepatitis B vaccination series was previously received, or (b) antibody testing shows the employee to be immune, or (c) the vaccine cannot be given

for medical reasons, the series does not have to be made available. If the employer claims one of these exemptions, it must be documented in the employee's medical record.

(a) The hepatitis B vaccination must be given in the standard dose and through the standard route of administration as recommended in the USPHS/CDC guidelines. At the time of publication of this standard, intradermal inoculation of 0.1 of the normal dose of the hepatitis B vaccine is not recommended by the USPHS and therefore is not an acceptable administration method.

(b) Current USPHS guidelines do not recommend routine post-vaccination testing. Therefore, employers are not currently required to routinely test immune status after vaccination has been completed.

(2) **Section (f)(2)(ii).** Prevaccination screening for antibody status cannot be required of an employee, although if an employer wishes, he/she can make it available at no cost to employees. An employee may decline the prescreening, and the employer must still make the vaccination series available to the employee.

(3) **Section (f)(2)(iii).** The signing of the hepatitis B vaccine declination form by the employee, at the time the vaccination is made available, does not relieve the employer from the requirement to provide the vaccine at a later date if the employee so chooses.

(4) **Section (f)(2)(iv).** Although the declination form set forth in **29 CFR 1910.1030, Appendix A**, does not have to be reproduced, the declination statement used by the employer must contain the same language as that found in **Appendix A**--no words may be added or subtracted.

(5) **Section (f)(2)(v).** At the time of this publication, the possible need for booster doses of the hepatitis B vaccine is still being assessed. There is no current requirement to provide boosters unless the USPHS recommends it at a later date.

c. **Post-Exposure Evaluation and Followup - (f)(3).** This section requires the employer to make immediately available a confidential medical evaluation and followup to an employee reporting an exposure incident.

NOTE: Employees who do not fall within the scope of this standard may still experience a specific exposure incident at work that is unrelated to the performance of their job duties. In such a case, OSHA strongly encourages their employer to offer them the followup procedures set forth in this section.

INSPECTION GUIDELINES. The compliance officer must determine if the employer's plan provides for immediate and confidential procedures. At sites where an exposure incident has occurred it should be determined if the procedures were properly followed through interviews, incident report reviews, and, if necessary, medical records reviews.

- The word "immediately" is used in the standard to emphasize the importance of prompt medical evaluation and prophylaxis. An exact time was not given in the standard since medical knowledge concerning the effectiveness of post-exposure prophylactic measures is constantly changing. OSHA requires the evaluation and followup procedures to be given as soon as possible after exposure.

- If the compliance officer believes that an employer is not properly following accepted post-exposure procedures, or needs specific information about current accepted procedures, the Regional bloodborne pathogens coordinator should be contacted. A health care professional in the National Office will then be consulted.

- The employer must also have established a system that maintains the required medical records in a way that protects the confidentiality of the employee's identity and test results. If the employer has contracted with a clinic or other health care facility to provide the followup programs, the confidentiality requirements must be part of the contract.

(1) **Section (f)(3)(i).** Documentation of the circumstances surrounding an exposure incident will help the employer and the compliance officer determine, for example, if PPE is being used or if training is lacking.

(2) **Section (f)(3)(ii).** This section requires the employer to identify the source individual in an exposure incident, unless this is infeasible. The employer must document in writing the identity of, or infeasibility of identifying, the source individual. Examples of when it may not be feasible to identify the source individual include incidents of needlesticks by unmarked syringes left in laundry or those involving blood samples which are not properly labeled, as well as prohibition by State or local law.

(a) **Section (f)(3)(ii)(A).** This section requires testing of the source individual's blood after consent is obtained. The employer must ask for consent from the source individual or anyone legally authorized to give consent on his/her behalf. If consent is not obtained, the employer must document this in writing. The compliance officer shall ensure that the employer's plan includes this provision.

<u>1</u> For those jurisdictions that do not require consent of the individual, available blood must be tested.

The term "if available" applies to blood samples that have already been drawn from the source individual.

2 OSHA does not require redrawing of blood specifically for HBV and HIV testing without consent of the source individual.

(b) **Section (f)(3)(ii)(C).** This section does not authorize the employer to be informed of the results of source individual or exposed employee testing. However, the results of the source individual's testing must be made available to the exposed employee.

1 The boundary between employer and health care professional may be blurred in a medical setting in which, for example, the physician is both the employer and the evaluating health care professional. In such cases, the compliance officer shall ensure that requirements for consent and confidentiality have been followed.

2 "Applicable laws and regulations concerning disclosure" refers to State and Federal laws that specifically cover medical privacy and confidentiality.

(c) **Section (f)(3)(iii).** The compliance officer must determine if the employer's program offers covered employees all of the listed requirements, in the event of an exposure incident. Counseling and evaluation of reported illnesses is not dependent on the employee's electing to have baseline HBV and HIV serological testing.

1 **Section (f)(3)(iii)(A).** Although the consent of the employee must also be obtained before collection of blood and before hepatitis B serological testing, the 90-day holding requirement in section (f)(3)(iii)(B) does not apply.

2 **Section (f)(3)(iii)(B).** This section allows employees the opportunity for future testing without the need for an immediate decision.

a Employees involved in an exposure incident have at least 90 days following baseline blood collection to decide if they wish to have their blood tested for HIV.

b Employers are required to preserve the blood the employee consented to have drawn, if it was not tested for HIV initially, for at least the 90-day period. Compliance officers shall check that if the employer contracts for post-exposure followup, the contractor has been informed of the 90-day requirement.

(d) **Section (f)(3)(iv).** See Appendices A and B for CDC's current guidelines on management of occupational exposure to HIV and HBV.

d. **Information Provided to the Health Care Professional - (f)(4).** This section requires the employer to provide information to the health care professional responsible for the employee's hepatitis B vaccination and post-exposure incident followup.

INSPECTION GUIDELINES. The compliance officer must determine if the employer's plan includes providing a copy of this standard to the health care professional responsible for the employee's hepatitis B vaccination.

(1) In the case of an exposure incident, the plan must provide for the transmission of the information required by **(f)(4)(ii)(A-C) and (E)** to the health care professional. The information required by **(f)(4)(ii)(D)** must be provided only if available.

(2) The employer does not have a specific right to know the actual results of the source individual's blood testing, but must ensure that the information is provided to the evaluating health care professional.

(3) If the evaluating health care professional is also the employer, the information must still be in the employee's record and made available at the time of a post-exposure incident. All applicable laws and standards of confidentiality apply in this situation.

e. **Health Care Professional's Written Opinion - (f)(5).** The employer is required to obtain and provide a written opinion to the employee within 15 working days of completion of the original evaluation. Employer access is allowed to the health care professional's written opinion.

(1) **Section (f)(5)(i)** limits the health care professional's written opinion to very specific information regarding the employee's hepatitis B vaccine status, including indication for vaccine and whether such vaccination was completed.

(2) **Section (f)(5)(ii)** requires documentation that a post-exposure evaluation was performed and that the exposed employee was informed of the results as well as any medical conditions resulting from exposure which require further evaluation and treatment.

7. **Employee Information and Training - 1910.1030(g).** Section (g) ensures that employees receive sufficient warning through labels, signs, and training to eliminate or minimize their exposure to bloodborne pathogens.

a. **Labels - (g)(1).** Labels must be provided on containers of regulated waste, on refrigerators and freezers that are used to store blood or OPIM, and on containers used to store, dispose of, transport, or ship blood or OPIM. This requirement alerts employees to possible exposure since the nature of the material or contents will not always be readily identifiable as blood or OPIM. (See Appendix E.)

NOTE: This does not preempt either the U.S. Postal Service labeling requirements (39 CFR Part III) or the Department of Transportation's Hazardous Materials Regulations (49 CFR Parts 171-180).

INSPECTION AND CITATION GUIDELINES. The compliance officer shall determine that the warning labels in the facility are used as required by sections **(g)(1)(i)(A) through (D)** and include the term "BIOHAZARD". OSHA does not require nor prohibit the use of warning signs or labels indicating source individuals' or specimens' known infectivity status although, in accordance with universal precautions, the agency strongly recommends against such warning signs.

(1) **Sections (g)(1)(i)(E) through (G).** These sections list exemptions from the labeling requirements which are additional to those exemptions listed for specimens in section **(d)(2)(xiii)(A)** and for laundry in section **(d)(4)(iv)(A)(2)**. (See M.4.b.(8)(a) and M.4.d.(4)(a) of this instruction.)

(a) Blood and blood products bearing an identifying label as specified by the Food and Drug Administration, which have been screened for HBV and HIV antibodies and released for transfusion or other clinical uses, are exempted from the labeling requirements.

(b) When blood is being drawn or laboratory procedures are being performed on blood samples, then the individual containers housing the blood or OPIM do not have to be labeled provided the larger container into which they are placed for storage, transport, shipment, or disposal (e.g., test tube rack) is labeled.

(2) **Section (g)(1)(i)(I).** Regulated waste that has been decontaminated by incineration, autoclaving, or chemical means, prior to disposal is not required to bear the BIOHAZARD warning label.

(a) Decontamination is discussed at M.4.d.(3)(i)(2) of this instruction.

(b) Failure to ensure adequate decontamination procedures prior to removal of the hazard label shall be cited under (g)(1)(i)(A), since the material would still be regulated waste.

b. **Information and Training - (g)(2).** All employees with occupational exposure must receive initial and annual training on the hazards associated with blood and OPIM, and the protective measures to be taken to minimize the risk of occupational exposure. Retraining shall take place when changes in procedures or tasks occur which affect occupational exposure. While the provisions for employee training are performance oriented, with flexibility allowed to tailor the program to, for example, the employee's background and responsibilities, the categories of information listed in section (g)(2)(vii) must be covered at a minimum. These requirements include some site-specific information.

INSPECTION GUIDELINES. The compliance officer shall verify that the training is provided at the time of initial employment or on or before June 4, 1992, and at least annually thereafter as well as whenever a change in an employee's responsibilities, procedures, or work situation is such that an employee's occupational exposure is affected. "At the time of initial assignment to tasks where occupational exposure may take place" means that employees shall be trained prior to being placed in positions where occupational exposure may occur.

- Employees who received training on bloodborne pathogens within the year preceding March 6, 1992, shall receive information on the sections of the standard which were not included in their training. The annual retraining for these employees shall be provided within one year of their original training.

- Part-time and temporary employees, and health care employees known as "per diem" employees are covered and are also to be trained on company time.

- The compliance officer shall interview a representative number of employees from different work areas to determine that the training (including written material, oral presentations, films, videos, computer programs, or audiotapes) was presented in a manner that was appropriate to the employee's education, literacy level, and language, and also that the trainer was able to answer questions as needed. If an employee is only proficient in a foreign language, the trainer or an interpreter must convey the information in that foreign language.

(1) **Sections (g)(2)(vii)(B) and (C).** These sections require that HIV and HBV and other bloodborne diseases be described. The employer must convey the idea that a number of bloodborne diseases other than HIV and HBV exist, such as hepatitis C or syphilis. At the same time, the employer need not cover such uncommon diseases as Cruetzfeld-Jacob disease unless, for example, it is appropriate for employees working in a research facility with that particular virus.

(2) **Section (g)(2)(vii)(J).** The word "emergency" in this section refers to blood exposure outside the normal scope of work. This does not refer to hospital emergency rooms or emergency medical technicians' work.

(3) **Section (g)(2)(vii)(N).** This section requires that there be an opportunity for interactive questions and answers with the person conducting the training session.

(a) Training the employees solely by means of a film or video without the opportunity for a discussion period would constitute a violation of this section.

(b) Similarly, a generic computer program, even an interactive one, is not considered appropriate unless the employer supplements such training with the site-specific information required (e.g., the location of the exposure control plan and the procedures to be followed if an exposure incident occurs) and a person is accessible for interaction.

(4) **Section (g)(2)(viii).** The person conducting the training is required to be knowledgeable in the subject matter covered by the elements contained in the training program as it relates to the workplace that the training will address. In addition to demonstrating expertise in the area of the occupational hazard of bloodborne pathogens, the trainer must be familiar with the manner in which the elements in the training program relate to the particular workplace.

(a) The compliance officer shall verify the competency of the trainer based on the completion of specialized courses, degree programs, or work experience, if he/she determines that deficiencies in training exist.

(b) Possible trainers include a variety of health care professionals such as infection control practitioners, nurse practitioners, registered nurses, physician's assistants, or emergency medical technicians.

(c) Non-health care professionals, such as industrial hygienists, epidemiologists, or professional trainers, may conduct the training provided they can demonstrate evidence of specialized training in the area of bloodborne pathogens.

(d) In some workplaces, such as dental or physicians' offices, the individual employer may conduct the training provided he or she is familiar with bloodborne pathogen exposure control and the subject matter required by sections **(g)(2)(vii)(A) through (N)**.

(5) **Section (g)(2)(ix)(A)-(C).** "Standard microbiological practices" in these sections refer to procedures outlined in "Biosafety in Microbiological and Biomedical Laboratories." (See D.9. of this instruction.)

(a) The requirement that "proficiency" be demonstrated means that employees who are experienced laboratorians may not need to be retrained in accordance with these sections.

(b) Education such as a graduate degree in the study of HIV or HBV, or another closely related subject area with a period of related laboratory research experience, would also constitute "proficiency".

(c) The employer is responsible for evaluating the employee's proficiency and for documenting the mechanism used to determine proficiency.

8. **Recordkeeping - 1910.1030(h).** Records are required to be kept for each employee covered by this standard for

training, as well as for medical evaluations, treatment, and surveillance.

a. Medical records required by section **(h)(1)** will be of particular importance to the health care professional in determining vaccination status and courses of treatment to follow in the event of an exposure incident. Although the employer is required to establish and maintain medical records, he/she may contract for the services of a health care professional located off-site and that person or company may retain the records.

NOTE: While section **(h)(1)(iii)** requires that medical records are to be kept confidential, section **(h)(1)(iii)(B)** stipulates that disclosure is permitted when required by this standard or other Federal, State, or local regulations.

INSPECTION GUIDELINES. All medical records required to be kept by this standard are also required to be made available to OSHA. The compliance officer must protect the confidentiality of these records. If they are copied for the case file, the provisions of 29 CFR 1913.10 must be followed.

- The compliance officer shall review the employer's recordkeeping program to ensure that the required information is collected, and provision has been made to ensure the confidentiality of the medical records in accordance with 29 CFR 1910.20.

b. **Section (h)(2)** requires accurate recordkeeping of training sessions, including titles of the employees who attend. The records are necessary to assist the employer and OSHA in determining whether the training program adequately addresses the risks involved in each job. Additionally, this information is helpful in tracking the relationship between exposure incidents (e.g., needlesticks) and various jobs and the corresponding level of training.

(1) Training records may be stored on-site and therefore the actual documents will be easily accessible for review. In order to ensure

that the employee training is complete, all the components of the program required by section **(g)(2)(vii)** must be covered.

(2) Training records are not considered to be confidential and may be maintained in any file. They must be retained for 3 years from the training date.

9. **Dates - 1910.1030(i).** The effective dates of the requirements of the standard appear in Appendix F of this instruction.

NOTE: OSHA Instruction CPL 2-2.44B shall remain in effect until the effective dates of the requirements of **29 CFR 1910.1030.**

N. Interface With Other Standards.

1. The hazard communication standard, 29 CFR 1910.1200, applies only to the hazards of chemicals in the workplace and does not apply to biological hazards such as bloodborne diseases.

2. Records concerning employee exposure to bloodborne pathogens and records about HIV and/or HBV status are considered employee medical records within the meaning of 29 CFR 1910.20. Under 29 CFR 1913.10, the compliance officer may review these records for purposes of determining compliance with 29 CFR 1910.20.

3. Generally, the respiratory protection standard, 29 CFR 1910.134 does not apply since there are no respirators approved for biohazards. However, placing respirators in areas where they could be contaminated by body fluids constitutes a violation of 29 CFR 1910.134 (b)(6).

4. The Hazardous Waste Operations and Emergency Response (HAZWOPER) standard, 29 CFR 1910.120, covers three groups of employees--workers at uncontrolled hazardous waste remediation sites; workers at Resource Conservation and Recovery Act (RCRA) permitted hazardous waste treatment, storage and disposal facilities; and those workers expected to respond to emergencies caused by the uncontrolled release of a hazardous substance.

a. The definition of hazardous substance includes any biological agent or infectious material which may cause disease or death. There are potential scenarios where the bloodborne and HAZWOPER standards may interface such as:

(1) Workers involved in cleanup operations at hazardous waste sites involving infectious waste;

(2) Workers responding to an emergency caused by the uncontrolled release of infectious material; e.g., a transportation accident; and

(3) Workers at RCRA permitted incinerators that burn infectious waste.

b. Employers of employees engaged in these types of activities must comply with the requirements in 29 CFR 1910.120 as well as the bloodborne pathogens standard. If there is a conflict or overlap, the provision that is more protective of employee safety and health applies.

O. Recording in the IMIS. Current instructions for completing the appropriate inspection classification boxes on the OSHA-1, Inspection Report, as found in the IMIS Manual, shall be applied when recording bloodborne pathogens inspections:

1. For any inspection which includes an evaluation of the hazards of bloodborne pathogens, Item 42 of the OSHA-1 shall be recorded as follows:

N 02 Blood

2. If local emphasis programs are approved at a later date, Item 25C of the OSHA-1 shall be completed with the appropriate value.

P. Referrals. When a complaint or inquiry regarding occupational exposure to bloodborne disease in a State or local government facility is received in a State without an OSHA approved State plan, the Regional Administrator should refer it to the appropriate State public health agency or local health agency with jurisdiction over the facility.

Dorothy L. Strunk
Acting Assistant Secretary

DISTRIBUTION: National, Regional and Area Offices
Compliance Officers
State Designees
NIOSH Regional Program Directors
7(c)(1) Project Managers

APPENDIX A

TEXT OF THE OSHA BLOODBORNE PATHOGENS STANDARD

XI. The Standard

General Industry

Part 1910 of title 29 of the Code of Federal Regulations is amended as follows:

PART 1910—[AMENDED]

Subpart Z—[Amended]

1. The general authority citation for subpart Z of 29 CFR part 1910 continues to read as follows and a new citation for § 1910.1030 is added:

Authority: Secs. 6 and 8, Occupational Safety and Health Act, 29 U.S.C. 655, 657, Secretary of Labor's Orders Nos. 12-71 (36 FR 8754), 8-76 (41 FR 25059), or 9-83 (48 FR 35736), as applicable; and 29 CFR part 1911.

* * * * *

Section 1910.1030 also issued under 29 U.S.C. 653.

* * * * *

2. Section 1910.1030 is added to read as follows:

§ 1910.1030 Bloodborne Pathogens.

(a) *Scope and Application.* This section applies to all occupational exposure to blood or other potentially infectious materials as defined by paragraph (b) of this section.

(b) *Definitions.* For purposes of this section, the following shall apply:

Assistant Secretary means the Assistant Secretary of Labor for Occupational Safety and Health, or designated representative.

Blood means human blood, human blood components, and products made from human blood.

Bloodborne Pathogens means pathogenic microorganisms that are present in human blood and can cause disease in humans. These pathogens include, but are not limited to, hepatitis B virus (HBV) and human immunodeficiency virus (HIV).

Clinical Laboratory means a workplace where diagnostic or other screening procedures are performed on blood or other potentially infectious materials.

Contaminated means the presence or the reasonably anticipated presence of blood or other potentially infectious materials on an item or surface.

Contaminated Laundry means laundry which has been soiled with blood or other potentially infectious materials or may contain sharps.

Contaminated Sharps means any contaminated object that can penetrate the skin including, but not limited to, needles, scalpels, broken glass, broken capillary tubes, and exposed ends of dental wires.

Decontamination means the use of physical or chemical means to remove, inactivate, or destroy bloodborne pathogens on a surface or item to the point where they are no longer capable of transmitting infectious particles and the surface or item is rendered safe for handling, use, or disposal.

Director means the Director of the National Institute for Occupational Safety and Health, U.S. Department of Health and Human Services, or designated representative.

Engineering Controls means controls (e.g., sharps disposal containers, self-sheathing needles) that isolate or remove the bloodborne pathogens hazard from the workplace.

Exposure Incident means a specific eye, mouth, other mucous membrane, non-intact skin, or parenteral contact with blood or other potentially infectious materials that results from the performance of an employee's duties.

Handwashing Facilities means a facility providing an adequate supply of running potable water, soap and single use towels or hot air drying machines.

Licensed Healthcare Professional is a person whose legally permitted scope of practice allows him or her to independently perform the activities required by paragraph (f) Hepatitis B Vaccination and Post-exposure Evaluation and Follow-up.

HBV means hepatitis B virus.

HIV means human immunodeficiency virus.

Occupational Exposure means reasonably anticipated skin, eye, mucous membrane, or parenteral contact with blood or other potentially infectious materials that may result from the performance of an employee's duties.

Other Potentially Infectious Materials means

(1) The following human body fluids: semen, vaginal secretions, cerebrospinal fluid, synovial fluid, pleural fluid, pericardial fluid, peritoneal fluid, amniotic fluid, saliva in dental procedures, any body fluid that is visibly contaminated with blood, and all body fluids in situations where it is difficult or impossible to differentiate between body fluids;

(2) Any unfixed tissue or organ (other than intact skin) from a human (living or dead); and

(3) HIV-containing cell or tissue cultures, organ cultures, and HIV- or HBV-containing culture medium or other solutions; and blood, organs, or other tissues from experimental animals infected with HIV or HBV.

Parenteral means piercing mucous membranes or the skin barrier through such events as needlesticks, human bites, cuts, and abrasions.

Personal Protective Equipment is specialized clothing or equipment worn by an employee for protection against a hazard. General work clothes (e.g., uniforms, pants, shirts or blouses) not intended to function as protection against a hazard are not considered to be personal protective equipment.

Production Facility means a facility engaged in industrial-scale, large-volume or high concentration producti[on] of HIV or HBV.

Regulated Waste means liquid or semi-liquid blood or other potentially infectious materials; contaminated ite[ms] that would release blood or other potentially infectious materials in a liquid or semi-liquid state if compress[ed]; items that are caked with dried blood [or] other potentially infectious materials and are capable of releasing these materials during handling; contaminat[ed] sharps; and pathological and microbiological wastes containing blo[od] or other potentially infectious materia[ls].

Research Laboratory means a laboratory producing or using researc[h] laboratory-scale amounts of HIV or HBV. Research laboratories may produce high concentrations of HIV o[r] HBV but not in the volume found in production facilities.

Source Individual means any individual, living or dead, whose bloo[d] or other potentially infectious materi[als] may be a source of occupational exposure to the employee. Examples include, but are not limited to, hospit[al] and clinic patients; clients in instituti[ons] for the developmentally disabled; trauma victims; clients of drug and alcohol treatment facilities; residents [of] hospices and nursing homes; human remains; and individuals who donate [or] sell blood or blood components.

Sterilize means the use of a physic[al] or chemical procedure to destroy all microbial life including highly resista[nt] bacterial endospores.

Universal Precautions is an approa[ch] to infection control. According to the concept of Universal Precautions, all human blood and certain human bod[y] fluids are treated as if known to be infectious for HIV, HBV, and other bloodborne pathogens.

Work Practice Controls means controls that reduce the likelihood of exposure by altering the manner in which a task is performed (e.g., prohibiting recapping of needles by a two-handed technique).

(c) *Exposure control*—(1) *Exposure Control Plan.* (i) Each employer havi[ng] an employee(s) with occupational exposure as defined by paragraph (b) [of] this section shall establish a written Exposure Control Plan designed to eliminate or minimize employee exposure.

(ii) The Exposure Control Plan shall contain at least the following elements:

(A) The exposure determination required by paragraph(c)(2),

(B) The schedule and method of implementation for paragraphs (d) Methods of Compliance, (e) HIV and HBV Research Laboratories and Production Facilities, (f) Hepatitis B Vaccination and Post-Exposure Evaluation and Follow-up, (g) Communication of Hazards to Employees, and (h) Recordkeeping, of this standard, and

(C) The procedure for the evaluation of circumstances surrounding exposure incidents as required by paragraph (f)(3)(i) of this standard.

(iii) Each employer shall ensure that a copy of the Exposure Control Plan is accessible to employees in accordance with 29 CFR 1910.20(e).

(iv) The Exposure Control Plan shall be reviewed and updated at least annually and whenever necessary to reflect new or modified tasks and procedures which affect occupational exposure and to reflect new or revised employee positions with occupational exposure.

(v) The Exposure Control Plan shall be made available to the Assistant Secretary and the Director upon request for examination and copying.

(2) *Exposure determination.* (i) Each employer who has an employee(s) with occupational exposure as defined by paragraph (b) of this section shall prepare an exposure determination. This exposure determination shall contain the following:

(A) A list of all job classifications in which all employees in those job classifications have occupational exposure;

(B) A list of job classifications in which some employees have occupational exposure, and

(C) A list of all tasks and procedures or groups of closely related task and procedures in which occupational exposure occurs and that are performed by employees in job classifications listed in accordance with the provisions of paragraph (c)(2)(i)(B) of this standard.

(ii) This exposure determination shall be made without regard to the use of personal protective equipment.

(d) *Methods of compliance*—(1) *General*—Universal precautions shall be observed to prevent contact with blood or other potentially infectious materials. Under circumstances in which differentiation between body fluid types is difficult or impossible, all body fluids shall be considered potentially infectious materials.

(2) *Engineering and work practice controls.* (i) Engineering and work practice controls shall be used to eliminate or minimize employee exposure. Where occupational exposure remains after institution of these controls, personal protective equipment shall also be used.

(ii) Engineering controls shall be examined and maintained or replaced on a regular schedule to ensure their effectiveness.

(iii) Employers shall provide handwashing facilities which are readily accessible to employees.

(iv) When provision of handwashing facilities is not feasible, the employer shall provide either an appropriate antiseptic hand cleanser in conjunction with clean cloth/paper towels or antiseptic towelettes. When antiseptic hand cleansers or towelettes are used, hands shall be washed with soap and running water as soon as feasible.

(v) Employers shall ensure that employees wash their hands immediately or as soon as feasible after removal of gloves or other personal protective equipment.

(vi) Employers shall ensure that employees wash hands and any other skin with soap and water, or flush mucous membranes with water immediately or as soon as feasible following contact of such body areas with blood or other potentially infectious materials.

(vii) Contaminated needles and other contaminated sharps shall not be bent, recapped, or removed except as noted in paragraphs (d)(2)(vii)(A) and (d)(2)(vii)(B) below. Shearing or breaking of contaminated needles is prohibited.

(A) Contaminated needles and other contaminated sharps shall not be recapped or removed unless the employer can demonstrate that no alternative is feasible or that such action is required by a specific medical procedure.

(B) Such recapping or needle removal must be accomplished through the use of a mechanical device or a one-handed technique.

(viii) Immediately or as soon as possible after use, contaminated reusable sharps shall be placed in appropriate containers until properly reprocessed. These containers shall be:

(A) Puncture resistant;

(B) Labeled or color-coded in accordance with this standard;

(C) Leakproof on the sides and bottom; and

(D) In accordance with the requirements set forth in paragraph (d)(4)(ii)(E) for reusable sharps.

(ix) Eating, drinking, smoking, applying cosmetics or lip balm, and handling contact lenses are prohibited i[n] work areas where there is a reasonable likelihood of occupational exposure.

(x) Food and drink shall not be kept i[n] refrigerators, freezers, shelves, cabinets or on countertops or benchtops where blood or other potentially infectious materials are present.

(xi) All procedures involving blood or other potentially infectious materials shall be performed in such a manner as to minimize splashing, spraying, spattering, and generation of droplets of these substances.

(xii) Mouth pipetting/suctioning of blood or other potentially infectious materials is prohibited.

(xiii) Specimens of blood or other potentially infectious materials shall be placed in a container which prevents leakage during collection, handling, processing, storage, transport, or shipping.

(A) The container for storage, transport, or shipping shall be labeled or color-coded according to paragraph (g)(1)(i) and closed prior to being stored, transported, or shipped. When a facility utilizes Universal Precautions in the handling of all specimens, the labeling/color-coding of specimens is not necessary provided containers are recognizable as containing specimens. This exemption only applies while such specimens/containers remain within the facility. Labeling or color-coding in accordance with paragraph (g)(1)(i) is required when such specimens/containers leave the facility.

(B) If outside contamination of the primary container occurs, the primary container shall be placed within a second container which prevents leakage during handling, processing, storage, transport, or shipping and is labeled or color-coded according to the requirements of this standard.

(C) If the specimen could puncture the primary container, the primary container shall be placed within a secondary container which is puncture-resistant in addition to the above characteristics.

(xiv) Equipment which may become contaminated with blood or other potentially infectious materials shall be examined prior to servicing or shipping and shall be decontaminated as necessary, unless the employer can demonstrate that decontamination of such equipment or portions of such equipment is not feasible.

(A) A readily observable label in accordance with paragraph (g)(1)(i)(H) shall be attached to the equipment stating which portions remain contaminated.

(B) The employer shall ensure that this information is conveyed to all affected employees, the servicing representative, and/or the manufacturer, as appropriate, prior to handling, servicing, or shipping so that appropriate precautions will be taken.

(3) Personal protective equipment—(i) Provision. When there is occupational exposure, the employer shall provide, at no cost to the employee, appropriate personal protective equipment such as, but not limited to, gloves, gowns, laboratory coats, face shields or masks and eye protection, and mouthpieces, resuscitation bags, pocket masks, or other ventilation devices. Personal protective equipment will be considered "appropriate" only if it does not permit blood or other potentially infectious materials to pass through to or reach the employee's work clothes, street clothes, undergarments, skin, eyes, mouth, or other mucous membranes under normal conditions of use and for the duration of time which the protective equipment will be used.

(ii) Use. The employer shall ensure that the employee uses appropriate personal protective equipment unless the employer shows that the employee temporarily and briefly declined to use personal protective equipment when, under rare and extraordinary circumstances, it was the employee's professional judgment that in the specific instance its use would have prevented the delivery of health care or public safety services or would have posed an increased hazard to the safety of the worker or co-worker. When the employee makes this judgement, the circumstances shall be investigated and documented in order to determine whether changes can be instituted to prevent such occurences in the future.

(iii) Accessibility. The employer shall ensure that appropriate personal protective equipment in the appropriate sizes is readily accessible at the worksite or is issued to employees. Hypoallergenic gloves, glove liners, powderless gloves, or other similar alternatives shall be readily accessible to those employees who are allergic to the gloves normally provided.

(iv) Cleaning, Laundering, and Disposal. The employer shall clean, launder, and dispose of personal protective equipment required by paragraphs (d) and (e) of this standard, at no cost to the employee.

(v) Repair and Replacement. The employer shall repair or replace personal protective equipment as needed to maintain its effectiveness, at no cost to the employee.

(vi) If a garment(s) is penetrated by blood or other potentially infectious materials, the garment(s) shall be removed immediately or as soon as feasible.

(vii) All personal protective equipment shall be removed prior to leaving the work area.

(viii) When personal protective equipment is removed it shall be placed in an appropriately designated area or container for storage, washing, decontamination or disposal.

(ix) Gloves. Gloves shall be worn when it can be reasonably anticipated that the employee may have hand contact with blood, other potentially infectious materials, mucous membranes, and non-intact skin; when performing vascular access procedures except as specified in paragraph (d)(3)(ix)(D); and when handling or touching contaminated items or surfaces.

(A) Disposable (single use) gloves such as surgical or examination gloves, shall be replaced as soon as practical when contaminated or as soon as feasible if they are torn, punctured, or when their ability to function as a barrier is compromised.

(B) Disposable (single use) gloves shall not be washed or decontaminated for re-use.

(C) Utility gloves may be decontaminated for re-use if the integrity of the glove is not compromised. However, they must be discarded if they are cracked, peeling, torn, punctured, or exhibit other signs of deterioration or when their ability to function as a barrier is compromised.

(D) If an employer in a volunteer blood donation center judges that routine gloving for all phlebotomies is not necessary then the employer shall:

(*1*) Periodically reevaluate this policy;

(*2*) Make gloves available to all employees who wish to use them for phlebotomy;

(*3*) Not discourage the use of gloves for phlebotomy; and

(*4*) Require that gloves be used for phlebotomy in the following circumstances:

(*i*) When the employee has cuts, scratches, or other breaks in his or her skin;

(*ii*) When the employee judges that hand contamination with blood may occur, for example, when performing phlebotomy on an uncooperative source individual; and

(*iii*) When the employee is receiving training in phlebotomy.

(x) Masks, Eye Protection, and Face Shields. Masks in combination with eye protection devices, such as goggles or glasses with solid side shields, or chin-length face shields, shall be worn whenever splashes, spray, spatter, or droplets of blood or other potentially infectious materials may be generated and eye, nose, or mouth contamination can be reasonably anticipated.

(xi) Gowns, Aprons, and Other Protective Body Clothing. Appropriate protective clothing such as, but not limited to, gowns, aprons, lab coats, clinic jackets, or similar outer garments shall be worn in occupational exposure situations. The type and characteristics will depend upon the task and degree of exposure anticipated.

(xii) Surgical caps or hoods and/or shoe covers or boots shall be worn in instances when gross contamination can reasonably be anticipated (e.g., autopsies, orthopaedic surgery).

(4) *Housekeeping*. (i) General. Employers shall ensure that the worksite is maintained in a clean and sanitary condition. The employer shall determine and implement an appropriate written schedule for cleaning and method of decontamination based upon the location within the facility, type of surface to be cleaned, type of soil present, and tasks or procedures being performed in the area.

(ii) All equipment and environmental and working surfaces shall be cleaned and decontaminated after contact with blood or other potentially infectious materials.

(A) Contaminated work surfaces shall be decontaminated with an appropriate disinfectant after completion of procedures; immediately or as soon as feasible when surfaces are overtly contaminated or after any spill of blood or other potentially infectious materials; and at the end of the work shift if the surface may have become contaminated since the last cleaning.

(B) Protective coverings, such as plastic wrap, aluminum foil, or imperviously-backed absorbent paper used to cover equipment and environmental surfaces, shall be removed and replaced as soon as feasible when they become overtly contaminated or at the end of the workshift if they may have become contaminated during the shift.

(C) All bins, pails, cans, and similar receptacles intended for reuse which have a reasonable likelihood for becoming contaminated with blood or other potentially infectious materials shall be inspected and decontaminated on a regularly scheduled basis and cleaned and decontaminated immediately or as soon as feasible upon visible contamination.

(D) Broken glassware which may be contaminated shall not be picked up directly with the hands. It shall be cleaned up using mechanical means, such as a brush and dust pan, tongs, or forceps.

(E) Reusable sharps that are contaminated with blood or other potentially infectious materials shall not be stored or processed in a manner that requires employees to reach by hand into the containers where these sharps have been placed.

(iii) Regulated Waste.

(A) Contaminated Sharps Discarding and Containment. (*1*) Contaminated sharps shall be discarded immediately or as soon as feasible in containers that are:

(*i*) Closable;

(*ii*) Puncture resistant;

(*iii*) Leakproof on sides and bottom; and

(*iv*) Labeled or color-coded in accordance with paragraph (g)(1)(i) of this standard.

(*2*) During use, containers for contaminated sharps shall be:

(*i*) Easily accessible to personnel and located as close as is feasible to the immediate area where sharps are used or can be reasonably anticipated to be found (e.g., laundries);

(*ii*) Maintained upright throughout use; and

(*iii*) Replaced routinely and not be allowed to overfill.

(*3*) When moving containers of contaminated sharps from the area of use, the containers shall be:

(*i*) Closed immediately prior to removal or replacement to prevent spillage or protrusion of contents during handling, storage, transport, or shipping;

(*ii*) Placed in a secondary container if leakage is possible. The second container shall be:

(*A*) Closable;

(*B*) Constructed to contain all contents and prevent leakage during handling, storage, transport, or shipping; and

(*C*) Labeled or color-coded according to paragraph (g)(1)(i) of this standard.

(*4*) Reusable containers shall not be opened, emptied, or cleaned manually or in any other manner which would expose employees to the risk of percutaneous injury.

(B) Other Regulated Waste Containment.(*1*) Regulated waste shall be placed in containers which are:

(*i*) Closable;

(*ii*) Constructed to contain all contents and prevent leakage of fluids during handling, storage, transport or shipping;

(*iii*) Labeled or color-coded in accordance with paragraph (g)(1)(i) this standard; and

(*iv*) Closed prior to removal to prevent spillage or protrusion of contents during handling, storage, transport, or shipping.

(*2*) If outside contamination of the regulated waste container occurs, it shall be placed in a second container. The second container shall be:

(*i*) Closable;

(*ii*) Constructed to contain all contents and prevent leakage of fluids during handling, storage, transport or shipping;

(*iii*) Labeled or color-coded in accordance with paragraph (g)(1)(i) of this standard; and

(*iv*) Closed prior to removal to prevent spillage or protrusion of contents during handling, storage, transport, or shipping.

(C) Disposal of all regulated waste shall be in accordance with applicable regulations of the United States, States and Territories, and political subdivisions of States and Territories.

(iv) Laundry.

(A) Contaminated laundry shall be handled as little as possible with a minimum of agitation. (1) Contaminated laundry shall be bagged or containerized at the location where it was used and shall not be sorted or rinsed in the location of use.

(2) Contaminated laundry shall be placed and transported in bags or containers labeled or color-coded in accordance with paragraph (g)(1)(i) of this standard. When a facility utilizes Universal Precautions in the handling of all soiled laundry, alternative labeling or color-coding is sufficient if it permits all employees to recognize the containers as requiring compliance with Universal Precautions.

(3) Whenever contaminated laundry is wet and presents a reasonable likelihood of soak-through of or leakage from the bag or container, the laundry shall be placed and transported in bags or containers which prevent soak-through and/or leakage of fluids to the exterior.

(B) The employer shall ensure that employees who have contact with contaminated laundry wear protective gloves and other appropriate personal protective equipment.

(C) When a facility ships contaminated laundry off-site to a second facility which does not utilize Universal Precautions in the handling of all laundry, the facility generating the contaminated laundry must place such laundry in bags or containers which are labeled or color-coded in accordance with paragraph (g)(1)(i).

(e) *HIV and HBV Research Laboratories and Production Facilities.* (1) This paragraph applies to research laboratories and production facilities engaged in the culture, production, concentration, experimentation, and manipulation of HIV and HBV. It does not apply to clinical or diagnostic laboratories engaged solely in the analysis of blood, tissues, or organs. These requirements apply in addition to the other requirements of the standard.

(2) Research laboratories and production facilities shall meet the following criteria:

(i) Standard microbiological practices. All regulated waste shall either be incinerated or decontaminated by a method such as autoclaving known to effectively destroy bloodborne pathogens.

(ii) Special practices.

(A) Laboratory doors shall be kept closed when work involving HIV or HBV is in progress.

(B) Contaminated materials that are to be decontaminated at a site away from the work area shall be placed in a durable, leakproof, labeled or color-coded container that is closed before being removed from the work area.

(C) Access to the work area shall be limited to authorized persons. Written policies and procedures shall be established whereby only persons who have been advised of the potential biohazard, who meet any specific entry requirements, and who comply with all entry and exit procedures shall be allowed to enter the work areas and animal rooms.

(D) When other potentially infectious materials or infected animals are present in the work area or containment module, a hazard warning sign incorporating the universal biohazard symbol shall be posted on all access doors. The hazard warning sign shall comply with paragraph (g)(1)(ii) of this standard.

(E) All activities involving other potentially infectious materials shall be conducted in biological safety cabinets or other physical-containment devices within the containment module. No work with these other potentially infectious materials shall be conducted on the open bench.

(F) Laboratory coats, gowns, smocks, uniforms, or other appropriate protective clothing shall be used in the work area and animal rooms. Protective clothing shall not be worn outside of the work area and shall be decontaminated before being laundered.

(G) Special care shall be taken to avoid skin contact with other potentially infectious materials. Gloves shall be worn when handling infected animals and when making hand contact with other potentially infectious materials is unavoidable.

(H) Before disposal all waste from work areas and from animal rooms shall either be incinerated or decontaminated by a method such as autoclaving known to effectively destroy bloodborne pathogens.

(I) Vacuum lines shall be protected with liquid disinfectant traps and high-efficiency particulate air (HEPA) filters or filters of equivalent or superior efficiency and which are checked routinely and maintained or replaced as necessary.

(J) Hypodermic needles and syringes shall be used only for parenteral injection and aspiration of fluids from laboratory animals and diaphragm bottles. Only needle-locking syringes or disposable syringe-needle units (i.e., the needle is integral to the syringe) shall be used for the injection or aspiration of other potentially infectious materials. Extreme caution shall be used when handling needles and syringes. A needle shall not be bent, sheared, replaced in the sheath or guard, or removed from the syringe following use. The needle and syringe shall be promptly placed in a puncture-resistant container and autoclaved or decontaminated before reuse or disposal.

(K) All spills shall be immediately contained and cleaned up by appropriate professional staff or others properly trained and equipped to work with potentially concentrated infectious materials.

(L) A spill or accident that results in an exposure incident shall be immediately reported to the laboratory director or other responsible person.

(M) A biosafety manual shall be prepared or adopted and periodically reviewed and updated at least annually or more often if necessary. Personnel shall be advised of potential hazards, shall be required to read instructions on practices and procedures, and shall be required to follow them.

(iii) Containment equipment. (A) Certified biological safety cabinets (Class I, II, or III) or other appropriate combinations of personal protection or physical containment devices, such as special protective clothing, respirators, centrifuge safety cups, sealed centrifuge rotors, and containment caging for animals, shall be used for all activities with other potentially infectious materials that pose a threat of exposure to droplets, splashes, spills, or aerosols.

(B) Biological safety cabinets shall be certified when installed, whenever they are moved and at least annually.

(3) HIV and HBV research laboratories shall meet the following criteria:

(i) Each laboratory shall contain a facility for hand washing and an eye wash facility which is readily available within the work area.

(ii) An autoclave for decontamination of regulated waste shall be available.

(4) HIV and HBV production facilities shall meet the following criteria:

(i) The work areas shall be separated from areas that are open to unrestricted traffic flow within the building. Passage through two sets of doors shall be the basic requirement for entry into the work area from access corridors or other contiguous areas. Physical separation of the high-containment work area from access corridors or other areas or activities may also be provided by a double-doored clothes-change room (showers may be included), airlock, or other access facility that requires passing through two sets of doors before entering the work area.

(ii) The surfaces of doors, walls, floors and ceilings in the work area shall be water resistant so that they can be easily cleaned. Penetrations in these surfaces shall be sealed or capable of being sealed to facilitate decontamination.

(iii) Each work area shall contain a sink for washing hands and a readily available eye wash facility. The sink shall be foot, elbow, or automatically operated and shall be located near the exit door of the work area.

(iv) Access doors to the work area or containment module shall be self-closing.

(v) An autoclave for decontamination of regulated waste shall be available within or as near as possible to the work area.

(vi) A ducted exhaust-air ventilation system shall be provided. This system shall create directional airflow that draws air into the work area through the entry area. The exhaust air shall not be recirculated to any other area of the building, shall be discharged to the outside, and shall be dispersed away from occupied areas and air intakes. The proper direction of the airflow shall be verified (i.e., into the work area).

(5) *Training Requirements.* Additional training requirements for employees in HIV and HBV research laboratories and HIV and HBV production facilities are specified in paragraph (g)(2)(ix).

(f) *Hepatitis B vaccination and post-exposure evaluation and follow-up—(1) General.* (i) The employer shall make available the hepatitis B vaccine and vaccination series to all employees who have occupational exposure, and post-exposure evaluation and follow-up to all employees who have had an exposure incident.

(ii) The employer shall ensure that all medical evaluations and procedures including the hepatitis B vaccine and vaccination series and post-exposure evaluation and follow-up, including prophylaxis, are:

(A) Made available at no cost to the employee;

(B) Made available to the employee at a reasonable time and place;

(C) Performed by or under the supervision of a licensed physician or by or under the supervision of another licensed healthcare professional; and

(D) Provided according to recommendations of the U.S. Public Health Service current at the time these evaluations and procedures take place, except as specified by this paragraph (f).

(iii) The employer shall ensure that all laboratory tests are conducted by an accredited laboratory at no cost to the employee.

(2) *Hepatitis B Vaccination.* (i) Hepatitis B vaccination shall be made available after the employee has received the training required in paragraph (g)(2)(vii)(I) and within 10 working days of initial assignment to all employees who have occupational exposure unless the employee has previously received the complete hepatitis B vaccination series, antibody testing has revealed that the employee is immune, or the vaccine is contraindicated for medical reasons.

(ii) The employer shall not make participation in a prescreening program a prerequisite for receiving hepatitis B vaccination.

(iii) If the employee initially declines hepatitis B vaccination but at a later date while still covered under the standard decides to accept the vaccination, the employer shall make available hepatitis B vaccination at that time.

(iv) The employer shall assure that employees who decline to accept hepatitis B vaccination offered by the employer sign the statement in appendix A.

(v) If a routine booster dose(s) of hepatitis B vaccine is recommended by the U.S. Public Health Service at a future date, such booster dose(s) shall be made available in accordance with section (f)(1)(ii).

(3) *Post-exposure Evaluation and Follow-up.* Following a report of an exposure incident, the employer shall make immediately available to the exposed employee a confidential medical evaluation and follow-up, including at least the following elements:

(i) Documentation of the route(s) of exposure, and the circumstances under which the exposure incident occurred;

(ii) Identification and documentation of the source individual, unless the employer can establish that identification is infeasible or prohibited by state or local law;

(A) The source individual's blood shall be tested as soon as feasible and after consent is obtained in order to determine HBV and HIV infectivity. If consent is not obtained, the employer shall establish that legally required consent cannot be obtained. When the source individual's consent is not required by law, the source individual's blood, if available, shall be tested and the results documented.

(B) When the source individual is already known to be infected with HBV or HIV, testing for the source individual's known HBV or HIV status need not be repeated.

(C) Results of the source individual's testing shall be made available to the exposed employee, and the employee shall be informed of applicable laws and regulations concerning disclosure of the identity and infectious status of the source individual.

(iii) Collection and testing of blood for HBV and HIV serological status;

(A) The exposed employee's blood shall be collected as soon as feasible and tested after consent is obtained.

(B) If the employee consents to baseline blood collection, but does not give consent at that time for HIV serologic testing, the sample shall be preserved for at least 90 days. If, within 90 days of the exposure incident, the employee elects to have the baseline sample tested, such testing shall be done as soon as feasible.

(iv) Post-exposure prophylaxis, when medically indicated, as recommended by the U.S. Public Health Service;

(v) Counseling; and

(vi) Evaluation of reported illnesses.

(4) *Information Provided to the Healthcare Professional.* (i) The employer shall ensure that the healthcare professional responsible for the employee's Hepatitis B vaccination is provided a copy of this regulation.

(ii) The employer shall ensure that the healthcare professional evaluating an employee after an exposure incident is provided the following information:

(A) A copy of this regulation;

(B) A description of the exposed employee's duties as they relate to the exposure incident;

(C) Documentation of the route(s) of exposure and circumstances under which exposure occurred;

(D) Results of the source individual's blood testing, if available; and

(E) All medical records relevant to the appropriate treatment of the employee including vaccination status which are the employer's responsibility to maintain.

(5) *Healthcare Professional's Written Opinion.* The employer shall obtain and provide the employee with a copy of the evaluating healthcare professional's written opinion within 15 days of the completion of the evaluation.

(i) The healthcare professional's written opinion for Hepatitis B vaccination shall be limited to whether Hepatitis B vaccination is indicated for an employee, and if the employee has received such vaccination.

(ii) The healthcare professional's written opinion for post-exposure evaluation and follow-up shall be limited to the following information:

(A) That the employee has been informed of the results of the evaluation; and

(B) That the employee has been told about any medical conditions resulting from exposure to blood or other potentially infectious materials which require further evaluation or treatment.

(iii) All other findings or diagnoses shall remain confidential and shall not be included in the written report.

(6) *Medical recordkeeping.* Medical records required by this standard shall be maintained in accordance with paragraph (h)(1) of this section.

(g) *Communication of hazards to employees*— (1) *Labels and signs.* (i) Labels. (A) Warning labels shall be affixed to containers of regulated waste, refrigerators and freezers containing blood or other potentially infectious material; and other containers used to store, transport or ship blood or other potentially infectious materials, except as provided in paragraph (g)(1)(i)(E), (F) and (G).

(B) Labels required by this section shall include the following legend:

BIOHAZARD

BIOHAZARD

(C) These labels shall be fluorescent orange or orange-red or predominantly so, with lettering or symbols in a contrasting color.

(D) Labels required by affixed as close as feasible to the container by string, wire, adhesive, or other method that prevents their loss or unintentional removal.

(E) Red bags or red containers may be substituted for labels.

(F) Containers of blood, blood components, or blood products that are labeled as to their contents and have been released for transfusion or other clinical use are exempted from the labeling requirements of paragraph (g).

(G) Individual containers of blood or other potentially infectious materials that are placed in a labeled container during storage, transport, shipment or disposal are exempted from the labeling requirement.

(H) Labels required for contaminated equipment shall be in accordance with this paragraph and shall also state which portions of the equipment remain contaminated.

(I) Regulated waste that has been decontaminated need not be labeled or color-coded.

(ii) Signs. (A) The employer shall post signs at the entrance to work areas specified in paragraph (e), HIV and HBV Research Laboratory and Production Facilities, which shall bear the following legend:

BIOHAZARD

BIOHAZARD

(Name of the Infectious Agent)
(Special requirements for entering the area)
(Name, telephone number of the laboratory director or other responsible person.)

(B) These signs shall be fluorescent orange-red or predominantly so, with lettering or symbols in a contrasting color.

(2) *Information and Training.* (i) Employers shall ensure that all employees with occupational exposure participate in a training program which must be provided at no cost to the employee and during working hours.

(ii) Training shall be provided as follows:

(A) At the time of initial assignment to tasks where occupational exposure may take place;

(B) Within 90 days after the effective date of the standard; and

(C) At least annually thereafter.

(iii) For employees who have received training on bloodborne pathogens in the year preceding the effective date of the standard, only training with respect to the provisions of the standard which were not included need be provided.

(iv) Annual training for all employees shall be provided within one year of their previous training.

(v) Employers shall provide additional training when changes such as modification of tasks or procedures or institution of new tasks or procedures affect the employee's occupational exposure. The additional training may be limited to addressing the new exposures created.

(vi) Material appropriate in content and vocabulary to educational level, literacy, and language of employees shall be used.

(vii) The training program shall contain at a minimum the following elements:

(A) Anaccessible copy of the regulatory text of this standard and an explanation of its contents;

(B) A general explanation of the epidemiology and symptoms of bloodborne diseases;

(C) An explanation of the modes of transmission of bloodborne pathogens;

(D) An explanation of the employer's exposure control plan and the means by which the employee can obtain a copy of the written plan;

(E) An explanation of the appropriate methods for recognizing tasks and other activities that may involve exposure to blood and other potentially infectious materials;

(F) An explanation of the use and limitations of methods that will prevent or reduce exposure including appropriate engineering controls, work practices, and personal protective equipment;

(G) Information on the types, proper use, location, removal, handling, decontamination and disposal of personal protective equipment;

(H) An explanation of the basis for selection of personal protective equipment;

(I) Information on the hepatitis B vaccine, including information on its efficacy, safety, method of administration, the benefits of being vaccinated, and that the vaccine and vaccination will be offered free of charge;

(J) Information on the appropriate actions to take and persons to contact in an emergency involving blood or other potentially infectious materials;

(K) An explanation of the procedure to follow if an exposure incident occurs, including the method of reporting the incident and the medical follow-up that will be made available;

(L) Information on the post-exposure evaluation and follow-up that the employer is required to provide for the employee following an exposure incident;

(M) An explanation of the signs and labels and/or color coding required by paragraph (g)(1); and

(N) An opportunity for interactive questions and answers with the person conducting the training session.

(viii) The person conducting the training shall be knowledgeable in the subject matter covered by the elements contained in the training program as it relates to the workplace that the training will address.

(ix) Additional Initial Training for Employees in HIV and HBV Laboratories and Production Facilities. Employees in HIV or HBV research laboratories and HIV or HBV production facilities shall receive the following initial training in addition to the above training requirements.

(A) The employer shall assure that employees demonstrate proficiency in standard microbiological practices and techniques and in the practices and operations specific to the facility before being allowed to work with HIV or HBV.

(B) The employer shall assure that employees have prior experience in the handling of human pathogens or tissue cultures before working with HIV or HBV.

(C) The employer shall provide a training program to employees who have no prior experience in handling human pathogens. Initial work activities shall not include the handling of infectious agents. A progression of work activities shall be assigned as techniques are learned and proficiency is developed. The employer shall assure that employees participate in work activities involving infectious agents only after proficiency has been demonstrated.

(h) *Recordkeeping—(1) Medical Records.* (i) The employer shall establish and maintain an accurate record for each employee with occupational exposure, in accordance with 29 CFR 1910.20.

(ii) This record shall include:

(A) The name and social security number of the employee;

(B) A copy of the employee's hepatitis B vaccination status including the dates of all the hepatitis B vaccinations and any medical records relative to the employee's ability to receive vaccination as required by paragraph (f)(2);

(C) A copy of all results of examinations, medical testing, and follow-up procedures as required by paragraph (f)(3);

(D) The employer's copy of the healthcare professional's written opinion as required by paragraph (f)(5); and

(E) A copy of the information provided to the healthcare professional as required by paragraphs (f)(4)(ii)(B)(C) and (D).

(iii) Confidentiality. The employer shall ensure that employee medical records required by paragraph (h)(1) are:

(A) Kept confidential; and

(B) Are not disclosed or reported without the employee's express written consent to any person within or outside the workplace except as required by this section or as may be required by law.

(iv) The employer shall maintain the records required by paragraph (h) for at least the duration of employment plus 30 years in accordance with 29 CFR 1910.20.

(2) *Training Records. (i) Training records shall include the following information:*

(A) The dates of the training sessions;

(B) The contents or a summary of the training sessions;

(C) The names and qualifications of persons conducting the training; and

(D) The names and job titles of all persons attending the training sessions.

(ii) Training records shall be maintained for 3 years from the date on which the training occurred.

(3) *Availability.* (i) The employer shall ensure that all records required to be maintained by this section shall be made available upon request to the Assistant Secretary and the Director for examination and copying.

(ii) Employee training records required by this paragraph shall be provided upon request for examination and copying to employees, to employee representatives, to the Director, and to the Assistant Secretary in accordance with 29 CFR 1910.20.

(iii) Employee medical records required by this paragraph shall be provided upon request for examination and copying to the subject employee, to anyone having written consent of the subject employee, to the Director, and to the Assistant Secretary in accordance with 29 CFR 1910.20.

(4) *Transfer of Records.* (i) The employer shall comply with the requirements involving transfer of records set forth in 29 CFR 1910.20(h).

(ii) If the employer ceases to do business and there is no successor employer to receive and retain the records for the prescribed period, the employer shall notify the Director, at least three months prior to their disposal and transmit them to the Director, if required by the Director to do so, within that three month period.

(i) *Dates—(1) Effective Date.* The standard shall become effective on March 6, 1992.

(2) The Exposure Control Plan required by paragraph (c)(2) of this section shall be completed on or before May 5, 1992.

(3) Paragraph (g)(2) Information and Training and (h) Recordkeeping shall take effect on or before June 4, 1992.

(4) Paragraphs (d)(2) Engineering and Work Practice Controls, (d)(3) Personal Protective Equipment, (d)(4) Housekeeping, (e) HIV and HBV Research Laboratories and Production Facilities, (f) Hepatitis B Vaccination and Post-Exposure Evaluation and Follow-up, and (g) (1) Labels and Signs, shall take effect July 6, 1992.

Appendix A to Section 1910.1030—Hepatitis B Vaccine Declination (Mandatory)

I understand that due to my occupational exposure to blood or other potentially infectious materials I may be at risk of acquiring hepatitis B virus (HBV) infection. I have been given the opportunity to be vaccinated with hepatitis B vaccine, at no charge to myself. However, I decline hepatitis B vaccination at this time. I understand that by declining this vaccine, I continue to be at risk of acquiring hepatitis B, a serious disease. If in the future I continue to have occupational exposure to blood or other potentially infectious materials and I want to be vaccinated with hepatitis B vaccine, I can receive the vaccination series at no charge to me.

[FR Doc. 91-28886 Filed 12-2-91; 8:45 am]
BILLING CODE 4510-26-M

APPENDIX B

EXAMPLE OF A FORM

THAT COULD BE USED AS

AN INJURY/ILLNESS

QUESTIONNAIRE

WORK INJURY-ILLNESS QUESTIONNAIRE

In order to maintain a careful account of every actual or reported incident that could trigger the OSHA injury/illness recordkeeping requirements, employers should consider the use of a printed form to be executed at the time such an incident is reported. The form would be filled in by the involved employee, his immediate supervisor and, if applicable, the treating physician or other medical personnel. The information to be gathered by the form is keyed to the 1986 Guidelines issued by the Labor Department's Bureau of Labor Statistics (BLS) and the definitions that are included in the OSHA Regulations.

A suggested format follows:

INCIDENT REPORT

Information has been obtained by this company that an incident involving an employee has occurred that may trigger the OSHA injury/illness recordkeeping requirements. In order to assist us in making the correct determination, please supply the following information. If you do not know the answer, please write "unknown."

1. Name of employee:
2. Your name:
3. Calendar date of incident:
4. Specific place it happened:
5. Cause:
6. Was the incident work-related?
7. Do you think it caused an injury?
8. If so, what injury?
9. Do you think it caused an illness?
10. If so, what illness?
11. Was medical attention received?
12. From whom?
13. Where?
14. When?
15. If there was medical attention of any kind, answer "yes" or "no" to whether or not it included the following.[1/]

1/ For the information of readers of this book, the first 15 subparts that begin on the next page (each number is in parenthesis) indicate that the treatment was

(1) Application of **ANTISEPTICS during first visit** to medical personnel.
(2) Treatment of **FIRST DEGREE BURN(S)**
(3) Application of **BANDAGE(S)** during any visit to medical personnel.
(4) Use of **ELASTIC BANDAGE(S) during first visit** to medical personnel.
(5) Removal of **FOREIGN BODIES NOT EMBEDDED IN EYE** if only irrigation is required.
(6) Removal of **FOREIGN BODIES FROM WOUND**; where procedure was **UNCOMPLICATED**, for example, by tweezers or other simple technique.
(7) Use of **NONPRESCRIPTION MEDICATIONS AND** administration of **single does of PRESCRIPTION MEDICATION** on first visit for minor injury or discomfort.
(8) **SOAKING THERAPY on initial visit** to medical personnel or removal of bandages by **SOAKING**.
(9) Application of hot or cold **COMPRESS(ES) during first visit** to medical personnel.
(10) Application of **OINTMENTS** to abrasions to prevent drying or cracking.
(11) Application of **HEAT THERAPY during first visit** to medical personnel.
(12) Use of **WHIRLPOOL BATH THERAPY during first visit** to medical personnel.
(13) **NEGATIVE X-RAY DIAGNOSIS**
(14) **OBSERVATION** of injury during visit to medical personnel.
(15) Administration of **TETANUS SHOT(S) OR BOOSTER(S).**
(16) Treatment of **INFECTION.**
(17) Application of **ANTISEPTICS during second or subsequent visit** to medical personnel.
(18) Treatment of **SECOND OR THIRD DEGREE BURN(S).**
(19) Application of **SUTURES** (stitches).
(20) Application of **BUTTERFLY ADHESIVE DRESSING(S) or STERI STRIP(S)** in lieu of sutures.
(21) Removal of **FOREIGN BODIES EMBEDDED IN EYE.**
(22) Removal of **FOREIGN BODIES FROM WOUND:** where procedure was **COMPLICATED** because of depth of the embodiment, size or location.
(23) Use of **PRESCRIPTION MEDICATIONS** (except a single does administered on first visit for minor injury or discomfort).

FIRST AID while "(16)" through "(30)" indicate that it was ***MEDICAL TREATMENT***. Consequently, if the incident was work-related (entry no. 6), an affirmative answer to <u>any</u> question numbered "(16)" through "(30)" indicates that the incident <u>***is recordable***</u>.

(24) Use of hot or cold **SOAKING THERAPY during second or subsequent visit** to medical personnel.
(25) Application of hot or cold **COMPRESS(ES) during second or subsequent visit** to medical personnel.
(26) **CUTTING AWAY DEAD SKIN** (surgical debridement).
(27) Application of **HEAT THERAPY during second or subsequent visit** to medical personnel.
(28) Use of **WHIRLPOOL BATH THERAPY during second or subsequent visit** to medical personnel.
(29) **POSITIVE X-RAY DIAGNOSIS** (fractures, broken bones, etc.)
(30) **ADMISSION TO A HOSPITAL** or equivalent medical facility **FOR TREATMENT**

16. Did the incident cause loss of consciousness?
17. If so, why? How long?
18. Was the involved employee unable to perform any part of his normal job assignment?
19. If so, what part?
20. State calendar date(s) of this inability.
21. Did the incident cause any restriction of motion in the employee?
22. If so, what motions were restricted?
23. State all calendar dates of this restriction of motion.
24. Did the incident result in transfer to another job?
25. If so, to what job?
26. State calendar date of this transfer.
27. Did incident result in full days (or shifts) of lost work time?
28. If so, state calendar date of each.
29. Did the incident result in termination of employment?
30. If so, state calendar date of termination.
31. Was the incident diagnosed as an occupational illness?
32. If so, by whom?
33. What was the "illness" that was diagnosed?
34. State calendar date such illness was first diagnosed.
35. Was the employee admitted to a hospital as a patient?
36. What hospital?
37. Date of admission
38. Date of discharge
39. Treatment received at hospital?
40. In your opinion, is this incident required to be recorded as a work-related injury or illness?
41. State today's calendar date.
42. Print your name.
43. Sign your name.

*** * * * * END OF FORM * * * * ***

Use of a form like the foregoing will be useful only if the information is obtained from the persons most likely to know the answers to the questions. That would almost always include the involved employee and his immediate supervisor, and if medical attention was provided, those who rendered medical assistance. Obtaining first-hand information in the handwriting of such people is always preferable to that recorded by a clerk, investigator or interviewer.

If the information obtained through this form indicates that the incident resulted in any of the nine matters that make it "recordable" for OSHA recordkeeping purposes,[2/] record it on the OSHA 200 Form. That should be done even if several different people report on the same incident but only one of them provided information that indicated that it was recordable.

One more action should be taken by the employer in order to ensure that no recordable incident is overlooked. There should be a mandatory work rule that every employee who is injured or hurt, becomes ill or develops symptoms of any illness as a result of his work, must immediately notify his supervisor.

Employers have nothing to lose by listing questionable incidents on the OSHA 200 Form -- and nothing to gain by not listing them -- at least so long as OSHA continues its post-1985 practice of seeking multi-million dollar fines for injury/illness recordkeeping citations.

In view of the matters discussed above, employers should not confuse incidents listed on the OSHA 200 with the company's actual employee injury/illness experience.

All of the latter cases should, of course, appear on the OSHA 200 but that form should also include cases that, in the employer's opinion, are not work-related injuries or illnesses if someone else (such as the involved employee, his immediate supervisor, or any person who provided medical assistance) provides information that indicates the incident is recordable under the OSHA recordkeeping guidelines.

2/ The term "recordable" means an occupational injury or illness which results in one or more of the following: 1. A fatality. 2. One or more lost workdays. 3. Transfer to another job. 4. Termination of employment. 5. Medical treatment other than first aid. 6. Loss of consciousness. 7. Restriction on performance of normal job functions. 8. Restriction of motion. 9. A diagnosed "occupational illness" which is reported to the employer.

APPENDIX C

OSHA'S 1988 RECOMMENDATIONS FOR PREVENTION OF HIV TRANSMISSION IN HEALTH-CARE SETTINGS

Recommendations for Prevention of HIV Transmission in Health-Care Settings

Introduction

Human immunodeficiency virus (HIV), the virus that causes acquired immunodeficiency syndrome (AIDS), is transmitted through sexual contact and exposure to infected blood or blood components and perinatally from mother to neonate. HIV has been isolated from blood, semen, vaginal secretions, saliva, tears, breast milk, cerebrospinal fluid, amniotic fluid, and urine and is likely to be isolated from other body fluids, secretions, and excretions. However, epidemiologic evidence has implicated only blood, semen, vaginal secretions, and possibly breast milk in transmission.

The increasing prevalence of HIV increases the risk that health-care workers will be exposed to blood from patients infected with HIV, especially when blood and body-fluid precautions are not followed for all patients. Thus, this document emphasizes the need for health-care workers to consider all patients as potentially infected with HIV and/or other blood-borne pathogens and to adhere rigorously to infection-control precautions for minimizing the risk of exposure to blood and body fluids of all patients.

The recommendations contained in this document consolidate and update CDC recommendations published earlier for preventing HIV transmission in health-care settings: precautions for clinical and laboratory staffs (*1*) and precautions for health-care workers and allied professionals (*2*); recommendations for preventing HIV transmission in the workplace (*3*) and during invasive procedures (*4*); recommendations for preventing possible transmission of HIV from tears (*5*); and recommendations for providing dialysis treatment for HIV-infected patients (*6*). These recommendations also update portions of the "Guideline for Isolation Precautions in Hospitals" (*7*) and reemphasize some of the recommendations contained in "Infection Control Practices for Dentistry" (*8*). The recommendations contained in this document have been developed for use in health-care settings and emphasize the need to treat blood and other body fluids from all patients as potentially infective. These same prudent precautions also should be taken in other settings in which persons may be exposed to blood or other body fluids.

Definition of Health-Care Workers

Health-care workers are defined as persons, including students and trainees, whose activities involve contact with patients or with blood or other body fluids from patients in a health-care setting.

Health-Care Workers with AIDS

As of July 10, 1987, a total of 1,875 (5.8%) of 32,395 adults with AIDS, who had been reported to the CDC national surveillance system and for whom occupational information was available, reported being employed in a health-care or clinical laboratory setting. In comparison, 6.8 million persons—representing 5.6% of the U.S. labor force—were employed in health services. Of the health-care workers with AIDS, 95% have been reported to exhibit high-risk behavior; for the remaining 5%, the means of HIV acquisition was undetermined. Health-care workers with AIDS were significantly more likely than other workers to have an undetermined risk (5% versus 3%, respectively). For both health-care workers and non-health-care workers with AIDS, the proportion with an undetermined risk has not increased since 1982.

AIDS patients initially reported as not belonging to recognized risk groups are investigated by state and local health departments to determine whether possible risk factors exist. Of all health-care workers with AIDS reported to CDC who were initially characterized as not having an identified risk and for whom follow-up information was available, 66% have been reclassified because risk factors were identified or because the patient was found not to meet the surveillance case definition for AIDS. Of the 87 health-care workers currently categorized as having no identifiable risk, information is incomplete on 16 (18%) because of death or refusal to be interviewed; 38 (44%) are still being investigated. The remaining 33 (38%) health-care workers were interviewed or had other follow-up information available. The occupations of these 33 were as follows: five physicians (15%), three of whom were surgeons; one dentist (3%); three nurses (9%); nine nursing assistants (27%); seven housekeeping or maintenance workers (21%); three clinical laboratory technicians (9%); one therapist (3%); and four others who did not have contact with patients (12%). Although 15 of these 33 health-care workers reported parenteral and/or other non-needlestick exposure to blood or body fluids from patients in the 10 years preceding their diagnosis of AIDS, none of these exposures involved a patient with AIDS or known HIV infection.

Risk to Health-Care Workers of Acquiring HIV in Health-Care Settings

Health-care workers with documented percutaneous or mucous-membrane exposures to blood or body fluids of HIV-infected patients have been prospectively evaluated to determine the risk of infection after such exposures. As of June 30, 1987, 883 health-care workers have been tested for antibody to HIV in an ongoing surveillance project conducted by CDC (9). Of these, 708 (80%) had percutaneous exposures to blood, and 175 (20%) had a mucous membrane or an open wound contaminated by blood or body fluid. Of 396 health-care workers, each of whom had only a convalescent-phase serum sample obtained and tested ≥90 days post-exposure, one—for whom heterosexual transmission could not be ruled out—was seropositive for HIV antibody. For 425 additional health-care workers, both acute- and convalescent-phase serum samples were obtained and tested; none of 74 health-care workers with nonpercutaneous exposures seroconverted, and three (0.9%) of 351 with percutaneous exposures seroconverted. None of these three health-care workers had other documented risk factors for infection.

Two other prospective studies to assess the risk of nosocomial acquisition of HIV infection for health-care workers are ongoing in the United States. As of April 30, 1987, 332 health-care workers with a total of 453 needlestick or mucous-membrane exposures to the blood or other body fluids of HIV-infected patients were tested for HIV antibody at the National Institutes of Health (*10*). These exposed workers included 103 with needlestick injuries and 229 with mucous-membrane exposures; none had seroconverted. A similar study at the University of California of 129 health-care workers with documented needlestick injuries or mucous-membrane exposures to blood or other body fluids from patients with HIV infection has not identified any seroconversions (*11*). Results of a prospective study in the United Kingdom identified no evidence of transmission among 150 health-care workers with parenteral or mucous-membrane exposures to blood or other body fluids, secretions, or excretions from patients with HIV infection (*12*).

In addition to health-care workers enrolled in prospective studies, eight persons who provided care to infected patients and denied other risk factors have been reported to have acquired HIV infection. Three of these health-care workers had needlestick exposures to blood from infected patients (*13-15*). Two were persons who provided nursing care to infected persons; although neither sustained a needlestick, both had extensive contact with blood or other body fluids, and neither observed recommended barrier precautions (*16,17*). The other three were health-care workers with non-needlestick exposures to blood from infected patients (*18*). Although the exact route of transmission for these last three infections is not known, all three persons had direct contact of their skin with blood from infected patients, all had skin lesions that may have been contaminated by blood, and one also had a mucous-membrane exposure.

A total of 1,231 dentists and hygienists, many of whom practiced in areas with many AIDS cases, participated in a study to determine the prevalence of antibody to HIV; one dentist (0.1%) had HIV antibody. Although no exposure to a known HIV-infected person could be documented, epidemiologic investigation did not identify any other risk factor for infection. The infected dentist, who also had a history of sustaining needlestick injuries and trauma to his hands, did not routinely wear gloves when providing dental care (*19*).

Precautions To Prevent Transmission of HIV

Universal Precautions

Since medical history and examination cannot reliably identify all patients infected with HIV or other blood-borne pathogens, blood and body-fluid precautions should be consistently used for all patients. This approach, previously recommended by CDC (*3,4*), and referred to as "universal blood and body-fluid precautions" or "universal precautions," should be used in the care of all patients, especially including those in emergency-care settings in which the risk of blood exposure is increased and the infection status of the patient is usually unknown (*20*).

1. All health-care workers should routinely use appropriate barrier precautions to prevent skin and mucous-membrane exposure when contact with blood or other body fluids of any patient is anticipated. Gloves should be worn for touching blood and body fluids, mucous membranes, or non-intact skin of all patients, for handling items or surfaces soiled with blood or body fluids, and for performing venipuncture and other vascular access procedures. Gloves should be changed after contact with each patient. Masks and protective eyewear or face shields should be worn during procedures that are likely to generate droplets of blood or other body fluids to prevent exposure of mucous membranes of the mouth, nose, and eyes. Gowns or aprons should be worn during procedures that are likely to generate splashes of blood or other body fluids.
2. Hands and other skin surfaces should be washed immediately and thoroughly if contaminated with blood or other body fluids. Hands should be washed immediately after gloves are removed.
3. All health-care workers should take precautions to prevent injuries caused by needles, scalpels, and other sharp instruments or devices during procedures; when cleaning used instruments; during disposal of used needles; and when handling sharp instruments after procedures. To prevent needlestick injuries, needles should not be recapped, purposely bent or broken by hand, removed from disposable syringes, or otherwise manipulated by hand. After they are used, disposable syringes and needles, scalpel blades, and other sharp items should be placed in puncture-resistant containers for disposal; the puncture-resistant containers should be located as close as practical to the use area. Large-bore reusable needles should be placed in a puncture-resistant container for transport to the reprocessing area.
4. Although saliva has not been implicated in HIV transmission, to minimize the need for emergency mouth-to-mouth resuscitation, mouthpieces, resuscitation bags, or other ventilation devices should be available for use in areas in which the need for resuscitation is predictable.
5. Health-care workers who have exudative lesions or weeping dermatitis should refrain from all direct patient care and from handling patient-care equipment until the condition resolves.
6. Pregnant health-care workers are not known to be at greater risk of contracting HIV infection than health-care workers who are not pregnant; however, if a health-care worker develops HIV infection during pregnancy, the infant is at risk of infection resulting from perinatal transmission. Because of this risk, pregnant health-care workers should be especially familiar with and strictly adhere to precautions to minimize the risk of HIV transmission.

Implementation of universal blood and body-fluid precautions for <u>all</u> patients eliminates the need for use of the isolation category of "Blood and Body Fluid Precautions" previously recommended by CDC (7) for patients known or suspected to be infected with blood-borne pathogens. Isolation precautions (e.g., enteric, "AFB" [7]) should be used as necessary if associated conditions, such as infectious diarrhea or tuberculosis, are diagnosed or suspected.

Precautions for Invasive Procedures

In this document, an invasive procedure is defined as surgical entry into tissues, cavities, or organs or repair of major traumatic injuries 1) in an operating or delivery room, emergency department, or outpatient setting, including both physicians' and dentists' offices; 2) cardiac catheterization and angiographic procedures; 3) a vaginal or cesarean delivery or other invasive obstetric procedure during which bleeding may occur; or 4) the manipulation, cutting, or removal of any oral or perioral tissues, including tooth structure, during which bleeding occurs or the potential for bleeding exists. The universal blood and body-fluid precautions listed above, combined with the precautions listed below, should be the minimum precautions for <u>all</u> such invasive procedures.

1. All health-care workers who participate in invasive procedures must routinely use appropriate barrier precautions to prevent skin and mucous-membrane contact with blood and other body fluids of all patients. Gloves and surgical masks must be worn for all invasive procedures. Protective eyewear or face shields should be worn for procedures that commonly result in the generation of droplets, splashing of blood or other body fluids, or the generation of bone chips. Gowns or aprons made of materials that provide an effective barrier should be worn during invasive procedures that are likely to result in the splashing of blood or other body fluids. All health-care workers who perform or assist in vaginal or cesarean deliveries should wear gloves and gowns when handling the placenta or the infant until blood and amniotic fluid have been removed from the infant's skin and should wear gloves during post-delivery care of the umbilical cord.
2. If a glove is torn or a needlestick or other injury occurs, the glove should be removed and a new glove used as promptly as patient safety permits; the needle or instrument involved in the incident should also be removed from the sterile field.

Precautions for Dentistry*

Blood, saliva, and gingival fluid from <u>all</u> dental patients should be considered infective. Special emphasis should be placed on the following precautions for preventing transmission of blood-borne pathogens in dental practice in both institutional and non-institutional settings.

1. In addition to wearing gloves for contact with oral mucous membranes of all patients, all dental workers should wear surgical masks and protective eyewear or chin-length plastic face shields during dental procedures in which splashing or spattering of blood, saliva, or gingival fluids is likely. Rubber dams, high-speed evacuation, and proper patient positioning, when appropriate, should be utilized to minimize generation of droplets and spatter.
2. Handpieces should be sterilized after use with each patient, since blood, saliva, or gingival fluid of patients may be aspirated into the handpiece or waterline. Handpieces that cannot be sterilized should at least be flushed, the outside surface cleaned and wiped with a suitable chemical germicide, and then rinsed. Handpieces should be flushed at the beginning of the day and after use with each patient. Manufacturers' recommendations should be followed for use and maintenance of waterlines and check valves and for flushing of handpieces. The same precautions should be used for ultrasonic scalers and air/water syringes.

*General infection-control precautions are more specifically addressed in previous recommendations for infection-control practices for dentistry (*8*).

3. Blood and saliva should be thoroughly and carefully cleaned from material that has been used in the mouth (e.g., impression materials, bite registration), especially before polishing and grinding intra-oral devices. Contaminated materials, impressions, and intra-oral devices should also be cleaned and disinfected before being handled in the dental laboratory and before they are placed in the patient's mouth. Because of the increasing variety of dental materials used intra-orally, dental workers should consult with manufacturers as to the stability of specific materials when using disinfection procedures.
4. Dental equipment and surfaces that are difficult to disinfect (e.g., light handles or X-ray-unit heads) and that may become contaminated should be wrapped with impervious-backed paper, aluminum foil, or clear plastic wrap. The coverings should be removed and discarded, and clean coverings should be put in place after use with each patient.

Precautions for Autopsies or Morticians' Services

In addition to the universal blood and body-fluid precautions listed above, the following precautions should be used by persons performing postmortem procedures:

1. All persons performing or assisting in postmortem procedures should wear gloves, masks, protective eyewear, gowns, and waterproof aprons.
2. Instruments and surfaces contaminated during postmortem procedures should be decontaminated with an appropriate chemical germicide.

Precautions for Dialysis

Patients with end-stage renal disease who are undergoing maintenance dialysis and who have HIV infection can be dialyzed in hospital-based or free-standing dialysis units using conventional infection-control precautions (*21*). Universal blood and body-fluid precautions should be used when dialyzing <u>all</u> patients.

Strategies for disinfecting the dialysis fluid pathways of the hemodialysis machine are targeted to control bacterial contamination and generally consist of using 500-750 parts per million (ppm) of sodium hypochlorite (household bleach) for 30-40 minutes or 1.5%-2.0% formaldehyde overnight. In addition, several chemical germicides formulated to disinfect dialysis machines are commercially available. None of these protocols or procedures need to be changed for dialyzing patients infected with HIV.

Patients infected with HIV can be dialyzed by either hemodialysis or peritoneal dialysis and do not need to be isolated from other patients. The type of dialysis treatment (i.e., hemodialysis or peritoneal dialysis) should be based on the needs of the patient. The dialyzer may be discarded after each use. Alternatively, centers that reuse dialyzers—i.e., a specific single-use dialyzer is issued to a specific patient, removed, cleaned, disinfected, and reused several times on the same patient only—may include HIV-infected patients in the dialyzer-reuse program. An individual dialyzer must never be used on more than one patient.

Precautions for Laboratories†

Blood and other body fluids from <u>all</u> patients should be considered infective. To supplement the universal blood and body-fluid precautions listed above, the following precautions are recommended for health-care workers in clinical laboratories.

†Additional precautions for research and industrial laboratories are addressed elsewhere (*22,23*).

1. All specimens of blood and body fluids should be put in a well-constructed container with a secure lid to prevent leaking during transport. Care should be taken when collecting each specimen to avoid contaminating the outside of the container and of the laboratory form accompanying the specimen.
2. All persons processing blood and body-fluid specimens (e.g., removing tops from vacuum tubes) should wear gloves. Masks and protective eyewear should be worn if mucous-membrane contact with blood or body fluids is anticipated. Gloves should be changed and hands washed after completion of specimen processing.
3. For routine procedures, such as histologic and pathologic studies or microbiologic culturing, a biological safety cabinet is not necessary. However, biological safety cabinets (Class I or II) should be used whenever procedures are conducted that have a high potential for generating droplets. These include activities such as blending, sonicating, and vigorous mixing.
4. Mechanical pipetting devices should be used for manipulating all liquids in the laboratory. Mouth pipetting must not be done.
5. Use of needles and syringes should be limited to situations in which there is no alternative, and the recommendations for preventing injuries with needles outlined under universal precautions should be followed.
6. Laboratory work surfaces should be decontaminated with an appropriate chemical germicide after a spill of blood or other body fluids and when work activities are completed.
7. Contaminated materials used in laboratory tests should be decontaminated before reprocessing or be placed in bags and disposed of in accordance with institutional policies for disposal of infective waste (*24*).
8. Scientific equipment that has been contaminated with blood or other body fluids should be decontaminated and cleaned before being repaired in the laboratory or transported to the manufacturer.
9. All persons should wash their hands after completing laboratory activities and should remove protective clothing before leaving the laboratory.

Implementation of universal blood and body-fluid precautions for <u>all</u> patients eliminates the need for warning labels on specimens since blood and other body fluids from all patients should be considered infective.

Environmental Considerations for HIV Transmission

No environmentally mediated mode of HIV transmission has been documented. Nevertheless, the precautions described below should be taken routinely in the care of <u>all</u> patients.

Sterilization and Disinfection

Standard sterilization and disinfection procedures for patient-care equipment currently recommended for use (*25,26*) in a variety of health-care settings—including hospitals, medical and dental clinics and offices, hemodialysis centers, emergency-care facilities, and long-term nursing-care facilities—are adequate to sterilize or disinfect instruments, devices, or other items contaminated with blood or other body fluids from persons infected with blood-borne pathogens including HIV (*21,23*).

Instruments or devices that enter sterile tissue or the vascular system of any patient or through which blood flows should be sterilized before reuse. Devices or items that contact intact mucous membranes should be sterilized or receive high-level disinfection, a procedure that kills vegetative organisms and viruses but not necessarily large numbers of bacterial spores. Chemical germicides that are registered with the U.S. Environmental Protection Agency (EPA) as "sterilants" may be used either for sterilization or for high-level disinfection depending on contact time.

Contact lenses used in trial fittings should be disinfected after each fitting by using a hydrogen peroxide contact lens disinfecting system or, if compatible, with heat (78 C-80 C [172.4 F-176.0 F]) for 10 minutes.

Medical devices or instruments that require sterilization or disinfection should be thoroughly cleaned before being exposed to the germicide, and the manufacturer's instructions for the use of the germicide should be followed. Further, it is important that the manufacturer's specifications for compatibility of the medical device with chemical germicides be closely followed. Information on specific label claims of commercial germicides can be obtained by writing to the Disinfectants Branch, Office of Pesticides, Environmental Protection Agency, 401 M Street, SW, Washington, D.C. 20460.

Studies have shown that HIV is inactivated rapidly after being exposed to commonly used chemical germicides at concentrations that are much lower than used in practice (*27-30*). Embalming fluids are similar to the types of chemical germicides that have been tested and found to completely inactivate HIV. In addition to commercially available chemical germicides, a solution of sodium hypochlorite (household bleach) prepared daily is an inexpensive and effective germicide. Concentrations ranging from approximately 500 ppm (1:100 dilution of household bleach) sodium hypochlorite to 5,000 ppm (1:10 dilution of household bleach) are effective depending on the amount of organic material (e.g., blood, mucus) present on the surface to be cleaned and disinfected. Commercially available chemical germicides may be more compatible with certain medical devices that might be corroded by repeated exposure to sodium hypochlorite, especially to the 1:10 dilution.

Survival of HIV in the Environment

The most extensive study on the survival of HIV after drying involved greatly concentrated HIV samples, i.e., 10 million tissue-culture infectious doses per milliliter (*31*). This concentration is at least 100,000 times greater than that typically found in the blood or serum of patients with HIV infection. HIV was detectable by tissue-culture techniques 1-3 days after drying, but the rate of inactivation was rapid. Studies performed at CDC have also shown that drying HIV causes a rapid (within several hours) 1-2 log (90%-99%) reduction in HIV concentration. In tissue-culture fluid, cell-free HIV could be detected up to 15 days at room temperature, up to 11 days at 37 C (98.6 F), and up to 1 day if the HIV was cell-associated.

When considered in the context of environmental conditions in health-care facilities, these results do not require any changes in currently recommended sterilization, disinfection, or housekeeping strategies. When medical devices are contaminated with blood or other body fluids, existing recommendations include the cleaning of these instruments, followed by disinfection or sterilization, depending on the type of medical device. These protocols assume "worst-case" conditions of extreme virologic and microbiologic contamination, and whether viruses have been inactivated after drying plays no role in formulating these strategies. Consequently, no changes in published procedures for cleaning, disinfecting, or sterilizing need to be made.

Housekeeping

Environmental surfaces such as walls, floors, and other surfaces are not associated with transmission of infections to patients or health-care workers. Therefore, extraordinary attempts to disinfect or sterilize these environmental surfaces are not necessary. However, cleaning and removal of soil should be done routinely.

Cleaning schedules and methods vary according to the area of the hospital or institution, type of surface to be cleaned, and the amount and type of soil present. Horizontal surfaces (e.g., bedside tables and hard-surfaced flooring) in patient-care areas are usually cleaned on a regular basis, when soiling or spills occur, and when a patient is discharged. Cleaning of walls, blinds, and curtains is recommended only if they are visibly soiled. Disinfectant fogging is an unsatisfactory method of decontaminating air and surfaces and is not recommended.

Disinfectant-detergent formulations registered by EPA can be used for cleaning environmental surfaces, but the actual physical removal of microorganisms by scrubbing is probably at least as important as any antimicrobial effect of the cleaning agent used. Therefore, cost, safety, and acceptability by housekeepers can be the main criteria for selecting any such registered agent. The manufacturers' instructions for appropriate use should be followed.

Cleaning and Decontaminating Spills of Blood or Other Body Fluids

Chemical germicides that are approved for use as "hospital disinfectants" and are tuberculocidal when used at recommended dilutions can be used to decontaminate spills of blood and other body fluids. Strategies for decontaminating spills of blood and other body fluids in a patient-care setting are different than for spills of cultures or other materials in clinical, public health, or research laboratories. In patient-care areas, visible material should first be removed and then the area should be decontaminated. With large spills of cultured or concentrated infectious agents in the laboratory, the contaminated area should be flooded with a liquid germicide before cleaning, then decontaminated with fresh germicidal chemical. In both settings, gloves should be worn during the cleaning and decontaminating procedures.

Laundry

Although soiled linen has been identified as a source of large numbers of certain pathogenic microorganisms, the risk of actual disease transmission is negligible. Rather than rigid procedures and specifications, hygienic and common-sense storage and processing of clean and soiled linen are recommended (*26*). Soiled linen should be handled as little as possible and with minimum agitation to prevent gross microbial contamination of the air and of persons handling the linen. All soiled linen should be bagged at the location where it was used; it should not be sorted or rinsed in patient-care areas. Linen soiled with blood or body fluids should be placed and transported in bags that prevent leakage. If hot water is used, linen should be washed with detergent in water at least 71 C (160 F) for 25 minutes. If low-temperature($\leq$70 C [158 F]) laundry cycles are used, chemicals suitable for low-temperature washing at proper use concentration should be used.

Infective Waste

There is no epidemiologic evidence to suggest that most hospital waste is any more infective than residential waste. Moreover, there is no epidemiologic evidence that hospital waste has caused disease in the community as a result of improper disposal. Therefore, identifying wastes for which special precautions are indicated is largely a matter of judgment about the relative risk of disease transmission. The most practical approach to the management of infective waste is to identify those wastes with the potential for causing infection during handling and disposal and for which some special precautions appear prudent. Hospital wastes for which special precautions appear prudent include microbiology laboratory waste, pathology waste, and blood specimens or blood products. While any item that has had contact with blood, exudates, or secretions may be potentially infective, it is not usually considered practical or necessary to treat all such waste as infective (*23,26*). Infective waste, in general, should either be incinerated or should be autoclaved before disposal in a sanitary landfill. Bulk blood, suctioned fluids, excretions, and secretions may be carefully poured down a drain connected to a sanitary sewer. Sanitary sewers may also be used to dispose of other infectious wastes capable of being ground and flushed into the sewer.

Implementation of Recommended Precautions

Employers of health-care workers should ensure that policies exist for:

1. Initial orientation and continuing education and training of all health-care workers—including students and trainees—on the epidemiology, modes of transmission, and prevention of HIV and other blood-borne infections and the need for routine use of universal blood and body-fluid precautions for <u>all</u> patients.
2. Provision of equipment and supplies necessary to minimize the risk of infection with HIV and other blood-borne pathogens.
3. Monitoring adherence to recommended protective measures. When monitoring reveals a failure to follow recommended precautions, counseling, education, and/or re-training should be provided, and, if necessary, appropriate disciplinary action should be considered.

Professional associations and labor organizations, through continuing education efforts, should emphasize the need for health-care workers to follow recommended precautions.

Serologic Testing for HIV Infection

Background

A person is identified as infected with HIV when a sequence of tests, starting with repeated enzyme immunoassays (EIA) and including a Western blot or similar, more specific assay, are repeatedly reactive. Persons infected with HIV usually develop antibody against the virus within 6-12 weeks after infection.

The sensitivity of the currently licensed EIA tests is at least 99% when they are performed under optimal laboratory conditions on serum specimens from persons infected for ≥12 weeks. Optimal laboratory conditions include the use of reliable reagents, provision of continuing education of personnel, quality control of procedures, and participation in performance-evaluation programs. Given this performance, the probability of a false-negative test is remote except during the first several weeks after infection, before detectable antibody is present. The proportion of infected persons with a false-negative test attributed to absence of antibody in the early stages of infection is dependent on both the incidence and prevalence of HIV infection in a population (Table 1).

The specificity of the currently licensed EIA tests is approximately 99% when repeatedly reactive tests are considered. Repeat testing of initially reactive specimens by EIA is required to reduce the likelihood of laboratory error. To increase further the specificity of serologic tests, laboratories must use a supplemental test, most often the Western blot, to validate repeatedly reactive EIA results. Under optimal laboratory conditions, the sensitivity of the Western blot test is comparable to or greater than that of a repeatedly reactive EIA, and the Western blot is highly specific when strict criteria are used to interpret the test results. The testing sequence of a repeatedly reactive EIA and a positive Western blot test is highly predictive of HIV infection, even in a population with a low prevalence of infection (Table 2). If the Western blot test result is indeterminant, the testing sequence is considered equivocal for HIV infection.

TABLE 1. Estimated annual number of patients infected with HIV not detected by HIV-antibody testing in a hypothetical hospital with 10,000 admissions/year*

Beginning prevalence of HIV infection	Annual incidence of HIV infection	Approximate number of HIV-infected patients	Approximate number of HIV-infected patients not detected
5.0%	1.0%	550	17-18
5.0%	0.5%	525	11-12
1.0%	0.2%	110	3-4
1.0%	0.1%	105	2-3
0.1%	0.02%	11	0-1
0.1%	0.01%	11	0-1

*The estimates are based on the following assumptions: 1) the sensitivity of the screening test is 99% (i.e., 99% of HIV-infected persons with antibody will be detected); 2) persons infected with HIV will not develop detectable antibody (seroconvert) until 6 weeks (1.5 months) after infection; 3) new infections occur at an equal rate throughout the year; 4) calculations of the number of HIV-infected persons in the patient population are based on the mid-year prevalence, which is the beginning prevalence plus half the annual incidence of infections.

When this occurs, the Western blot test should be repeated on the same serum sample, and, if still indeterminant, the testing sequence should be repeated on a sample collected 3-6 months later. Use of other supplemental tests may aid in interpreting of results on samples that are persistently indeterminant by Western blot.

Testing of Patients

Previous CDC recommendations have emphasized the value of HIV serologic testing of patients for: 1) management of parenteral or mucous-membrane exposures of health-care workers, 2) patient diagnosis and management, and 3) counseling and serologic testing to prevent and control HIV transmission in the community. In addition, more recent recommendations have stated that hospitals, in conjunction with state and local health departments, should periodically determine the prevalence of HIV infection among patients from age groups at highest risk of infection (*32*).

Adherence to universal blood and body-fluid precautions recommended for the care of all patients will minimize the risk of transmission of HIV and other blood-borne pathogens from patients to health-care workers. The utility of routine HIV serologic testing of patients as an adjunct to universal precautions is unknown. Results of such testing may not be available in emergency or outpatient settings. In addition, some recently infected patients will not have detectable antibody to HIV (Table 1).

Personnel in some hospitals have advocated serologic testing of patients in settings in which exposure of health-care workers to large amounts of patients' blood may be anticipated. Specific patients for whom serologic testing has been advocated include those undergoing major operative procedures and those undergoing treatment in critical-care units, especially if they have conditions involving uncontrolled bleeding. Decisions regarding the need to establish testing programs for patients should be made by physicians or individual institutions. In addition, when deemed appropriate, testing of individual patients may be performed on agreement between the patient and the physician providing care.

In addition to the universal precautions recommended for all patients, certain additional precautions for the care of HIV-infected patients undergoing major surgical operations have been proposed by personnel in some hospitals. For example, surgical procedures on an HIV-infected patient might be altered so that hand-to-hand passing of sharp instruments would be eliminated; stapling instruments rather than

TABLE 2. Predictive value of positive HIV-antibody tests in hypothetical populations with different prevalences of infection

	Prevalence of infection	Predictive value of positive test*
Repeatedly reactive enzyme immunoassay (EIA)†	0.2%	28.41%
	2.0%	80.16%
	20.0%	98.02%
Repeatedly reactive EIA followed by positive Western blot (WB)§	0.2%	99.75%
	2.0%	99.97%
	20.0%	99.99%

*Proportion of persons with positive test results who are actually infected with HIV.
†Assumes EIA sensitivity of 99.0% and specificity of 99.5%.
§Assumes WB sensitivity of 99.0% and specificity of 99.9%.

hand-suturing equipment might be used to perform tissue approximation; electrocautery devices rather than scalpels might be used as cutting instruments; and, even though uncomfortable, gowns that totally prevent seepage of blood onto the skin of members of the operative team might be worn. While such modifications might further minimize the risk of HIV infection for members of the operative team, some of these techniques could result in prolongation of operative time and could potentially have an adverse effect on the patient.

Testing programs, if developed, should include the following principles:

- Obtaining consent for testing.
- Informing patients of test results, and providing counseling for seropositive patients by properly trained persons.
- Assuring that confidentiality safeguards are in place to limit knowledge of test results to those directly involved in the care of infected patients or as required by law.
- Assuring that identification of infected patients will not result in denial of needed care or provision of suboptimal care.
- Evaluating prospectively 1) the efficacy of the program in reducing the incidence of parenteral, mucous-membrane, or significant cutaneous exposures of health-care workers to the blood or other body fluids of HIV-infected patients and 2) the effect of modified procedures on patients.

Testing of Health-Care Workers

Although transmission of HIV from infected health-care workers to patients has not been reported, transmission during invasive procedures remains a possibility. Transmission of hepatitis B virus (HBV)—a blood-borne agent with a considerably greater potential for nosocomial spread—from health-care workers to patients has been documented. Such transmission has occurred in situations (e.g., oral and gynecologic surgery) in which health-care workers, when tested, had very high concentrations of HBV in their blood (at least 100 million infectious virus particles per milliliter, a concentration much higher than occurs with HIV infection), and the health-care workers sustained a puncture wound while performing invasive procedures or had exudative or weeping lesions or microlacerations that allowed virus to contaminate instruments or open wounds of patients (*33,34*).

The hepatitis B experience indicates that only those health-care workers who perform certain types of invasive procedures have transmitted HBV to patients. Adherence to recommendations in this document will minimize the risk of transmission of HIV and other blood-borne pathogens from health-care workers to patients during invasive procedures. Since transmission of HIV from infected health-care workers performing invasive procedures to their patients has not been reported and would be expected to occur only very rarely, if at all, the utility of routine testing of such health-care workers to prevent transmission of HIV cannot be assessed. If consideration is given to developing a serologic testing program for health-care workers who perform invasive procedures, the frequency of testing, as well as the issues of consent, confidentiality, and consequences of test results—as previously outlined for testing programs for patients—must be addressed.

Management of Infected Health-Care Workers

Health-care workers with impaired immune systems resulting from HIV infection or other causes are at increased risk of acquiring or experiencing serious complications of infectious disease. Of particular concern is the risk of severe infection following exposure to patients with infectious diseases that are easily transmitted if appropriate precautions are not taken (e.g., measles, varicella). Any health-care worker with an impaired immune system should be counseled about the potential risk associated with taking care of patients with any transmissible infection and should continue to follow existing recommendations for infection control to minimize risk of exposure to other infectious agents (*7,35*). Recommendations of the Immunization Practices Advisory Committee (ACIP) and institutional policies concerning requirements for vaccinating health-care workers with live-virus vaccines (e.g., measles, rubella) should also be considered.

The question of whether workers infected with HIV—especially those who perform invasive procedures—can adequately and safely be allowed to perform patient-care duties or whether their work assignments should be changed must be determined on an individual basis. These decisions should be made by the health-care worker's personal physician(s) in conjunction with the medical directors and personnel health service staff of the employing institution or hospital.

Management of Exposures

If a health-care worker has a parenteral (e.g., needlestick or cut) or mucous-membrane (e.g., splash to the eye or mouth) exposure to blood or other body fluids or has a cutaneous exposure involving large amounts of blood or prolonged contact with blood—especially when the exposed skin is chapped, abraded, or afflicted with dermatitis—the source patient should be informed of the incident and tested for serologic evidence of HIV infection after consent is obtained. Policies should be developed for testing source patients in situations in which consent cannot be obtained (e.g., an unconscious patient).

If the source patient has AIDS, is positive for HIV antibody, or refuses the test, the health-care worker should be counseled regarding the risk of infection and evaluated clinically and serologically for evidence of HIV infection as soon as possible after the exposure. The health-care worker should be advised to report and seek medical evaluation for any acute febrile illness that occurs within 12 weeks after the exposure. Such an illness—particularly one characterized by fever, rash, or lymphadenopathy—may be indicative of recent HIV infection. Seronegative health-care workers should be retested 6 weeks post-exposure and on a periodic basis thereafter (e.g., 12 weeks and 6 months after exposure) to determine whether transmission has occurred. During this follow-up period—especially the first 6-12 weeks after exposure, when most infected persons are expected to seroconvert—exposed health-care workers should follow U.S. Public Health Service (PHS) recommendations for preventing transmission of HIV (*36,37*).

No further follow-up of a health-care worker exposed to infection as described above is necessary if the source patient is seronegative unless the source patient is at high risk of HIV infection. In the latter case, a subsequent specimen (e.g., 12 weeks following exposure) may be obtained from the health-care worker for antibody testing. If the source patient cannot be identified, decisions regarding appropriate follow-up should be individualized. Serologic testing should be available to all health-care workers who are concerned that they may have been infected with HIV.

If a patient has a parenteral or mucous-membrane exposure to blood or other body fluid of a health-care worker, the patient should be informed of the incident, and the same procedure outlined above for management of exposures should be followed for both the source health-care worker and the exposed patient.

References

1. CDC. Acquired immunodeficiency syndrome (AIDS): Precautions for clinical and laboratory staffs. MMWR 1982;31:577-80.
2. CDC. Acquired immunodeficiency syndrome (AIDS): Precautions for health-care workers and allied professionals. MMWR 1983;32:450-1.
3. CDC. Recommendations for preventing transmission of infection with human T-lymphotropic virus type III/lymphadenopathy-associated virus in the workplace. MMWR 1985;34:681-6, 691-5.
4. CDC. Recommendations for preventing transmission of infection with human T-lymphotropic virus type III/lymphadenopathy-associated virus during invasive procedures. MMWR 1986;35:221-3.
5. CDC. Recommendations for preventing possible transmission of human T-lymphotropic virus type III/lymphadenopathy-associated virus from tears. MMWR 1985;34:533-4.
6. CDC. Recommendations for providing dialysis treatment to patients infected with human T-lymphotropic virus type III/lymphadenopathy-associated virus infection. MMWR 1986;35:376-8, 383.
7. Garner JS, Simmons BP. Guideline for isolation precautions in hospitals. Infect Control 1983;4 (suppl) :245-325.
8. CDC. Recommended infection control practices for dentistry. MMWR 1986;35:237-42.
9. McCray E, The Cooperative Needlestick Surveillance Group. Occupational risk of the acquired immunodeficiency syndrome among health care workers. N Engl J Med 1986;314:1127-32.
10. Henderson DK, Saah AJ, Zak BJ, et al. Risk of nosocomial infection with human T-cell lymphotropic virus type III/lymphadenopathy-associated virus in a large cohort of intensively exposed health care workers. Ann Intern Med 1986;104:644-7.
11. Gerberding JL, Bryant-LeBlanc CE, Nelson K, et al. Risk of transmitting the human immunodeficiency virus, cytomegalovirus, and hepatitis B virus to health care workers exposed to patients with AIDS and AIDS-related conditions. J Infect Dis 1987;156:1-8.
12. McEvoy M, Porter K, Mortimer P, Simmons N, Shanson D. Prospective study of clinical, laboratory, and ancillary staff with accidental exposures to blood or other body fluids from patients infected with HIV. Br Med J 1987;294:1595-7.
13. Anonymous. Needlestick transmission of HTLV-III from a patient infected in Africa. Lancet 1984;2:1376-7.
14. Oksenhendler E, Harzic M, Le Roux JM, Rabian C, Clauvel JP. HIV infection with seroconversion after a superficial needlestick injury to the finger. N Engl J Med 1986;315:582.
15. Neisson-Vernant C, Arfi S, Mathez D, Leibowitch J, Monplaisir N. Needlestick HIV seroconversion in a nurse. Lancet 1986;2:814.
16. Grint P, McEvoy M. Two associated cases of the acquired immune deficiency syndrome (AIDS). PHLS Commun Dis Rep 1985;42:4.
17. CDC. Apparent transmission of human T-lymphotropic virus type III/lymphadenopathy-associated virus from a child to a mother providing health care. MMWR 1986;35:76-9.
18. CDC. Update: Human immunodeficiency virus infections in health-care workers exposed to blood of infected patients. MMWR 1987;36:285-9.
19. Kline RS, Phelan J, Friedland GH, et al. Low occupational risk for HIV infection for dental professionals [Abstract]. In: Abstracts from the III International Conference on AIDS, 1-5 June 1985. Washington, DC: 155.
20. Baker JL, Kelen GD, Sivertson KT, Quinn TC. Unsuspected human immunodeficiency virus in critically ill emergency patients. JAMA 1987;257:2609-11.
21. Favero MS. Dialysis-associated diseases and their control. In: Bennett JV, Brachman PS, eds. Hospital infections. Boston: Little, Brown and Company, 1985:267-84.

22. Richardson JH, Barkley WE, eds. Biosafety in microbiological and biomedical laboratories, 1984. Washington, DC: US Department of Health and Human Services, Public Health Service. HHS publication no. (CDC) 84-8395.
23. CDC. Human T-lymphotropic virus type III/lymphadenopathy-associated virus: Agent summary statement. MMWR 1986;35:540-2, 547-9.
24. Environmental Protection Agency. EPA guide for infectious waste management. Washington, DC: U.S. Environmental Protection Agency, May 1986 (Publication no. EPA/530-SW-86-014).
25. Favero MS. Sterilization, disinfection, and antisepsis in the hospital. In: Manual of clinical microbiology. 4th ed. Washington, DC: American Society for Microbiology, 1985;129-37.
26. Garner JS, Favero MS. Guideline for handwashing and hospital environmental control, 1985. Atlanta: Public Health Service, Centers for Disease Control, 1985. HHS publication no. 99-1117.
27. Spire B, Montagnier L, Barré-Sinoussi F, Chermann JC. Inactivation of lymphadenopathy associated virus by chemical disinfectants. Lancet 1984;2:899-901.
28. Martin LS, McDougal JS, Loskoski SL. Disinfection and inactivation of the human T lymphotropic virus type III/lymphadenopathy-associated virus. J Infect Dis 1985; 152:400-3.
29. McDougal JS, Martin LS, Cort SP, et al. Thermal inactivation of the acquired immunodeficiency syndrome virus-III/lymphadenopathy-associated virus, with special reference to antihemophilic factor. J Clin Invest 1985;76:875-7.
30. Spire B, Barré-Sinoussi F, Dormont D, Montagnier L, Chermann JC. Inactivation of lymphadenopathy-associated virus by heat, gamma rays, and ultraviolet light. Lancet 1985;1:188-9.
31. Resnik L, Veren K, Salahuddin SZ, Tondreau S, Markham PD. Stability and inactivation of HTLV-III/LAV under clinical and laboratory environments. JAMA 1986;255:1887-91.
32. CDC. Public Health Service (PHS) guidelines for counseling and antibody testing to prevent HIV infection and AIDS. MMWR 1987;3:509-15..
33. Kane MA, Lettau LA. Transmission of HBV from dental personnel to patients. J Am Dent Assoc 1985;110:634-6.
34. Lettau LA, Smith JD, Williams D, et. al. Transmission of hepatitis B with resultant restriction of surgical practice. JAMA 1986;255:934-7.
35. Williams WW. Guideline for infection control in hospital personnel. Infect Control 1983;4 (suppl) :326-49.
36. CDC. Prevention of acquired immune deficiency syndrome (AIDS): Report of inter-agency recommendations. MMWR 1983;32:101-3.
37. CDC. Provisional Public Health Service inter-agency recommendations for screening donated blood and plasma for antibody to the virus causing acquired immunodeficiency syndrome. MMWR 1985;34:1-5.

MMWR: Centers for Disease Control: August 21, 1987; Vol 36, No. 2s.

APPENDIX D

GRAPHIC REPRESENTATION OF THE STANDARD'S REQUIREMENTS FOR:

1. Labelling
2. Hepatitis B Vaccination
3. Post-Exposure Evaluation and Follow-up

LABELING REQUIREMENTS

Item	No Label Required		Biohazard Label		Red Color-coded Container
Regulated waste container			X	or	X
Reusable contaminated sharps.			X	or	X
Refrigerator/freezer holding blood or other potentially infectious material (opim).			X		
Containers used for storage, transport, or shipping of blood or opim.			X	or	X
Blood/blood products released for clinical use.	X				
Individual specimen containers of blood or opim remaining in facility.	X[1]	or	X	or	X
Specimens shipped from the primary facility to another facility.			X	or	X
Individual containers of blood or opim placed in labeled container during storage, transport, shipment, or disposal.	X				
Contaminated equipment needing servicing or shipping.			X[2]		
Contaminated laundry.	X[3]	or	X	or	X
Laundry sent to another facility that does not use universal precautions.			X	or	X

[1] Labels are not be required if universal precautions are used in handling all specimens and containers are recognizable as containing specimens.
[2] Specifying, in addition, the location of the contamination.
[3] Alternative label or color code must be used when facility uses UP in handling all soiled laundry and employees can recognize containers as requiring compliance with UP.

HEPATITIS B VACCINATION

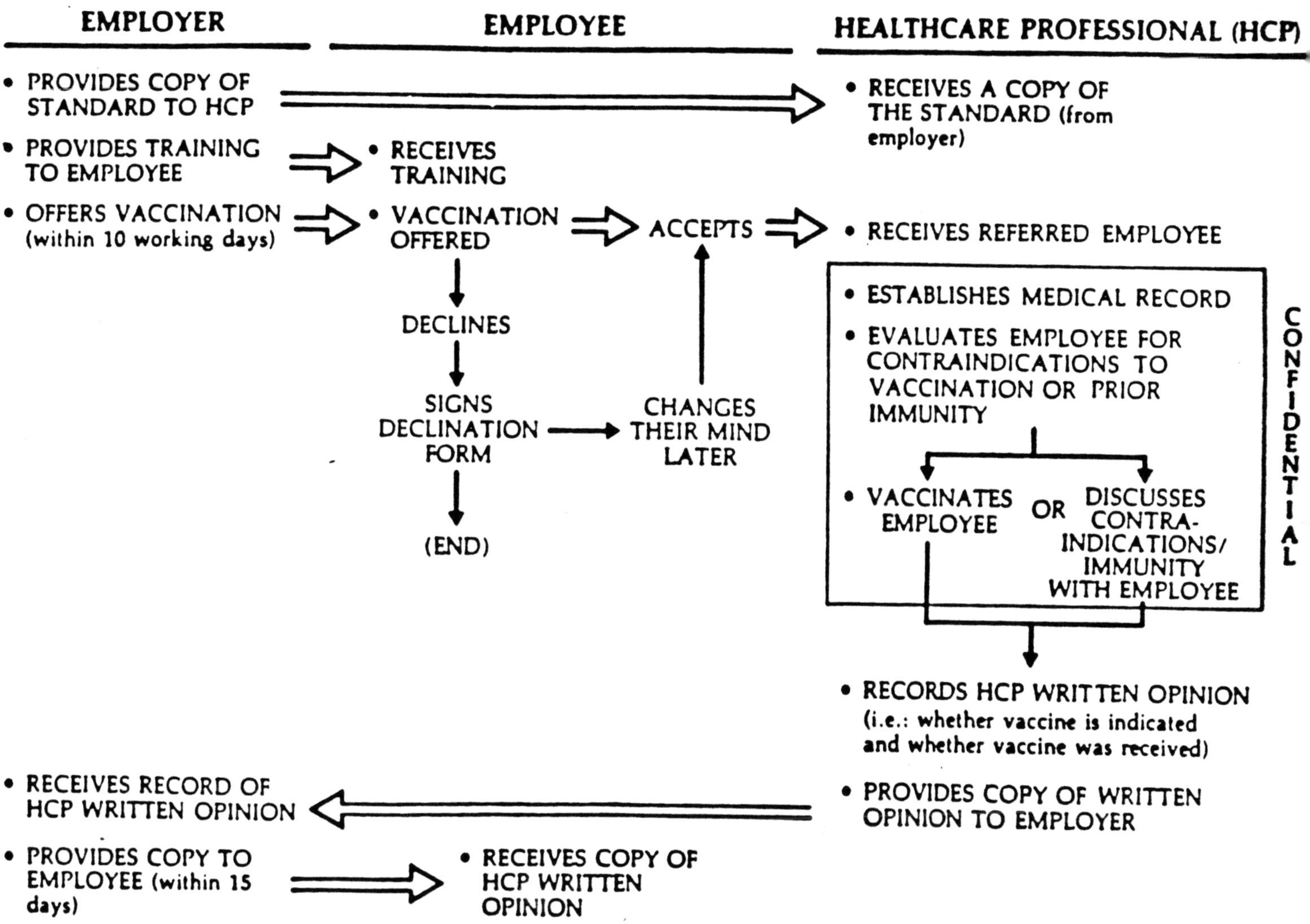

POST-EXPOSURE EVALUATION AND FOLLOW-UP

EXPOSURE INCIDENT OCCURS

EMPLOYEE

- REPORTS INCIDENT TO EMPLOYER

EMPLOYER

- DIRECTS EMPLOYEE TO HCP
- SENDS TO HCP
  - — COPY OF STANDARD
  - — JOB DESCRIPTION OF EMPLOYEE
  - — INCIDENT REPORT (route, circumstances, etc.)
  - — SOURCE INDIVIDUAL'S HBV/HIV STATUS (if known)
  - — EMPLOYEE'S HEPATITIS B VACCINE STATUS AND OTHER RELEVANT MEDICAL INFORMATION

HEALTH CARE PROFESSIONAL (HCP)

CONFIDENTIAL

- EVALUATES EXPOSURE INCIDENT
- ARRANGES FOR TESTING OF EMPLOYEE AND SOURCE INDIVIDUAL (if not already known)
- NOTIFIES EMPLOYEE OF RESULTS OF ALL TESTING
- PROVIDES COUNSELING
- PROVIDES POST-EXPOSURE PROPHYLAXIS
- EVALUATES REPORTED ILLNESSES

HCP:

- SENDS (ONLY) THE HCP WRITTEN OPINION TO EMPLOYER:
  - — Documentation that employee was informed of evaluation results and the need for any further follow-up;

    and

  - — Whether hepatitis B vaccine is indicated and if vaccine was received.

EMPLOYER:

- DOCUMENTS EVENTS ON OSHA 200 AND 101 (if applicable)
- RECEIVES HCP'S WRITTEN OPINION
- PROVIDES COPY OF HCP'S WRITTEN OPINION TO EMPLOYEE (within 15 days of completed evaluation)

EMPLOYEE:

- RECEIVES COPY OF HCP'S WRITTEN OPINION

APPENDIX E

ONE-PAGE FACT SHEETS ON:

1. Holding the Line on Contamination
2. Personal Protective Equipment
3. Hepatitis B Vaccination
4. Handling Sharps

Bloodborne facts

Holding the Line on Contamination

U.S. Department of Labor
Occupational Safety and Health Administration

Keeping work areas in a clean and sanitary condition reduces employees' risk of exposure to bloodborne pathogens. Each year about 8,700 health care workers are infected with hepatitis B virus, and 200 die from contracting hepatitis B through their work. The chance of contracting human immunodeficiency virus (HIV), the bloodborne pathogen which causes AIDS, from occupational exposure is small, yet a good housekeeping program can minimize this risk as well.

DECONTAMINATION

Every employer whose employees are exposed to blood or other potentially infectious materials must develop a written schedule for cleaning each area where exposures occur. The methods of decontaminating different surfaces must be specified, determined by the type of surface to be cleaned, the soil present and the tasks or procedures that occur in that area.

For example, different cleaning and decontamination measures would be used for a surgical operatory and a patient room. Similarly, hard surfaced flooring and carpeting require separate cleaning methods. More extensive efforts will be necessary for gross contamination than for minor spattering. Likewise, such varied tasks as laboratory analyses and normal patient care would require different techniques for clean-up.

Employees must decontaminate working surfaces and equipment with an appropriate disinfectant after completing procedures involving exposure to blood. Many laboratory procedures are performed on a continual basis throughout a shift. Except as discussed below, it is not necessary to clean and decontaminate between procedures. However, if the employee leaves the area for a period of time, for a break or lunch, then contaminated work surfaces must be cleaned.

Employees also must clean (1) when surfaces become obviously contaminated; (2) after any spill of blood or other potentially infectious materials; and (3) at the end of the work shift if contamination might have occurred. Thus, employees need not decontaminate the work area after each patient care procedure, but only after those that actually result in contamination.

If surfaces or equipment are draped with protective coverings such as plastic wrap or aluminum foil, these coverings should be removed or replaced if they become obviously contaminated. Reusable receptacles such as bins, pails and cans that are likely to become contaminated must be inspected and decontaminated on a regular basis. If contamination is visible, workers must clean and decontaminate the item immediately, or as soon as feasible.

Should glassware that may be potentially contaminated break, workers need to use mechanical means such as a brush and dustpan or tongs or forceps to pick up the broken glass--never by hand, even when wearing gloves.

Before any equipment is serviced or shipped for repairing or cleaning, it must be decontaminated to the extent possible. The equipment must be labeled, indicating which portions are still contaminated. This enables employees and those who service the equipment to take appropriate precautions to prevent exposure.

REGULATED WASTE

In addition to effective decontamination of work areas, proper handling of regulated waste is essential to prevent unnecessary exposure to blood and other potentially infectious materials. Regulated waste must be handled with great care--i.e., liquid or semi-liquid blood and other potentially infectious materials, items caked with these materials, items that would release blood or other potentially infected materials if compressed, pathological or microbiological wastes containing them and contaminated sharps.

Containers used to store regulated waste must be closable and suitable to contain the contents and prevent leakage of fluids. Containers designed for sharps also must be puncture resistant. They must be labeled or color-coded to ensure that employees are aware of the potential hazards. Such containers must be closed before removal to prevent the contents from spilling. If the outside of a container becomes contaminated, it must be placed within a second suitable container.

Regulated waste must be disposed of in accordance with applicable state and local laws.

LAUNDRY

Laundry workers must wear gloves and handle contaminated laundry as little as possible, with a minimum of agitation. Contaminated laundry should be bagged or placed in containers at the location where it is used, but not sorted or rinsed there.

Laundry must be transported within the establishment or to outside laundries in labeled or red color-coded bags. If the facility uses Universal Precautions for handling all soiled laundry, then alternate labeling or color coding that can be recognized by the employees may be used. If laundry is wet and it might soak through laundry bags, then workers must use bags that prevent leakage to transport it.

RESEARCH FACILITIES

More stringent decontamination requirements apply to research laboratories and production facilities that work with concentrated strains of HIV and HBV.

Bloodborne *facts*

Personal Protective Equipment Cuts Risk

U.S. Department of Labor
Occupational Safety and Health Administration

Wearing gloves, gowns, masks, and eye protection can significantly reduce health risks for workers exposed to blood and other potentially infectious materials. The new OSHA standard covering bloodborne disease requires employers to provide appropriate personal protective equipment (PPE) and clothing free of charge to employees.

Workers who have direct exposure to blood and other potentially infectious materials on their jobs run the risk of contracting bloodborne infections from hepatitis B virus (HBV), human immunodeficiency virus (HIV) which causes AIDS, and other pathogens. About 8,700 health care workers each year are infected with HBV, and 200 die from the infection. Although the risk of contracting AIDS through occupational exposure is much lower, wearing proper personal protective equipment can greatly reduce potential exposure to all bloodborne infections.

SELECTING PPE

Personal protective clothing and equipment must be suitable. This means the level of protection must fit the expected exposure. For example, gloves would be sufficient for a laboratory technician who is drawing blood, whereas a pathologist conducting an autopsy would need considerably more protective clothing.

PPE may include gloves, gowns, laboratory coats, face shields or masks, eye protection, pocket masks, and other protective gear. The gear must be readily accessible to employees and available in appropriate sizes.

If an employee is expected to have hand contact with blood or other potentially infectious materials or contaminated surfaces, he or she must wear gloves. Single use gloves cannot be washed or decontaminated for reuse. Utility gloves may be decontaminated if they are not compromised. They should be replaced when they show signs of cracking, peeling, tearing, puncturing, or deteriorating. If employees are allergic to standard gloves, the employer must provide hypoallergenic gloves or similar alternatives.

Routine gloving is not required for phlebotomy in voluntary blood donation centers, though it is necessary for all other phlebotomies. In any case, gloves must be available in voluntary blood donation centers for employees who want to use them. Workers in voluntary blood donation centers must use gloves (1) when they have cuts, scratches or other breaks in their skin; (2) while they are in training; and (3) when they believe contamination might occur.

Employees should wear eye and mouth protection such as goggles and masks, glasses with solid side shields, and masks or chin-length face shields when splashes, sprays, splatters, or droplets of potentially infectious materials pose a hazard through the eyes, nose or mouth. More extensive coverings such as gowns, aprons, surgical caps and hoods, and shoe covers or boots are needed when gross contamination is expected. This often occurs, for example, during orthopedic surgery or autopsies.

AVOIDING CONTAMINATION

The key is that blood or other infectious materials must not reach an employee's work clothes, street clothes, undergarments, skin, eyes, mouth, or other mucous membranes under normal conditions for the duration of exposure.

Employers must provide the PPE and ensure that their workers wear it. This means that if a lab coat is considered PPE, it must be supplied by the employer rather than the employee. The employer also must clean or launder clothing and equipment and repair or replace it as necessary.

Additional protective measures such as using PPE in animal rooms and decontaminating PPE before laundering are essential in facilities that conduct research on HIV or HBV.

EXCEPTION

There is one exception to the requirement for protective gear. An employee may choose, temporarily and briefly, **under rare and extraordinary circumstances**, to forego the equipment. It must be the employee's professional judgment that using the protective equipment would prevent the delivery of health care or public safety services or would pose an increased hazard to the safety of the worker or co-worker. When one of these excepted situations occurs, employers are to investigate and document the circumstances to determine if there are ways to avoid it in the future. For example, if a firefighter's resuscitation device is damaged, perhaps another type of device should be used or the device should be carried in a different manner. Exceptions must be limited--this is not a blanket exemption.

DECONTAMINATING AND DISPOSING OF PPE

Employees must remove personal protective clothing and equipment before leaving the work area or when the PPE becomes contaminated. If a garment is penetrated, workers must remove it immediately or as soon as feasible. Used protective clothing and equipment must be placed in designated containers for storage, decontamination, or disposal.

OTHER PROTECTIVE PRACTICES

If an employee's skin or mucous membranes come into contact with blood, he or she is to wash with soap and water and flush eyes with water as soon as feasible. In addition, workers must wash their hands immediately or as soon as feasible after removing protective equipment. If soap and water are not immediately available, employers may provide other handwashing measures such as moist towelettes. Employees still must wash with soap and water as soon as possible.

Employees must refrain from eating, drinking, smoking, applying cosmetics or lip balm, and handling contact lenses in areas where they may be exposed to blood or other potentially infectious materials.

Bloodborne facts

Hepatitis B Vaccination--Protection For You

U.S. Department of Labor
Occupational Safety and Health Administration

WHAT IS HBV?

Hepatitis B virus (HBV) is a potentially life-threatening bloodborne pathogen. Centers for Disease Control estimates there are approximately 280,000 HBV infections each year in the U.S.

Approximately 8,700 health care workers each year contract hepatitis B, and about 200 will die as a result. In addition, some who contract HBV will become carriers, passing the disease on to others. Carriers also face a significantly higher risk for other liver ailments which can be fatal, including cirrhosis of the liver and primary liver cancer.

HBV infection is transmitted through exposure to blood and other infectious body fluids and tissues. Anyone with occupational exposure to blood is at risk of contracting the infection.

Employers must provide engineering controls; workers must use work practices and protective clothing and equipment to prevent exposure to potentially infectious materials. However, the best defense against hepatitis B is vaccination.

WHO NEEDS VACCINATION?

The new OSHA standard covering bloodborne pathogens requires employers to offer the three-injection vaccination series free to all employees who are exposed to blood or other potentially infectious materials as part of their job duties. This includes health care workers, emergency responders, morticians, first-aid personnel, law enforcement officers, correctional facilities staff, launderers, as well as others.

The vaccination must be offered within 10 days of initial assignment to a job where exposure to blood or other potentially infectious materials can be "reasonably anticipated." The requirements for vaccinations of those already on the job take effect July 6, 1992.

WHAT DOES VACCINATION INVOLVE?

The hepatitis B vaccination is a noninfectious, yeast-based vaccine given in three injections in the arm. It is prepared from recombinant yeast cultures, rather than human blood or plasma. Thus, there is no risk of contamination from other bloodborne pathogens nor is there any chance of developing HBV from the vaccine.

The second injection should be given one month after the first, and the third injection six months after the initial dose. More than 90 percent of those vaccinated will develop immunity to the hepatitis B virus. To ensure immunity, it is important for individuals to receive all three injections. At this point it is unclear how long the immunity lasts, so booster shots may be required at some point in the future.

The vaccine causes no harm to those who are already immune or to those who may be HBV carriers. Although employees may opt to have their blood tested for antibodies to determine need for the vaccine, employers may not make such screening a condition of receiving vaccination nor are employers required to provide prescreening.

Each employee should receive counseling from a health care professional when vaccination is offered. This discussion will help an employee determine whether inoculation is necessary.

WHAT IF I DECLINE VACCINATION?

Workers who decide to decline vaccination must complete a declination form. Employers must keep these forms on file so that they know the vaccination status of everyone who is exposed to blood. At any time after a worker initially declines to receive the vaccine, he or she may opt to take it.

WHAT IF I AM EXPOSED BUT HAVE NOT YET BEEN VACCINATED?

If a worker experiences an exposure incident, such as a needlestick or a blood splash in the eye, he or she must receive confidential medical evaluation from a licensed health care professional with appropriate follow-up. To the extent possible by law, the employer is to determine the source individual for HBV as well as human immunodeficiency virus (HIV) infectivity. The worker's blood will also be screened if he or she agrees.

The health care professional is to follow the guidelines of the U.S. Public Health Service in providing treatment. This would include hepatitis B vaccination. The health care professional must give a written opinion on whether or not vaccination is recommended and whether the employee received it. Only this information is reported to the employer. Employee medical records must remain confidential. HIV or HBV status must NOT be reported to the employer.

Bloodborne *facts*

Protect Yourself When Handling Sharps

U.S. Department of Labor
Occupational Safety and Health Administration

A needlestick or a cut from a contaminated scalpel can lead to infection from hepatitis B virus (HBV) or human immunodeficiency virus (HIV) which causes AIDS. Although few cases of AIDS have been documented from occupational exposure, approximately 8,700 health care workers each year contract hepatitis B. About 200 will die as a result. The new OSHA standard covering bloodborne pathogens specifies measures to reduce these risks of infection.

PROMPT DISPOSAL

The best way to prevent cuts and sticks is to minimize contact with sharps. That means disposing of them immediately after use. Puncture-resistant containers must be available nearby to hold contaminated sharps--either for disposal or, for reusable sharps, later decontamination for re-use. When reprocessing contaminated reusable sharps, employees must not reach by hand into the holding container. Contaminated sharps must never be sheared or broken.

Recapping, bending, or removing needles is permissible **only** if there is no feasible alternative or if required for a specific medical procedure such as blood gas analysis. If recapping, bending, or removal is necessary, workers must use either a mechanical device or a one-handed technique. If recapping is essential--for example, between multiple injections for the same patient--employees must avoid using both hands to recap. Employees might recap with a one-handed "scoop" technique, using the needle itself to pick up the cap, pushing cap and sharp together against a hard surface to ensure a tight fit. Or they might hold the cap with tongs or forceps to place it on the needle.

SHARPS CONTAINERS

Containers for used sharps must be puncture resistant. The sides and the bottom must be leakproof. They must be labeled or color coded red to ensure that everyone knows the contents are hazardous. Containers for disposable sharps must have a lid, and they must be maintained upright to keep liquids and the sharps inside.

Employees must never reach by hand into containers of contaminated sharps. Containers for reusable sharps could be equipped with wire basket liners for easy removal during reprocessing, or employees could use tongs or forceps to withdraw the contents. Reusable sharps disposal containers may not be opened, emptied, or cleaned manually.

Containers need to be located as near to as feasible the area of use. In some cases, they may be placed on carts to prevent access to mentally disturbed or pediatric patients. Containers also should be available wherever sharps may be found, such as in laundries. The containers must be replaced routinely and not be overfilled, which can increase the risk of needlesticks or cuts.

HANDLING CONTAINERS

When employees are ready to discard containers, they should first close the lids. If there is a chance of leakage from the primary container, the employees should use a secondary container that is closable, labeled, or color coded and leak resistant.

Careful handling of sharps can prevent injury and reduce the risk of infection. By following these work practices, employees can decrease their chances of contracting bloodborne illness.

APPENDIX F

ALPHABETICAL

INDEX

ALPHABETICAL INDEX

by subject matter (numbers are <u>page</u> numbers)

APPENDIX G

SECTION
BY
SECTION
INDEX
TO
29 C.F.R §1910.1030

SECTION-BY-SECTION INDEX

to C.F.R. §1910.1030 (numbers are <u>page</u> numbers)

HOW TO OBTAIN ADDITIONAL INFORMATION:

From time to time, MORAN ASSOCIATES sends out OSHA information and circulars to persons and organizations interested in OSHA matters. There is no charge for this service.

If you purchased this book directly from MORAN ASSOCIATES, your name was added to the mailing list used to make those distributions. If someone other than you purchased the book from MORAN ASSOCIATES or if you obtained this book in any other way, you can have your name added to the mailing list by tearing this page out of the book, filling out the information below, and mailing it to:

MORAN ASSOCIATES (Attention Mailing List)
919 18th Street, N.W.
Suite 800
Washington, D.C. 20006

(or you can reproduce this page -- or send a letter)

TO: Moran Associates' Mail Room

Please add the following information to your mailing list for upcoming OSHA information and circulars:

NAME/TITLE: ____________________

COMPANY/ORGANIZATION: ____________________

ADDRESS: ____________________

____

CITY/STATE/ZIP: ____________________

TELEPHONE: ( ) ____________________